Library of
Davidson College

US–WEST EUROPEAN RELATIONS DURING THE REAGAN YEARS

Also by Douglas A. Wertman and published by St. Martin's Press:

ITALIAN CHRISTIAN DEMOCRACY: The Politics of Dominance (*with Robert Leonardi*)

US–West European Relations during the Reagan Years

The Perspective of West European Publics

Steven K. Smith

and

Douglas A. Wertman

St. Martin's Press   New York

© Steven K. Smith and Douglas A. Wertman, 1992

All rights reserved. For information, write:
Scholarly and Reference Division,
St. Martin's Press, Inc., 175 Fifth Avenue,
New York, N.Y. 10010

First published in the United States of America in 1992

Printed in Hong Kong

ISBN 0–312–06838–7

Library of Congress Cataloging-in-Publication Data
Smith, Steven K.
US–West European relations during the Reagan years: the perspective of West European publics/Steven K. Smith and Douglas A. Wertman
  p. cm.
Includes bibliographical references and index.
ISBN 0–312–06838–7
1. Europe—Foreign relations—United States. 2. United States--Foreign relations—Europe. 3. Public opinion—Europe. 4. United States—Foreign public opinion, European. 5. United States—Foreign relations—1981–1898. I. Wertman, Douglas A. II. Title.
D1065.U5S66 1992
327.7304—dc20   91—23539
                                                            CIP

To Lauren, Colin, and Brendan
—S.K.S.

To Ellen, John, and Ann
– D.A.W.

Contents

List of Tables and Figures	viii
Preface: A Note on Data and Terminology	xii
Acknowledgements	xiv
1 Introduction	1
2 NATO and Western Security	9
3 INF Deployment in Western Europe	51
4 The American Image	91
5 The Soviet Image and Public Diplomacy	129
6 US–Soviet Relations	161
7 US Public Diplomacy Efforts in Western Europe	184
8 Combating International Terrorism	198
9 US–West European Economic Relations	218
10 Conclusions	248
Epilogue: The Gulf Conflict	254
Appendix 1: Chronology of Events in US–West European Relations, 1979–89	258
Appendix 2: List of USIA Surveys used in this Book, 1976–91	261
Appendix 3: Additional Data Tables	266
Notes and References	289
Select Bibliography	307
Index	315

List of Tables and Figures

Tables

2.1	Concern over Soviet and US political pressure on their country, April 1987	18
2.2	Support for NATO versus neutrality, 1981–87	22
2.3	Perceived essentiality of NATO, 1981–89	24
2.4	Perceived necessity of NATO, July 1989	26
2.5	Country which would come to their aid in case of attack, July 1988	29
2.6	Support for American troops in Western Europe, May–June 1984	31
2.7	Necessity of US military presence in Western Europe, October 1988	33
2.8	West German attitudes on withdrawal of US troops from Western Europe, 1956–89	34
2.9	Attitudes on the use of nuclear weapons, 1981–87	40
2.10	Attitudes on SDI research, 1985–87	44
2.11	Support for defence spending, 1968–88	48
3.1	Activities done to show position on INF stationing in their country, June 1983	60
3.2	Support for INF deployment when linked to arms talks, March 1981–April 1983	68
3.3	Support for INF deployment when information on Soviet missiles included in the question, 1981–82	71
3.4	Impact on support for INF deployment of information on Soviet INF missiles, October 1981	72
3.5	Support for INF deployment, 1983–85	74
3.6	British views on INF deployment, 1981–84	78
3.7	West German views on INF deployment, 1983	82
3.8	Why INF supporters favour deployment, May 1984	85
3.9	Why INF opponents oppose deployment, May 1984	86
4.1	Anti-Americanism in Western Europe, 1982–88	96
4.2	Favourable opinion of the USA, 1981–89	98
4.3	Favourable opinion of the USA in Western Europe, late 1980s	99
4.4	Good/Bad opinion of the USA, 1954–1984	102

List of Tables and Figures ix

4.5	Perception of whether American values are similar to or different from their own, June 1985	105
4.6	Attitudes on US society, September–October 1987	108
4.7	Trust in Americans, March–April 1986	110
4.8	Trust of Western Europeans in 18 different peoples, March–April 1986	112
4.9	Confidence in US foreign policy, 1960–89	117
4.10	Effects of US policies, 1982–89	119
4.11	How the USA and Soviet Union compare on various aspects of foreign policy, 1987	122
4.12	Overall opinion of President Reagan, Fall 1987	125
5.1	Soviet image in Western Europe, October 1989	134
5.2	Pro- and anti-Soviet feelings among West Europeans, 1983–89	136
5.3	Improvements in opinion toward the Soviet Union, 1987	138
5.4	European confidence in Soviet foreign policy, October 1989	141
5.5	Soviet policies promote peace, 1982–9	143
5.6	Gorbachev image in Western Europe, October 1989	145
5.7	Protection of human rights in the Soviet Union, 1977–89	148
5.8	Soviet protection of human rights, September 1987	149
5.9	West European relations with the Soviet Union, 1985–87	153
6.1	US–Soviet summits, 1955–90	162
6.2	US–Soviet relations, 1985–88	163
6.3	Geneva summit accomplishments, December 1985	169
6.4	SDI and arms control, November–December 1985	170
6.5	Western Europeans judge Geneva summit leaders, December 1985	171
6.6	Nuclear arms control accomplishments at Reykjavik, October 1986	174
6.7	US defence commitment to Western Europe in wake of INF Treaty, December 1987	177
6.8	West European support for INF Treaty, December 1987	178
6.9	Credit for progress on arms control negotiations, November 1987	179
6.10	Washington summit accomplishments, December 1987	179
6.11	Moscow summit accomplishments, June 1988	181

6.12	US protects West European interests at the summits, 1986–88	182
7.1	Perception of media coverage of Gorbachev and Reagan, September 1987	186
7.2	Selected VOA Europe 1988–89 listenership rates	189
7.3	WORLDNET interactive programs requested and produced and broadcast to Western Europe, 1986–90	191
7.4	Primary sources of information on US–European relations, October 1987	194
7.5	Source of information on arms control and international affairs, 1986–87	194
7.6	Media habits and education level, October 1987	195
7.7	Sources of information by attitudes toward the US, October 1987	196
8.1	Countries and organizations which promote international terrorism, February 1981	199
8.2	Attitudes on actions against countries which harbor or support terrorists, April 1985	200
8.3	Nations supporting terrorism in other countries, March–April 1985	203
8.4	Pre-raid support for US military action against Libya, April 1986	209
8.5	Support for US military action against Libya, April 1986	210
8.6	President Reagan too quick to employ US forces, April 1986	211
8.7	Actions against terrorist supporting countries, April 1987	213
8.8	Should governments negotiate for release of hostages, April 1987	215
8.9	Iran–Contra issue damages US credibility among informed Western Europeans, April 1987	217
9.1	Perceived economic health of their country, 1977–89	221
9.2	Co-ordination of economic policies with the US, 1987	224
9.3	How much the USA takes into account the views of Western Europe on economic decisions important to Europe, 1979–85	225
9.4	US goals in its economic dealings with Western Europe, 1977–84	227
9.5	US co-operativeness in resolving economic problems with Western Europe, 1983–88	228

9.6	Effects of US policies on their economy, 1982–89	230
9.7	Perceptions of the effects on their country's economy of US, Japanese, and EC policies, 1982–89	232
9.8	Support for free trade in the 1980s	235
9.9	US trade policy – free trade or protectionist?, 1976–89	236
9.10	Western European perceptions of US barriers to their country's manufactured products, 1979–85	239
A.1	Confidence in US foreign policy	267
A.2	Effects of US policies	273
A.3	Overall opinion of the Soviet Union, 1981–89	275
A.4	Confidence in Soviet foreign policy, 1982–89	278
A.5	Effects of Soviet foreign policies, 1982–89	281
A.6	US–Soviet relations, 1985–88	283
A.7	Effects of US economic policies	285

Figures

5.1	Favourable image of the Soviet Union, 1981–89	131
5.2	Confidence in Soviet foreign Policy, 1982–89	140

Preface: A Note on Data and Terminology

This book, which focuses on West European public opinion on the USA, the Soviet Union, security issues, economic issues, and terrorism, is based on a unique data source of more than 80 multi-country public opinion surveys conducted in Western Europe in the 1980s. In a few cases, longer-term trends going back as far as the 1950s are analysed. The bulk of the surveys used in this book were commissioned by the United States Information Agency's Office of Research. Any survey not specifically identified as to source is a USIA survey. USIA surveys are referred to in the text or tables by the month, year, and a brief title. Appendix 2 then gives a list of all these USIA surveys, including the names of all countries in which the survey was conducted and the number of cases in each country. The source for non-USIA surveys is given in the notes.

All USIA surveys done prior to late 1985 were personal interview surveys; since then, USIA has done both personal interview and telephone surveys. While the personal interview and telephone surveys were both based on national adult populations, the different sampling frames and techniques, the kind of weighting required in telephone surveys because telephone penetration is less than 100 per cent, and the fact that one cannot ask all questions in a telephone survey that can be asked in a personal interview survey argue for keeping the two separate. Therefore, we have been careful to identify whenever a survey was done by telephone (any survey not specifically so identified was done by personal interview), to report the findings from personal interview and telephone surveys in different tables, and to avoid using the two together in discussing trends.

When analysing an opinion, one can look at the direction (pro/con, for/against, favourable/unfavourable, etc.), the intensity (whether the opinion is held strongly or weakly), salience (how important the issue or opinion is to the individual), or informational content (the degree of knowledge on which the opinion is based). All of these aspects are examined in this book when the data permit. One important distinction, often confused, is between the extent of opinion and the intensity of an opinion. When we say feelings are broadly or widely or overwhelmingly held, we are talking about the extent, or how many people hold these views; when we say that feelings are strongly held, we are talking about the intensity of views.

Because all surveys involve sampling and measurement error, we have adopted the following conventions in our terminology. We only call something a majority when 54 per cent or more hold that view. A plurality means that a particular response is given to a question by more people than give any other response. However, if the margin in the number holding two different views is 3 per cent or less, we call opinion divided, and, if the margin is in the range of 4 to 6 per cent, we will normally say that opinion is roughly divided or close to divided.

STEVEN K. SMITH
DOUGLAS A. WERTMAN

Acknowledgements

The authors would like to acknowledge the work of several generations of analysts at the US Information Agency who have contributed to a greater understanding of foreign public opinion. Many of these individuals provided valuable assistance to our project: Kenneth Adler, Leo Crespi, Vello Ederma, Gunther Eyck, David Gibson, Steven Grant, Christine Kielpinski, Martha Mac Iver, Scott Righetti, Charles Spencer, Gordon Tubbs, and Nancy Walker. Ronald Hinckley, Director of USIA's Office of Research, also provided useful material. We would also like to thank Helen Crossley of the US Information Agency who has devoted a lifetime to safeguarding the integrity and history of survey research at USIA.

Disclaimer

The views expressed in this book are those of the authors and not necessarily those of the US Department of Justice, the US Information Agency, or the US Government.

S.K.S.
D.A.W.

1 Introduction

The 1980s, the last decade of the Cold War, were marked by great ups and downs in US–Soviet relations which directly impacted on the US–West European Alliance. In the early 1980s, a more confrontational atmosphere reigned as a result of the December 1979 Soviet invasion of Afghanistan; the harsher rhetoric toward the Soviet Union by President Ronald Reagan; the declaration of martial law in Poland in December 1981; the battle over the deployment of intermediate-range nuclear forces (INF) and an intensive Soviet 'peace offensive' to prevent this deployment; the US announcement of the Strategic Defence Initiative in March 1983; the Soviet shootdown of the Korean airliner in September 1983; and many other events. Characteristic of this confrontational environment, no US–Soviet Summit was held between June 1979 and November 1985, the longest period without such a meeting since the immediate postwar years. Between November 1982 and March 1985 three successive Soviet leaders died, and Soviet policy was marked by little or no innovation. During the first half of the 1980s, the USA and many West European countries did not always agree on how to deal with the Soviet Union, whether on the question of economic sanctions or on the tone of the rhetoric. In 1985, the key event which served as the catalyst to the vast changes in Eastern Europe and the Soviet Union occurred when Mikhail Gorbachev came to power. Indicative of the greatly changed world and the greatly improved US–Soviet relations, four Reagan–Gorbachev summits were held in the 1985–88 period, and several more took place in the first two years of the Bush Administration. In 1980 – or for that matter, in 1988 – no one predicted, or could have predicted, that German reunification would occur in 1990 or that there would be free elections across Eastern Europe in 1989 or 1990. The post-Cold War world is shaping a new form of US–Soviet relations. (See Appendix 1 for a chronology of the key events of the 1980s.)

In the early 1980s, the NATO Alliance underwent a major test of its internal cohesion as a result of the struggle over INF deployment, which was the last major battle of the Cold War. The anti-INF demonstrations in the 1981–83 period were the most serious mass-based challenge to a key NATO policy since the early 1960s and, arguably, in its entire history. At the same time, the early 1980s saw the breakdown in both Britain and West Germany of the elite consensus on defence shared by the two major parties in each country. In the late 1980s and early 1990s, as a function of the changed nature of East–West relations, NATO has faced a very different kind of challenge which has led to a substantial revision in key NATO doctrines, in particular flexible response, and, in essence, an identity crisis for the Alliance.

In the early 1980s, US–West European economic relations were frequently troubled as a result of disagreements over East–West trade and the US desire for economic sanctions against the Soviets; the uncontrolled growth in the value of the US dollar, which reached all-time highs against the German mark in February 1985; the high US interest rates; and the growing US budget and trade deficits. More recently, the USA and Western Europe have disagreed strongly on the issue of free trade in agriculture, a key factor in the GATT Uruguay Round. The inability of the USA, Japan, and West Europe to co-ordinate economic policies through the annual Economic Summits or the many other multilateral mechanisms continued unabated until September 1985, when the Plaza Agreement allowed for a co-ordinated downward movement in the dollar's value. However, despite the growth in mechanisms for US–West European economic co-operation, including the regularisation of US–European Community ministerial meetings, the 1980s were not marked by a high degree of co-ordination of economic policies. Economic issues will even more frequently be at the top of the agenda in the 1990s as a result of the changed East–West relations. International terrorism and the Western response to it became another divisive issue for the NATO Allies, particularly in the mid-1980s with the USA pressing for economic sanctions against Libya, then bombing Libya to punish it for sponsoring terrorism, and then being embarrassed by the revelations of the Iran–Contra Affair. These issues – US–Soviet relations and the images of the two superpowers; NATO; INF deployment; US–West European economic relations; and terrorism – are the major foci of this book.

WEST EUROPEAN PUBLIC OPINION AND THE REAGAN ADMINISTRATION

The Reagan Administration put a new emphasis on 'public diplomacy' aimed at both mass and elite audiences in Western Europe, while attacking the Soviet public diplomacy efforts, particularly the Soviet 'peace offensive' of the early 1980s, as propaganda and disinformation. The increased US emphasis on 'public diplomacy' was an outgrowth of two factors: the US fears about West European public opinion; and the nature of the Reagan Administration itself, which, even more than its predecessors, gave major importance to public relations. An official recognition of the importance of 'public diplomacy' came in January 1983 with National Security Decision Directive 77 (NSDD77) entitled 'Management of Public Diplomacy Relative to National Security'. In the 1980s, a greater effort was made to reach the *mass* publics than was ever before true of US public diplomacy in Western Europe, which had primarily stressed reaching the elite. Worldnet and VOA Europe, discussed in Chapter 7, were the two major examples of this attempt in the 1980s. Public diplomacy was seen as an important factor in the managing of American relations with West Europe. Two chapters in this book examine the US and Soviet efforts to persuade West European publics in the 1980s.

While it was recognised in Washington that the demonstrators in the streets protesting against INF deployment were not necessarily representative of the West European publics, many in the Reagan Administration (as well as many American journalists and other observers of Western Europe) nevertheless feared that a wave of anti-Americanism, neutralism, and pacifism was sweeping West Europe. The concerns in Washington matched those in the late 1950s and early 1960s when the 'Ban the Bomb' movement was at its height and in the late 1960s and early 1970s during the Vietnam War. Serious concern was also raised about the 'successor generation', those better-educated, younger West Europeans who would move into positions of leadership in the 1990s and after (Szabo, 1983).

Clearly, the catalyst for many of these fears about West European public opinion was the battle over INF deployment. Some of the pressure on the Reagan Administration to consider West European public opinion came also from the West European governments who had agreed to accept deployment on their soil but faced internal opposition as part of broadly anti-nuclear feelings. One result of these concerns was the numerous multi-country surveys on INF and related issues conducted by the United States Information Agency throughout Western Europe in the first half of the 1980s. Richard Bissell, Director of USIA's Office of Research for a year during the height of the INF controversy, wrote that 'the crisis in Alliance confidence over INF deployment created a policy-level need for frequent updating of European public opinion' (Bissell, 1986, p. 219). Similarly, Ronald Hinckley, who specialised in public opinion issues while on the National Security Council staff in the Reagan Administration, argued that 'during the early 1980s, the crisis in NATO nations' public confidence over INF deployment in Western Europe established a policy-level need for the continual review of the latest public opinion in those countries where deployment was being resisted by the native populations' (Hinckley, 1990, p. 51). Richard Wirthlin, President Reagan's private pollster, also said that the White House was interested in understanding the views of the West European publics on INF and related issues and that he at times wrote summary reports for the White House of the findings from USIA's Western European surveys. Furthermore, in Spring 1982 Wirthlin directly commissioned an in-depth survey in Britain, France, and West Germany to help in developing the themes for President Reagan's speeches, including the key one to the British Parliament, during his June 1982 trip to Western Europe (Wirthlin, 1990). President Reagan himself – the Great Communicator who was highly successful within the USA – was clearly seen by the White House as a major vehicle and the greatest asset for public diplomacy efforts.

The purposes of these efforts to study West European public opinion were probably two: (1) the primary motivation – and result – was a better understanding of how to market, or sell, US policy in Western Europe: in other words, the tactics of presenting the case for INF deployment, including the need for emphasising NATO's arms control efforts, and for other US policy initiatives; and (2) a by-product, though an important one, was an understanding of the importance to West European publics, and, therefore, of the pressure many West European governments felt, that the arms control track of the 'Dual Track' December 1979 NATO decision be pursued seriously (Thompson, 1987). This does not mean that the US Government, or President Reagan personally, was successful in making the US case for INF deployment to West European publics, but the Reagan Administration had a broad array of survey data available to help it in shaping its marketing efforts.

PUBLIC OPINION AND FOREIGN POLICY

A large body of literature on public opinion and foreign policy argues that the great bulk of the mass public of western democratic societies, including both the USA and Western Europe, have a low interest in foreign policy issues, are not well-informed about them, and consider them of low salience (Mueller, 1973; Kegley and Wittkopf, 1982; Adler, 1984a; Flynn, 1985; Flynn and Rattinger, 1985; Hinckley, 1988; Shapiro and Page, 1988). Only a limited minority, commonly referred to as the 'attentive public', are considered to have a higher interest and level of information about foreign policy questions. With few exceptions, foreign policy issues are fairly remote from the daily lives of most citizens, who have no personal experience with or involvement in these issues. Individuals are, therefore, more likely to have well-formed views on domestic than foreign policy issues. Some international economic issues may be of greater interest to mass publics than other foreign policy questions, at least to the limited extent that their domestic ramifications are understood.

The evidence presented in this book supports this view of a general public which is largely uninterested and poorly informed about foreign policy issues. For example, as Chapter 3 shows, even on such an important foreign policy issue as INF deployment which was in the headlines constantly for more than three years, the public was not very well-informed nor did most people consider it one of their major concerns among the problems facing their country. In addition, foreign policy issues normally do not have a great effect on election outcomes in the USA or Western Europe, and this was true of INF deployment in Italy and West Germany in 1983. An exception was the 1983 British General Election, in which, in the wake of the Falklands War, the Labour Party was hurt by its defence policies (Flynn and Rattinger, 1985).

Caution is necessary in interpreting public opinion data. Particular attention must be paid to how the question is worded, especially how much and what kind of information is provided to the respondents. As Ken Adler (1984a, p. 145) writes,

> the process of providing information to previously unaware or uninformed respondents is likely to make the sample unrepresentative of general public opinion. And the greater the segment of the general public who do not know or care about the issue, the more unrepresentative of the public will be the findings.

When pressed, people may give opinions without ever having previously thought about the issue or having much conviction one way or the other. In other words, particularly on complex, specific issues, polls may 'create' opinion rather than reflect it (Adler, 1984a).

At the same time, when a wide variety of question wordings are used within a short time-span, as was the case with INF deployment in Britain and West Germany in the 1982–83 period, the variation in question wording can provide useful information about what factors influence opinion on an issue.

The mass public is likely to have general orientations on or beliefs on things such as the United States, the Soviet Union, their foreign policies, their leaders, nuclear weapons, or terrorism, but less likely to have opinions, or at least well-developed opinions, on more specific issues. In many cases, there is also inconsistency between, on the one hand, the general orientations and, on the other, the opinions on specific issues directly related to those general orientations. For example, as Chapter 2 will discuss in detail, there is a gap within the West European publics between, on the one hand, widespread support for general principles such as NATO membership, deterrence, and having a strong defence and, on the other hand, limited support – or even broad opposition – on specific policies such as INF deployment, increasing defence spending, or NATO's flexible response strategy (when it was still NATO's strategy). Of course, another general orientation of many Western Europeans was a fear of nuclear weapons, which in this case may have overridden the general support for NATO and a strong defence. As another example, Chapter 8 shows that most Western Europeans strongly oppose international terrorism, but few favour their government responding forcefully with economic sanctions or military action against nations supporting terrorism.

The bottom line question is whether, and to what degree, public opinion influences the foreign policy of democratically-elected governments. Determining the impact of public opinion on foreign policy decisions is very difficult. Even if policy agrees with public opinion, there remain the questions which must be answered in each case in looking at causality:

1. was public opinion actually a factor in the government's foreign policy decision, or do they simply coincide without public opinion having been an influence?; and
2. if policy and public opinion agree, is that because public opinion was a key factor leading to the policy, or was it because political leaders mobilised public opinion to support the leaders' policies?

Most argue that public opinion has a very limited, at most indirect, impact on governmental foreign policy. Furthermore, the impact of public opinion may vary with a number of different factors, including the nature of the issue, the perception of policy-makers, and the international and domestic circumstances (Kegley and Wittkopf, 1982, pp. 287–91). Public opinion may act as a general constraint in placing broad limits on what foreign policy will be, but it is only very rarely the main reason, or even one of the principal reasons, for a foreign policy decision. At the same time, general orientations, such as anti-nuclear feelings, may have an impact on government leaders; the particular public revulsion against neutron weapons certainly was an important factor in complicating the possibilities of deployment in Western Europe. However, public opinion is just one part of the decision-maker's environment: it is one input into the equation, but in most cases not the most important one. INF deployment occurred despite the broad opposition to it in many of the basing countries. In addition, public opinion is often shaped, or 'led', by the elites, by the government leaders, and is usually mobilisable in a crisis by the leaders, as was the case for Margaret Thatcher during the Falklands War in 1982. At the same time, the greater division over defence issues within the British and West German elites in the early 1980s than in the previous two decades may have facilitated, or legitimised, the anti-INF protest movement. In sum, much remains uncertain about the public opinion-foreign policy relationship.

Beyond the issues raised here about the impact of public opinion on foreign policy, the US government was even one step further removed. In other words, the US government was not directly pressured by West European public opinion, but was instead concerned about the impact of public opinion on the policies of the West European governments. 'Public diplomacy' aimed at the West European mass publics was, therefore, considered by the USA as an important part of its overall diplomatic efforts to win the support of West European governments for US policies.

Despite the caveats presented in this introduction, the dimension of West European public opinion is certainly a key part of the history of US–Soviet relations, the changing image of the Soviet Union, the INF debate, and many other foreign policy issues in the 1980s. This book, using a larger amount of survey data covering a broader range of issues than any previous study, examines what is and is not true about West European public opinion; in other words, whether the American fears about West European opinion were justified or not. It also looks at how Western European public opinion has and has not changed through the historic events of the 1980s and, thereby, provides important insights into the Europe of the 1990s. Finally, West European opinion is often not monolithic, and this book will show the issues and images on which there was agreement and disagreement among the various West European publics.

2 NATO and Western Security

In the early 1990s, NATO faces an identity crisis as the sweeping changes in the Soviet Union and Eastern Europe have 'greatly reduced' the Soviet threat in Europe which was the Alliance's cement (US Department of Defense, 1990, p. 2). Clearly, the context of the security situation has been greatly altered from what was true for most of the 1980s and before, and NATO at more than 40 years of age is trying to re-define its role in the post-Cold War world. Among the events and changes which have brought about this need to re-define NATO are: the collapse of the Warsaw Pact; the reunification of Germany; the withdrawal of Soviet troops from much of Eastern Europe; the agreement for both sides to reduce conventional weapons and for both the USA and USSR to withdraw some of their troops from Europe; the clearly obsolete nature of NATO's 'flexible response doctrine' which led to its major revision in July 1990; and decisions by many NATO allies, including the USA, to cut their defence spending; and the dramatic upheaval in the Soviet Union in August and September 1991. The London NATO Summit in early July 1990, in effect, declared the end of the Cold War and began NATO on the process of re-defining itself with the goal of maintaining strong political and security ties between the USA and Western Europe even in the absence of a clear threat. The attitudes of West European publics in the 1980s on NATO, the US defence commitment to Western Europe, the Soviet threat, nuclear weapons, and other defence issues which are examined in this chapter inform us about the conflicts over Western security in the last decade of the Cold War. However, they also provide important insights about the public opinion environment in which NATO must re-shape its nature and role in the 1990s.

In the early 1980s, NATO also faced a major challenge – though a very different one. Many questioned the future of NATO in the early 1980s as many do in the early 1990s, but the test a decade ago was whether the Alliance would maintain its cohesion in the face of Soviet efforts to divide the USA and Western Europe. One can, of course, exaggerate the degree to which the 1980s were a departure from the past in terms of Alliance cohesion; there have been differences in

NATO since its beginning. But the NATO Alliance did face serious tensions in the 1980s. The battle over INF deployment was clearly one of the Alliance's most serious tests in its 40 year history and was the last great battle of the Cold War. After little public conflict over nuclear weapons from the early 1960s to the late 1970s, the issues of first neutron weapons and then INF deployment once again made nuclear weapons a public controversy in the late 1970s and early 1980s. The last time the peace movement was so vocal and active was in the late 1950s and early 1960s when the deployment of Thor missiles in Britain and Jupiters in Italy and Turkey occurred. Though the anti-INF demonstrators were only a small minority of Western Europeans, larger numbers in the mass publics – even majorities in many countries – held many of the same views about nuclear weapons.

Another factor which made the conflicts and tensions in the Alliance in the 1980s of great concern was that it was marked by a breakdown of elite consensus on security issues which, except for the fringes of the British Labour Party and the West German Social Democrats, had existed between the two major parties in both Britain and West Germany for two decades. In fact, in the 1980s, many within the British Labour Party and the West German Social Democratic Party opposed INF deployment and even questioned NATO and its reliance on nuclear weapons for deterrence.

Major NATO decisions in the Carter years – the 1977 agreement that all member countries would strive to achieve annual three per cent real increases in defence spending through to 1984, and the 1979 'dual track' decision to pursue INF deployment and arms control negotiations simultaneously – provided important challenges to NATO at the time that the Reagan Administration came into power and undertook a massive military build-up and a more confrontational course with the Soviet Union. The challenges of increasing defence spending in the wake of serious economic and budgetary problems as the USA called for Europe to share more of the burden; of bringing about INF deployment if no arms control agreement was achieved; and of maintaining Alliance solidarity as the USA and many of its West European Allies differed over the priority to be given to arms control, over how serious the Soviet threat was, and over East–West economic ties: all provided serious strains on the Alliance. In fact, the USA and its Western European allies differed over sanctions against the Soviet Union after its December 1979 invasion of Afghanistan, and even harsher disagreements occurred in the 1981–82 period over US efforts to enforce economic sanctions following the declaration of martial law in Poland. As Robert Tucker (1989, p. 17) argued, 'Reagan came to office at a time of considerable tension and disarray in the Western Alliance'. Within a period of two years, a period bounded by the invasion of Afghanistan and the imposition of military rule in Poland, almost every possible challenge to the cohesiveness of the Alliance had been made'.

The Reagan Administration emphasised the Soviet threat, undertook – certainly in its rhetoric – a confrontational policy toward the Soviet Union, wanted to negotiate from a position of strength, and pressured Western Europe to avoid any trade deals with the Soviets which could help strengthen them economically or militarily. The Soviet Union made a major propaganda effort to capitalise on West European concerns about the USA at a time when US credibility was decreasing following the Carter years and the fears about President Reagan. Many Western Europeans, both elites and publics, disagreed with the Reagan Administration's definition of the Soviet threat: a definition which put great emphasis on Soviet activities in the Third World and which called for NATO, against the wishes of many Europeans, to undertake more 'out-of-area' efforts. While the USA emphasised its concern over the Soviet threat, many West Europeans were worried that the cure, a military build-up and INF deployment, was worse than the disease.

The second half of the 1980s was marked by much better East–West relations, by the first US–Soviet Summit of the 1980s in November 1985 in Geneva, and by the INF Treaty to eliminate INF missiles rather than by the battle of deployment as in the first half of the 1980s. Many of the tensions within NATO itself in the 1980s were relieved by these changes in the international environment; at the same time, these changes in East–West relations have in turn led to NATO's identity crisis of the 1990s.

The West European publics, as discussed in the introductory chapter, are like publics in other democracies in that their interest in and knowledge of foreign policy and security issues are limited, meaning that there is at times inconsistency from one question to the next. Even in the first half of the 1980s, when security issues received great press attention, the publics did not usually consider them the most salient problems (Eichenberg, 1982; Rattinger, 1987). However, the large anti-INF, anti-nuclear demonstrations in the 1981–83 period gave the impression of a much broader public involvement in security issues than true for most of the postwar period and raised the spectre of widespread neutralism and pacifism, in other words, of calling into question the foundations of the NATO Alliance. Along with their concern about anti-Americanism discussed in Chapter 4, many American policymakers, elites, and media expressed their fears that neutralism and pacifism were growing in Western Europe.

As Flynn (1985) and Adler and Wertman (1981a; 1981b) argue and as the data presented in this chapter will show, there was in the 1980s a gap within the West European publics between the widespread support for general principles such as NATO membership, deterrence, and having a strong defence, and the much more limited support – or even broad opposition in some cases – on specific policies such as INF deployment, increasing defence spending, or NATO's flexible response strategy. This chapter and the next will together provide the full picture of West European public attitudes on security issues. This chapter focuses on NATO, neutrality, nuclear weapons, defence spending, and the US defence commitment to Western Europe and the next on INF deployment and the anti-INF movement.

PERCEPTIONS OF THE SOVIET THREAT

The definition of the nature and extent of the threat to the West from the Soviet Union and the Warsaw Pact is a major factor in the equation for Western leaders in making decisions on spending for defence, on deployment of nuclear weapons, and on NATO strategy. In the early 1980s, the Reagan Administration believed the Soviet threat to be extremely serious and multi-faceted given the growing Soviet capability to project its military power throughout the world; this Soviet threat was perceived to include support for conflicts in the Third World, conventional forces in Europe, theatre nuclear weapons in Europe and Asia, and strategic nuclear weapons. The issuance each year from 1981 of the glossy volume *Soviet Military Power*, which was full of graphics and pictures of Soviet weapons systems, the rhetoric of President Reagan and other US leaders, and the massive US military build-up in the first half of the 1980s all testify to the very deep concern of the Reagan Administration about the Soviet threat. Some West European leaders shared the American sense of the Soviet threat, but others did not. In fact, the broad foreign policy consensus among the major parties which had existed in Britain and West Germany for the previous two decades began to break down in the face of INF deployment and more confrontational American policies toward the Soviet Union.

A threat can be of many different kinds. To the USA the threat has been defined largely in terms of the Soviet Union, both a military threat and a threat of political intimidation. To many West Europeans, however, the sense of threat came in forms other than simply the Soviet Union. West Europeans were concerned about the threat from increased US–Soviet tensions in the first half of the 1980s, the threat from the military build-ups of *both* the USA and the Soviet Union, the threat of nuclear weapons, and the threat of one of the superpowers gaining superiority and acting on the basis of that superiority. The exaggerated press image of the USA led by a cowboy run wild who pushed confrontation with the Soviet Union created fears in Western Europe of an increased risk of war. These fears were exacerbated by the loose talk and misstatements by President Reagan and other US officials about concepts such as 'limited nuclear war' and 'war-fighting' – thereby leaving the impression of 'a casual attitude toward nuclear weapons' (Tucker, 1989, p. 23) and of a USA which considered limited nuclear war in Europe a possibility (Sigal, 1984, p. 67; Joffe, 1987, p. 16).

Majorities in five of six countries surveyed in late 1981/early 1982 believed the goal of both the USA and the USSR to be military superiority over the other superpower; only in West Germany, where a majority said this of the USSR, but opinion was evenly divided on the US goal, was this perception not held about *both* superpowers. This is clearly a negative evaluation of the security policies of both superpowers. In fact, while one might expect West European publics – as citizens of countries who are members of the NATO Alliance – to prefer that the USA (or NATO) have superiority, this has not been the view of Western Europeans for more than twenty years. In 1958, majorities in Britain, France, and West Germany still wanted the USA to be ahead, but this had changed somewhat by 1964, when only the Germans preferred US superiority. Since 1971, however, all surveys in West European countries have consistently found a majority preference for the two superpowers to be about equal in military strength. By 1988 no more than 17 per cent in any of the six countries surveyed (the four largest plus Belgium and the Netherlands) wanted NATO to be ahead. The preference for equality rather than US superiority is undoubtedly a feeling that the chances of war are reduced when both sides are about equal.[1]

Fears of a world war within the next decade peaked among the West European public in the early 1980s, declined by the mid-1980s, and dropped further to a very low level in the late 1980s. War fears were greatest in the 1980–83 period, the time of the most intense confrontation between the USA and the USSR since the era of detente began in the early 1970s, and were lowest in the late 1980s as the post-Cold War era began. Asked to rate the chances of a world war over the next ten years on a scale ranging from 0, no danger of war, to 100, war certain, the proportion in ten European countries saying there was a 50–50 or greater chance of war was 23 per cent in 1977 and peaked at 37 per cent in Fall 1981. This number gradually dropped to 21 per cent by Fall 1985 and then fell further to only 11 per cent by Fall 1989.[2] Parallel to these findings, the number saying there was *no* danger of war dropped from 31 per cent in 1977 to 20 per cent in 1981. It then slowly rose to the range of 31 to 35 per cent in the 1984 to 1987 period and climbed to 42 per cent in 1988 and 51 per cent in 1989. Findings for West Germany were the most dramatic of all; in fact, the West Germans, among the most fearful of war in the early 1980s, were among the the least fearful of war by the late 1980s. In West Germany, the number seeing *no* danger of war went from 30 per cent in 1971 to 21 per cent in 1977 to 13 per cent in 1981 before gradually rising to 30 per cent by 1987 and then jumping massively to 50 per cent in 1988 and 63 per cent by Fall 1989.[3]

While the general mood showed many with some fears of war in the early 1980s, more specific questions indicated that – little different from the results of surveys in the 1950s or 1960s – in the 1980s very few thought a Soviet attack on Western Europe likely within the next five years. In surveys in Belgium, Britain, Denmark, France, Italy, the Netherlands, and West Germany in the 1981–83 period, the proportion thinking a Soviet attack fairly or very likely ranged from only seven to 23 per cent in these countries; in West Germany, the key country in NATO's central front, only between 9 and 15 per cent believed an attack likely.[4] While few thought an attack likely, more in the early 1980s expressed at least a fair amount of concern over a Soviet attack within five years; in October 1981, between 26 per cent in Norway and 56 per cent in France were either fairly or very concerned. However, matching the small numbers considering an attack likely, few were *very* concerned – ranging from 6 per cent in Norway to 22 per cent in France and 23 per cent in Britain. By 1985, even the concern over a Soviet attack had dropped in all countries, with no more than a third in any country fairly concerned and no more than 13 per cent *very* concerned.[5] Furthermore, in a 1987 survey, few in the four major Western European countries thought the Soviet troops stationed in Eastern Europe were maintained there by the Soviets because of aggressive intentions toward Western Europe; in other words, the Soviet troops in Eastern Europe were generally not seen as a threat by Western Europeans. Specifically, only 23 to 29 per cent in these four countries thought that the major reason for the Soviets stationing their troops there was either to dominate Western Europe ultimately or to intimidate it politically. The most commonly selected purposes of the troops were to control East Europe or to prevent an attack against the USSR.[6]

Western Europeans have been asked to compare the overall military strength and the conventional strength of East and West, sometimes in terms of only the USA and the USSR, other times in terms of the USA and its NATO allies compared to the Soviet Union and its Warsaw Pact allies. Overall, views on the East–West balance have been uninformed and have varied over time and among countries. In the early 1980s, when the US engaged in a massive military build-up to counter what it argued was a substantial Soviet lead, there was no broad consensus among West European publics that the Soviet Union was ahead in overall military strength. In five surveys conducted in seven countries in 1981 and 1982, only in Britain (in all surveys) and in West Germany (in most surveys) was it the clearly prevailing view that the USSR was ahead; with the exception of one survey in Britain, this was a plurality rather than majority view. In Belgium, France, Italy, the Netherlands, and Norway, though more saw the USSR than the USA as ahead, the number seeing the USSR as ahead was in the range of between only one in five and one in three; in these five countries, the largest number in most surveys saw the USA and the USSR as equal in total military strength. Furthermore, in these seven countries few (ranging from 15 to 22 per cent in Britain and West Germany and from only two to nine per cent in the other five countries) saw the USSR as *considerably* ahead. In any case, the US military build-up in the first half of the 1980s did clearly have an impact on West European perceptions. By 1985 the prevailing view in all seven countries surveyed was that the two were about equal in total military strength, with opinion roughly divided over who was ahead among those not seeing the two as equal.[7]

By the early 1980s, the NATO governments and virtually all independent analysts had repeatedly argued for more than three decades that the NATO allies were considerably behind the Soviet Union and its Warsaw Pact allies in the conventional balance, i.e., soldiers, tanks, planes, etc. Even on this, however, there was no consensus among Western European publics. While a majority in

Britain (57 per cent) and large pluralities in Norway (44 per cent) and West Germany (42 per cent) in an October 1981 survey did see the USSR as ahead of the USA in conventional strength in Europe, this was not the clearly prevailing view in the four other countries surveyed. In Belgium, France and the Netherlands, more saw the USSR than the USA as ahead, but at least as many saw the two as equal. In Italy, opinion was roughly divided among the three views. Altogether in these four countries between 29 and 37 per cent considered the USSR to be ahead. By July 1988, there was no clear sense among the West European publics that the Soviet Union and its Warsaw Pact allies were ahead in conventional forces; only in Britain did a clear plurality consider the USSR ahead.[8]

The USA also stressed the threat of Soviet political intimidation in the early 1980s. This 'Finlandisation', that the Soviets would pressure the Western Europeans to take positions on foreign policy and security issues against the interests of Western Europe, was argued to be a Soviet effort to divide the USA and Western Europe and damage, or even destroy, the NATO Alliance. However, throughout the 1980s, parallel to findings on the military threat, very few Western Europeans – ranging from 5 to 17 per cent in five countries surveyed in 1981, from 8 to 19 per cent in seven countries surveyed in 1984, and from 4 to 25 per cent in 14 countries surveyed in 1987 – were *very* concerned about Soviet political intimidation.[9] Considering both those very and fairly concerned, concern over Soviet political intimidation was not the prevailing view in most countries. In 1981, between 25 per cent in the Netherlands and 43 per cent in Britain were at least fairly concerned that the Soviet Union would pressure their country into adopting policies against their country's interest; in May 1984, between 32 and 45 per cent were at least fairly concerned in the seven countries surveyed. Overall, in surveys between 1981 and 1987, the proportion at least fairly concerned over Soviet pressure ranged from 35 to 45 per cent in Britain, from 20 to 47 per cent in France, from 23 to 39 per cent in Italy, and from 11 to 44 per cent in West Germany. In all four cases, the lowest level of concern was registered in Fall 1987.

Underlining how limited West European fears of Soviet political intimidation were, in both 1985 and 1987 surveys more people in many Western European countries expressed concern that the USA would pressure their country into adopting policies against its interests than expressed such concerns about the Soviets. In a June 1985 survey, more in all six countries surveyed named the USA rather than the USSR in an open-ended question when asked which country or countries they thought most likely to pressure their own into adopting policies against its interests.[10] As Table 2.1 shows, in all 11 EC countries surveyed in April 1987, more or about as many were at least fairly concerned about US pressure as were concerned about Soviet pressure. Particularly striking are the results in Britain, where about 20 per cent more were concerned about US pressures.

At the same time, one should not exaggerate the level of concern over US pressure. While majorities in two countries (Britain and Greece) were at least fairly concerned over US pressure, this was not the prevailing view in the other nine countries surveyed; in four countries (France, Italy, the Netherlands, and Spain) opinion was roughly divided, while concern over the USA was the minority view of between 30 and 38 per cent in the remaining five (see Table 2.1). The higher level of concern over US than Soviet pressure found in many countries is largely because their country has much closer, much busier, more interdependent relations with the United States than with the Soviet Union. It parallels the finding, reported in Chapter 4, that many Western Europeans, while considering their country's bilateral relations with the USA to be good, see the relationship as unequal and think that the USA expects them to give into American wishes on matters of mutual concern.

In sum, in the 1980s few Western Europeans were greatly concerned about either a Soviet military threat or Soviet political intimidation. There was also no broad consensus in Western Europe that the Soviet Union was ahead in total military strength. In other words, the West European publics predominantly did not share the same sense of a Soviet threat that was the basis of the Reagan Administration's foreign and defence policies, as well as of its public diplomacy efforts, in the first half of the 1980s. As Leon Sigal (1984, p. 66) argues, 'American hyperbole about the magnitude and imminence of that threat was greeted with incredulity in much of Europe, where exposure to Soviet power has been a constant since World War II'.

NEUTRALISM

Neutralism is an oft-used word among journalists, politicians, and other observers of Western Europe and NATO. This was particularly true in the first half of the 1980s, when American policymakers and the American mass media frequently expressed concern that anti-Americanism, neutralism, and pacifism were sweeping Western

Table 2.1 Concern over Soviet and US political pressure on their country, April 1987

	Belgium	Britain	Denmark	France	Greece	Ireland	Italy	The Netherlands	Portugal	Spain	West Germany
Concern over Soviet pressure:											
Very/fairly concerned	28	43	23	47	52	34	33	29	33	30	21
Little/not at all concerned	59	53	66	45	35	54	56	63	42	51	76
Concern over US pressure:											
Very/fairly concerned	38	65	34	43	70	38	43	46	30	42	30
Little/not at all concerned	51	31	57	49	18	51	46	48	47	40	67

Question: How concerned are you that the (Soviet Union) (United States) will pressure (Survey Country) into adopting policies which are against the interests of our country – very concerned, fairly concerned, not very concerned, or not at all concerned?

Source: April 1987 Eurobarometer.

Europe. The term neutralism is, however, a rather vague one which, depending on who is speaking or writing, can be used to mean a number of different things; it was clearly overused and misused in the early 1980s. In the broadest sense, it is those who simply do not want their country to get involved in disputes between the United States and the Soviet Union, without necessarily opposing membership in NATO or wanting to remain neutral in the case of military conflict. In the most narrow sense, it is those who do not want their country to be part of any military alliance. Today, except in this more narrow military sense, the term neutralism is largely a concept of the past. As Robert E. Hunter (1990, p. 64) argues 'politically, economically, and culturally, the term neutrality has been drained of any practical meaning, save as an effort to preserve outdated modes of thinking and acting'.

Neutralism in the broadest sense was the view of many West Europeans in the 1980s, as surveys at both the beginning and the end of the Reagan era show. In July 1981, majorities in Britain, France, Italy, and the Netherlands preferred that their government 'do everything possible to stay out of disputes between the United States and the USSR' rather than 'generally side with the USA' in these disputes; only in West Germany, where opinion was divided, was neutrality not the prevailing view. In July 1988, majorities ranging from 59 to 71 per cent in the six countries surveyed (Belgium, Britain, France, Italy, The Netherlands, and West Germany) agreed with the following statement: 'Our country should remain strictly neutral in political disputes between the Soviet Union and the United States'. Between 24 per cent in West Germany and 42 per cent in Britain strongly agreed with this statement.[11] This type of neutralism is an expression of a general mood of wishing to avoid conflicts which could be harmful to their country; it may also be an expression of frequent disagreement with American foreign policy, for example, on East–West trade or on sanctions for Soviet behaviour in Afghanistan or the martial law in Poland. However, it does not speak to the fundamental security interests represented by the NATO Alliance nor does it predict the view of West European publics in specific disputes.

NATO MEMBERSHIP

Throughout the 1980s, NATO membership was broadly supported by the publics in every NATO country except Greece and Spain.[12] Support for NATO membership has remained widespread in most countries despite the strong challenges to NATO cohesion in the first half of the 1980s and NATO's identity crisis in the late 1980s/early 1990s following the major changes in Eastern Europe and the Soviet Union. Furthermore, despite these events, the level of support for NATO in the four largest countries (Britain, France, Italy, and West Germany) during the 1980s was at least as high as in previous decades; in these four countries perceived essentiality of NATO has varied up and down within the same range in the 1980s as it did in the 1967–1979 period.[13] Similarly, trend data reported elsewhere suggest that in at least three other countries (Denmark, the Netherlands, and Norway) the level of support for NATO was as high or higher in the 1980s as it was in the 1960s and 1970s.[14]

Neutralism in the narrow sense, that is, opposing a military alliance with the United States, is clearly a minority view in most NATO countries. In the 1980s, as Table 2.2 shows, support for neutrality was never higher than 29 per cent in Britain, 20 per cent in West Germany, and 25 per cent in the Netherlands; in Italy, where the large Communist electorate generally prefers neutrality despite the party's official support for NATO, support for neutralism varied between 28 and 42 per cent. Throughout the 1980s, large majorities in Britain and West Germany, and majorities or large pluralities in Italy preferred NATO to neutrality. In France, surveys since April 1982 have shown majority support for remaining in the Atlantic Alliance. Majorities in Belgium, Denmark, and the Netherlands also preferred NATO to neutrality, as have the plurality in Portugal (where the level of no opinion responses is very high). Greece and Spain, however, differ from the general pattern of predominant support for NATO over neutrality. In Greece, a 46 per cent to 30 per cent plurality wanted neutrality in October 1984, but, more recently, in April 1987, opinion was evenly divided. Only in Spain, where neutrality was the view of the majority in 1984 and of a plurality in 1987, has prevailing opinion consistently opposed membership. Nevertheless, in 1986 the Spanish, by a margin of 53 per cent to 40 per cent (with 7 per cent abstaining) voted to stay in NATO. An example of how a leader can mobilise public opinion, this support came after the strong endorsement of NATO membership by Socialist Prime Minister Felipe Gonzalez and the linkage of support for membership to the removal of some American bases.

Western European publics were also asked a variety of questions throughout the 1980s which allowed them to choose among a number of different options for a defence alliance. All of these questions included at least three options – NATO as currently structured, a

Europeanised Alliance without the USA, and no defence alliance – and others also included the option of NATO with a separate Western European command within it. Majorities in Belgium, Britain, Denmark, the Netherlands, Norway, and West Germany have consistently supported continuing a military alliance including the USA over a solely Western European alliance without the USA or no defence alliance. In France and Italy, majorities or large pluralities have supported an alliance with the United States over the alternatives. The Spanish once again stand out, with only 22 per cent in late 1989 preferring NATO over a solely European alliance or no defence alliance at all.[15]

Results on the perceived essentiality of NATO closely match those for the preference between NATO and neutrality. Throughout the 1980s, as Table 2.3 shows, NATO was viewed as essential to their country's security by majorities in Belgium, Britain, Denmark, the Netherlands, Norway, and West Germany. In Italy, majorities between 1981 and 1987 and pluralities in 1988 and 1989 called NATO essential. In France, pluralities considered NATO essential. Data for three countries is available only for 1988 and 1989: Portugal, in which pluralities consider NATO essential, and Greece and Spain, the two countries out of NATO's 16 in which NATO essentiality does not clearly prevail. In Greece, opinion was divided in both 1988 and 1989, while in Spain, NATO's newest member, large pluralities in both surveys saw NATO as not being essential. In the eight countries with trend data from 1984 or before, support for NATO remained as widespread or almost as widespread in Fall 1989 as earlier in the decade. In most Western European countries, only limited minorities thought NATO was no longer essential; in fact, apart from Greece and Spain, the number calling NATO no longer essential in Fall 1989 ranged from 17 to 30 per cent (see Table 2.3).

Other questions about NATO asked in the 1988–89 period produced largely the same results as the essentiality and NATO/neutrality questions. In July 1989 publics in eight of 10 Western European countries predominantly said that the NATO Alliance should be maintained rather than that it is not necessary anymore; only the Spanish, where opinion was divided, and the Portuguese, where most of those answering supported NATO but fully two-thirds had no opinion, were exceptions (see Table 2.4). Data from Luxembourg and Turkey, not included in the other surveys reported in this section, show broad majority support for NATO in Luxembourg and a large plurality in Turkey considering NATO necessary.

Table 2.2 Support for NATO versus neutrality, 1981–7 (per cent)

	Belgium		Britain				Greece		Portugal	
	Oct. 1984	Apr. 1987	Mar. 1981	Jul. 1981	Feb. 1982	Apr. 1982	Jul. 1983	Apr. 1987	Oct. 1984	Apr. 1987	Oct. 1984	Apr. 1987
NATO	67	57	67	59	63	73	72	74	30	36	29	48
Neutrality	18	26	20	29	25	21	19	16	46	37	15	11
Don't know	15	17	12	12	12	6	8	10	24	28	57	41
Total	100	100	99	100	100	100	99	100	100	101	101	100

	The Netherlands				Italy			Spain		West Germany			
	Mar. 1981	Jul. 1981	Oct. 1984	Apr. 1987	Mar. 1981	Jul. 1981	Apr. 1982	Jul. 1983	Oct. 1984	Apr. 1987	Jan. 1982	Feb. 1982	Apr. 1982	Jul. 1981	Mar. 1981
NATO	62	56	77	70	49	49	59	63	57	60	49				
Neutrality	17	25	17	20	42	34	28	35	30	36					
Don't know	21	18	7	10	8	7	9	9	9	15					
Total	100	99	101	100	99	100	100	101	99						

NATO	20	28	67	64	65	70	72	70	77	71
Neutrality	56	43	14	18	17	13	18	20	13	18
Don't know	24	29	19	19	17	17	10	10	10	12
Total	100	100	100	101	99	100	100	100	100	101

France[a]

	Mar. 1981	Feb. 1982	Apr. 1982	Oct. 1984	Apr. 1987
Atlantic Alliance	45	46	62	60	63
Neutrality	40	20	29	17	17
Don't know	15	34	10	23	20
Total	100	100	101	100	100

[a] The question for France was: All things considered, do you think it would be better for France to belong to the Atlantic Alliance, or would it be better for us to get out of the Atlantic Alliance and be neutral?

Question: Except in France, the question was: All things considered, do you think it is better for (Survey Country) to belong to NATO, that is, the North Atlantic Treaty Organization, or would it be better for us to get out of NATO and become a neutral country[a]

In July 1981, the question was slightly different: All things considered, do you think it is better for (Survey Country) to belong to NATO, that is, the Western Defence Alliance, or would it be better for us to get out of NATO and become a neutral country?

Sources: March 1981 Security Survey, July 1981 Security Survey, January 1982 West German Security Survey, February 1982 Poland–INF Survey, April 1982 Versailles Economic Summit Survey, July–August 1983 Intensive INF Survey, October–November 1984 Eurobarometer, April 1987 Eurobarometer.

Table 2.3 Perceived essentiality of NATO, 1981–89 (per cent)

	Belgium			Britain							
	May 1984	Oct. 1988	Oct 1989	Mar. 1981	Jul. 1982	Jul. 1983	May 1984	Feb. 1987	Sep. 1987	Oct. 1988	Oct 1989
Essential	60	66	55	70	65	72	76	72	72	72	67
No longer essential	20	22	30	15	25	16	12	17	16	17	17
Don't know	20	12	14	15	10	12	13	12	12	11	16
Total	100	100	99	100	100	100	101	101	100	100	100

	Denmark			France[a]					Greece	
	May 1984	Oct. 1987	Oct. 1988	Oct. 1989	Jul. 1982	Feb. 1987	Sep. 1987	Oct. 1988	Oct. 1989	Oct. 1988	Oct. 1989
Essential	63	61	70	68	34	49	48	58	41	36	39
No longer essential	19	22	23	24	26	28	19	22	28	35	36
Don't know	18	16	7	8	40	24	32	20	31	29	25
Total	100	99	100	100	100	101	99	100	100	100	100

	Italy						The Netherlands			
	Mar. 1981	Jul. 1982	Jul. 1983	May 1984	Feb. 1987	Sep. 1987	Oct. 1988	Oct. 1989	Mar. 1981	Jul. 1982	May 1984	Oct. 1988	Oct. 1989
Essential	62	55	61	63	58	65	53	48	62	67	58	64	58
No longer essential	27	31	26	24	29	23	31	28	15	16	20	25	30
Don't know	12	14	13	14	13	12	16	26	23	17	21	11	12
Total	101	100	100	101	100	100	100	100	100	100	99	100	100

	Norway			Portugal			Spain	
	Mar. 1981	May 1984	Oct. 1987	Oct. 1988	Oct. 1989	Oct. 1988	Oct. 1989
Essential	66	73	71	44	37	19	24
No longer essential	21	15	14	21	17	53	45
Don't know	13	13	15	35	46	28	31
Total	100	101	100	100	100	100	100

	West Germany							
	Mar. 1981	Jul. 1982	Jul. 1983	May 1984	Feb. 1987	Sep. 1987	Oct. 1988	Oct. 1989
Essential	62	66	86	87	71	70	76	59
No longer essential	20	18	12	10	11	15	13	24
Don't know	19	16	2	3	17	15	12	16
Total	101	100	100	100	99	100	100	99

[a] In France the question referred to the 'Atlantic Alliance'.

Question: Some people say that NATO is still essential to our country's security. Others say that it is no longer essential. Which of these views is closer to your own? In the September and October 1987 surveys, the word 'necessary' was used rather than 'essential'.

Sources: March 1981 Security Survey, July 1982 Security Survey, July–August 1983 INF Intensive Survey, May–June 1984 Security Survey, February 1987 Security Survey, September 1987 Security Survey, October 1987 Scandinavian Survey, October 1988 Eurobarometer, and, for the October 1989 results, *Eurobarometer*, No. 32 (December 1989), p. A41.

Table 2.4 Perceived necessity of NATO, July 1989

	Belgium	Britain	Denmark	Italy	Luxembourg	The Netherlands	Portugal	Spain	Turkey	West Germany
NATO should be kept	69	71	43	58	69	81	26	31	50	63
NATO not necessary	13	15	13	18	11	15	9	34	14	13
Don't know	18	14	45	25	21	4	65	36	36	24
Total	100	100	101	101	101	100	100	101	100	100

Question: Do you think the NATO Alliance should be maintained, or is the Alliance not necessary any more?
Source: Gallup International Survey.

Similarly, in an October 1989 survey, majorities in Belgium, Britain, Denmark, Italy, the Netherlands, and West Germany and pluralities in France and Portugal had a favourable opinion of NATO.[16] However, in France 40 per cent and in Portugal 50 per cent had no opinion or had not heard enough to say. Only from 8 to 22 per cent in these eight countries had an unfavourable opinion of NATO. Greece and Spain were again the exceptions; in Greece, as in other questions asked in the late 1980s, opinion on NATO was divided (with 39 per cent having a favourable opinion and 39 per cent an unfavourable one), while in Spain more had an unfavourable (40 per cent) than favourable (33 per cent) opinion. Though positive attitudes toward NATO were broadly held in most NATO member countries in October 1989, many of those with positive attitudes did not hold these views strongly. Apart from Britain, where 25 per cent had a *very* favourable opinion, and Denmark, where 28 per cent did, only between 7 and 16 per cent had a *very* favourable opinion of NATO.

Most West German proponents of reunification of the two Germanys appeared unwilling to give up NATO membership even if this would block reunification, which it ultimately did not. In Fall 1989, 78 per cent in West Germany supported reunification; among these, only one-quarter expressed their willingness to leave NATO even if this were a precondition for reunification.[17] Furthermore, in March 1990, only 23 per cent of West Germans wanted their country to leave NATO after reunification; 76 per cent supported NATO membership, though about two-thirds of these NATO supporters did not want NATO troops in the area of what was then East Germany after reunification. Support for NATO was less widespread, but nevertheless clearly the prevailing viewpoint, in two other surveys in 1990. In a June 1990 survey, after an introduction mentioning NATO, 51 per cent thought 'we must remain in a strong alliance so that our security will not be endangered'; 34 per cent believed: 'The military alliances are crumbling and will soon be unimportant. Therefore, Germany should be made neutral'.[18] In an April 1990 survey, 56 per cent of West Germans felt that peace could be guaranteed solely by NATO, while only 22 per cent thought that peace could be guaranteed only by the neutrality of West Europe without NATO. These April 1990 numbers were virtually unchanged from October 1986 and November 1989 findings (Veen, 1990). All of these results suggest that, however the question is phrased, neutrality continues to be the minority viewpoint of West Germans in the early 1990s.

Throughout the 1980s, NATO membership was broadly supported by the publics in most NATO countries, and neutralism and other alternatives to NATO were largely rejected. In most NATO countries, the publics generally hold favourable opinions of NATO and consider NATO essential to their security. The Greeks and Spanish are the two exceptions to these findings. As NATO re-defines itself in the early 1990s, support for a Western European military alliance with the United States continues to be widespread, though, at the same time, many of those supporting NATO do not hold strongly favourable views of it. During the Persian Gulf conflict, public support for NATO in Europe did not weaken, and, in fact, actually increased somewhat in a number of West European countries. According to the January 1991 USIA survey on the Persian Gulf, public backing for the US–West European Alliance remained solid during the first international crisis of the post-Cold War era.

THE AMERICAN FACTOR IN WEST EUROPEAN DEFENCE

Throughout the 1980s, most Western European NATO publics supported their country's NATO membership and, therefore, a military alliance with the United States. In most countries neutrality or other alternative defence arrangements not involving the USA were widely rejected. In the four largest countries, where this question was asked, the USA was generally considered the leader of NATO. The Soviet efforts to exploit the battle over INF deployment to divide the Alliance – to drive a wedge between the USA and its Western European allies – did not succeed at the level of governments and, as the data reported above show, did not succeed among the publics in Western Europe. In sum, the United States was viewed as a major part of the defence equation by most Western European publics.

The question remains about how much confidence the Western European publics actually have in the US commitment, which has existed under the NATO Treaty since 1949, to come to their aid if attacked and how much the West European publics want US bases and soldiers stationed on their soil as a tangible evidence of this United States defence commitment.

Western Europeans generally have confidence in the US defence commitment to them, though when the risk of destruction of US cities is included in the question this confidence drops somewhat. In a July 1988 survey in six European countries (see Table 2.5) considerably

Table 2.5 Country which would come to their aid in case of attack, July 1988

	Belgium	Britain	France	Italy	The Netherlands	West Germany
USA	41	75	58	61	39	53
2nd Most Often Named	10 (Fr)	12 (Fr)	21 (Brit)	4 (Fr)	13 (Brit)	18 (Fr)

Question: If our country were attacked with military force, which country, if any, do you think would come to our aid?
Source: July 1988 Security Survey.

more named the USA than any other country in an open-ended question asking 'if our country were attacked with military force, which country, if any, do you think would come to our aid'. In surveys in 1981 and again in the 1987–89 period, majorities in the four largest countries, the Netherlands and Norway expressed at least a fair amount of confidence 'that the United States would do whatever was necessary to defend our country in case of a Soviet attack'. In Belgium, a majority likewise expressed a fair amount of confidence in July 1988. Only the Danes, asked this question in October 1987, did not predominantly have such confidence in the US defence commitment. In the 1980s, confidence ranged from 60 to 74 per cent in Britain, from 58 to 78 per cent in France, from 65 to 77 per cent in Italy, and from 53 to 67 per cent in West Germany.[19] Looking at the longer trend going back to 1968, the publics in the four largest countries have always predominantly had at least a fair amount of confidence in the US defence commitment (Adler and Wertman, 1981a). In Britain and Italy, this confidence was always the majority view; in France and West Germany, this confidence fell slightly below the majority level only once: in a May 1975 survey immediately after the collapse of South Vietnam and the chaotic televised scenes of US helicopters ferrying thousands of people to US ships off the Vietnamese coast.

When the possible consequences to the USA are added into the equation, however, confidence in the United States drops. In fact, a different version of this confidence in the US defence commitment question, used in the July 1981–February 1987 period, asked about the degree of confidence 'that the USA would do whatever is necessary to defend our country, *even if this would risk the destruction of US cities*'. Since this version and the version without this phrase were never asked in the same survey, it is impossible to judge the exact impact of this phrase. However, comparing the most proximate pairs (March 1981 with July 1981 and February 1987 with September 1987) in which the two different questions were asked in the four largest countries, suggests that, depending on the country and the particular events of the time, this phrase could have as little an impact as 10 per cent and as much as 30 per cent in the level of confidence.[20] With the phrase about the risk of destruction of US cities included, little or no confidence prevailed five of eight times in West Germany and three of eight times in Britain; in Italy, it prevailed only once and in France no times. Little or no confidence never predominated in these countries with the version not including this phrase. The loose talk at times by President Reagan and other Administration officials, which included terms like 'theatre' nuclear weapons and somehow seemed to be suggesting that a war could be fought in Europe, may have also affected European confidence between mid-1981 and early 1987. It is very possible that, even without this phrase, confidence in the US defence commitment would have reached all-time lows in the mid-1980s, but clearly the idea of American cities suffering destruction directly when included in the question caused some West Europeans to express greater doubts about the US reliability as an ally.

As the concrete evidence of the US defence commitment to Western Europe and contribution to NATO's ability to deter an attack, the US military presence in Western Europe throughout the 1980s totalled over 300,000 soldiers as well as sizeable numbers of American planes, helicopters, tanks, tactical nuclear weapons, and other equipment. This does not, of course, count the American ships constantly patrolling off European coasts nor the substantial amounts of pre-positioned equipment stored in Europe ready for use by American divisions stationed in the USA but committed to fighting in Europe in the case of war. In May 1984, as Table 2.6 shows, majorities or large pluralities in all seven countries surveyed preferred keeping the number of US troops at least as high as its then current level. In other words, even though NATO had just gone through a major test over INF deployment which had resulted in initial stationing of some INF missiles in Britain, Italy, and West Germany despite substantial public opposition, the seven publics surveyed, including these three, did not want to see American troops withdrawn from Europe or even reduced in number.

Table 2.6 Support for American troops in Western Europe, May–June 1984 (per cent)

	Belgium	Britain	Denmark	Italy	Norway	The Netherlands	West Germany
US troops should be:							
Increased	9	7	3	10	7	4	4
Left at present level	44	58	49	44	55	51	62
Decreased	18	13	14	15	12	13	17
Withdrawn	12	12	14	23	16	12	7
Don't know	16	9	20	8	16	20	10
Total	99	99	100	100	100	100	100

Question: Do you think the number of American troops now stationed in Europe should be increased, left at their present level, decreased, or withdrawn completely?

Source: May–June 1984 Security Survey.

In the 1987–88 period, most, though not all, of the eleven NATO publics surveyed still predominantly considered the US military presence in Western Europe as necessary to their country's security, though many of the supporters thought this presence only 'somewhat' necessary.[21] (See Table 2.7 for October 1988 results in ten countries.) The publics in the four largest countries were asked about the US military presence four times altogether between Spring 1987 and Fall 1988. In all four surveys, the British, French, and West Germans predominantly considered the US military presence in West Europe necessary; opinion is Italy was less consistent, with pluralities in two surveys considering the US military presence necessary, opinion divided in one survey, and a plurality in the fourth considering US troops not necessary. Most of the other seven NATO publics surveyed either considered the American military presence necessary or were at worst divided. However, despite the support in most countries for the US military presence in West Europe, in October 1988, only between 5 and 27 per cent in the 10 NATO countries surveyed *strongly* regarded it as necessary. As with NATO membership, the two publics that stand out are the Greeks and the Spanish; in both the April 1987 and October 1988 surveys, these two publics predominantly considered the US military presence in Europe as *not* necessary. Strikingly, 45 per cent in Spain and 31 per cent in Greece *strongly* felt this way.

By the 1989–90 period, the security situation had changed greatly – with the United States reaching an agreement with the Soviets for a reduction of over 10 per cent in US troops in Europe, many in the US Congress arguing for even deeper cuts in response to budgetary pressures, and the USA willing to at least temporarily re-deploy its tank divisions from Western Europe to the Persian Gulf. In response to these changes in the post-Cold War world, larger numbers of Western Europeans are willing to see US troops reduced or even withdrawn completely. Most important are the findings for West Germany, where about two-thirds of the American ground forces in Europe are stationed. As Table 2.8 shows, majorities or near majorities in ten surveys in West Germany between 1962 and 1986 consistently said they would regret a withdrawal of US troops from Europe. However, in 1988, for the first time since 1957, opinion was divided on whether such a withdrawal would be welcomed or regrettable, and by late 1989 a plurality (38 per cent) said they would welcome it. In Britain, where surveys in 1981 and 1984 showed 29 per cent and 25 per cent respectively in favour of a decrease, or withdrawal of US troops, 40 per cent in January 1990 favoured a decrease, though 51 per cent of

Table 2.7 Necessity of US military presence in Western Europe, October 1988 (per cent)

	Belgium	Britain	Denmark	France	Greece	Ireland	Italy	The Netherlands	Portugal	Spain	West Germany
Strongly necessary	27	26	24	24	14	16	15	20	20	5	18
Somewhat necessary	36	34	36	31	20	40	32	28	36	14	47
Subtotal	63	60	60	55	34	56	47	48	56	19	65
Somewhat unnecessary	22	18	23	19	15	19	24	27	10	15	19
Strongly unnecessary	8	15	10	15	31	10	23	18	6	45	9
Subtotal	30	33	33	34	46	29	47	45	16	60	28
Don't know	7	8	8	11	20	14	7	8	28	21	7
Total	100	101	101	100	100	99	100	101	100	100	100

Question: As you may know, the United States maintains a substantial military presence in Western Europe. In your opinion, is this US military presence necessary in order to preserve peace in Europe, or is it not necessary? Do you feel that way strongly or somewhat?

Source: October 1988 Eurobarometer.

Table 2.8 West German attitudes on withdrawal of US troops from Western Europe, 1956–89 (per cent)

	1956	1957	1962	1970	1973	1976	1978	1979	1981	1982	1984	1986	1988	1989
Welcome	51	34	12	22	23	15	17	11	17	21	17	22	37	38
Regret	22	34	59	51	45	55	57	60	59	55	59	51	38	30
Don't know	27	32	29	27	32	30	26	29	24	24	24	28	25	32
Total	100	100	100	100	100	100	100	100	100	100	100	101	100	100

Question: If you read in the newspaper tomorrow that the Americans were withdrawing all of their troops from Europe, would you welcome it or regret it?

Sources: The 1956–88 data are contained in a report by Sinus Institute reporting a 1988 study commissioned by the Friedrich-Ebert-Stiftung and *Stern* magazine. The November 1989 data are from a survey by Allensbach Institute.

the British still wanted the American forces in Europe to remain at their present level.[22] Prior to the sweeping changes in Eastern Europe and the Soviet Union in the late 1980s, the US military presence in Western Europe was predominantly supported by most NATO publics. The most recent data suggest, however, that this support is much softer in the early 1990s. Unilateral American withdrawals or sizeable reductions, though still not favoured by a majority in most European countries in 1991, would draw substantially more support than in the 1980s. Bilateral US–Soviet withdrawals resulting from an agreement between the two superpowers would probably receive the support of large majorities in Western Europe. For example, in the same 1988 survey in which 37 per cent of West Germans said they would welcome the unilateral withdrawal of US troops, 76 per cent said they would welcome a US withdrawal if the Soviets at the same time withdrew their troops from East Germany, Poland, and Czechoslovakia.[23]

NATO AND NUCLEAR WEAPONS

With the battles over neutron weapons and then, more importantly, INF deployment; the resurgence of the anti-nuclear movement in Western Europe; the tensions between the United States and the Soviet Union; and the concern over loose talk by President Reagan and other top US officials which suggested 'a certain carelessness about the dangers of the nuclear age' (Mandelbaum, 1984), nuclear weapons once again became an important political issue in Europe in the first half of the 1980s. Chapter 3 will examine the INF question and the anti-nuclear movement in detail, while this chapter will look specifically at the attitudes of the NATO publics toward the Alliance's flexible response strategy, the NATO doctrine adopted in the 1960s which provided for retaliatory use of nuclear weapons in the face of Warsaw Pact conventional superiority. The end of the Cold War and the collapse of the Warsaw Pact led the July 1990 NATO Summit meeting to revise NATO doctrine to emphasise that nuclear weapons were to be 'truly weapons of last resort'. However, NATO deterrence strategy in the early 1990s still rests – in this modified, reduced dependence which was a compromise between those wanting to abandon flexible response and those wanting as little change in it as possible – on a willingness to be the first to use nuclear weapons if a Soviet conventional attack should threaten to overwhelm NATO defences. While this readiness to employ nuclear weapons as a retaliatory weapon was supported by most experts in the 1960s and 1970s, there was less expert consensus in the 1980s as some argued that flexible response was increasingly losing its deterrence credibility and that, instead, a beefed-up conventional defence was necessary (Huntington, 1983). Former top officials, including Secretary of Defense Robert S. McNamara, were among those calling for a revision in NATO doctrine (Bundy *et al.*, 1982).

While NATO governments did not alter the 'flexible response' strategy in the 1980s, the broad public opposition to reliance on nuclear weapons, coupled with the anti-nuclear activism of a much smaller number, was certainly one of the factors leading to the questioning of NATO strategy even prior to the major changes in East–West relations. The widespread public opposition is no surprise since using nuclear weapons in Western Europe threatens 'the complete destruction of precisely that which is defended: Western Europe, its territory, its population, and its society' (Hopmann and Barnaby, 1988, p. 183). NATO's retaliatory use of nuclear weapons against a Soviet conventional attack in Europe, in fact, would destroy in particular much of West Germany, where thousands of US tactical nuclear weapons are stationed as the country most likely to be the avenue of any Soviet attack. Interestingly, as part of a public relations effort to defuse West European concerns arising from the idea of 'theatre' nuclear weapons, in Fall 1981 the USA, at the urging of the Western European governments and the specific suggestion of Paul Nitze, decided to change the terminology for the missiles to be deployed there from Long-Range Theater Nuclear Forces (LRTNF) to Intermediate-Range Nuclear Forces (INF) (Nitze, 1989, pp. 369–70).

Most NATO publics have expressed their willingness to resist militarily any Soviet attack on their country. The degree to which Western Europeans actually hold pacifist feelings or believe 'better red than dead' seems to have been greatly exaggerated. For example, in February 1982, majorities or large pluralities in Belgium, Britain, Denmark, France, and West Germany said that it was better to fight in defence of their country than to risk Russian domination.[24] In October 1981, majorities in all seven countries surveyed (Belgium, Britain, France, Italy, the Netherlands, Norway, and West Germany) said their country should resist militarily against a conventional attack by the Soviets. In the next question on the same survey, however, when asked about whether they should resist a nuclear attack by the Soviets, between 12 and 26 per cent fewer in each of these countries favoured resistance. In Italy, a plurality actually opposed resistance under these circumstances, and, in Belgium, opinion was close to equally divided.[25] Furthermore, putting the retaliatory use of nuclear weapons, particularly on one's own territory, into the equation greatly decreases the willingness to support defence of their country. West German findings from a February–March 1980 survey dramatically make this point. In this survey, a 64 to 19 per cent majority said that West Germany should use 'military weapons' to defend itself against an attack. A 53 to 31 per cent majority believed that West Germany should defend itself against an attack 'even if the war is fought primarily on the soil of the Federal Republic'. Only 15 per cent, however, favoured the defence of West Germany 'if nuclear weapons have to be used on the soil of the FRG'. Seventy-one per cent were opposed.[26]

At the most general level, when the possibility of the retaliatory use of nuclear weapons or the actual deployment of nuclear weapons in their country is not mentioned, most NATO publics widely consider nuclear weapons important for NATO to be credible. For example, in July 1988, large majorities in five of six countries (Belgium, Britain, France, the Netherlands, and West Germany, but not Italy) agreed that 'NATO's nuclear weapons are an important reason that Western Europe has enjoyed more than 40 years of peace'. Also in July 1988 majorities of all six publics surveyed agreed that 'NATO should have as many nuclear weapons in Western Europe as the Soviet Union has in Eastern Europe'. Finally, once again in July 1988, majorities – and, in most of the six countries, large majorities – agreed that 'NATO must modernise its nuclear weapons so long as the Soviet Union continues to modernise its nuclear weapons'.[27] However, as the data presented here and in Chapter 3 will show, when it comes to the crunch – that is, a concrete commitment to give real teeth to NATO deterrence – opposition is widespread: first use of nuclear weapons against a conventional attack is overwhelmingly opposed; INF deployment was predominantly opposed; and deployment of enhanced radiation weapons was widely opposed.

NATO's flexible response strategy, which, even today in its modified form, provides for retaliatory use of nuclear weapons as a 'last resort' if a conventional attack on Western Europe threatens to overrun Western defences, is overwhelmingly opposed. This widespread opposition to NATO's fundamental doctrine actually pre-dates the doctrine itself; data from the mid-1950s and early 1960s show this opposition to first use of nuclear weapons to be longstanding and enduring (Crespi,

1983). In the 1980s when given the choice among three options – no use of nuclear weapons under any circumstance, use of nuclear weapons only if first used by the Soviets, or first use in the face of a Soviet conventional attack which threatens to overwhelm NATO defences – only between 6 and 24 per cent in the eight countries surveyed were willing to support first use (see Table 2.9). In most countries, a much larger number are actually 'nuclear pacifists', those who oppose any use of nuclear weapons by NATO whatever the circumstances. In the eight countries surveyed between 22 and 55 per cent were nuclear pacifists. This view was least common in Britain, where the proportion having this view ranged from 22 to 31 per cent; in most countries the number of nuclear pacifists never dipped below about 30 per cent. No first use, which the Soviets repeatedly urged from their position of conventional superiority, was clearly an effective propaganda theme among West European publics. In seven countries surveyed in May 1984, three-quarters or more – fully 92 per cent in the FRG – favoured a joint East–West no first use declaration; furthermore, 55 per cent or more in each country *strongly* favoured this.[28]

Even the doctrine that 'nuclear weapons are necessary to deter an attack against our country' is generally opposed by four of six publics surveyed.[29] Only the British and French publics, whose countries have their own nuclear weapons and who have generally opposed unilateral disarmament in surveys throughout the 1980s, have predominantly supported this view, although even in these countries it did not prevail in all five surveys in which the question was asked between March 1986 and July 1988. In these five surveys, between 36 and 47 per cent in France and 42 and 59 per cent in Britain, but only a quarter in West Germany and one in five in Italy, thought nuclear weapons necessary for deterrence. Pluralities in West Germany ranging from 39 to 51 per cent and large majorities in Italy ranging from 59 to 77 per cent preferred relying on conventional weapons for deterrence. In July 1988, the only time the question was asked in Belgium and the Netherlands, large pluralities in these two countries also held this view.

Clearly, despite these strongly anti-nuclear attitudes, NATO publics are poorly informed about NATO's nuclear weapons. In fact, in telephone surveys in May 1987 and September 1987, large numbers of Western Europeans did not know whether the USA would 'have any other nuclear weapons stationed in Western Europe with which to defend its allies' after all INF missiles were eliminated.[30] Despite the fact that there are thousands of other US nuclear weapons in Western Europe, in September 1987 fully 37 per cent in Belgium, 37 per cent in

Italy, 43 per cent in the Netherlands, 45 per cent in Britain, 50 per cent in France, and 62 per cent in West Germany either were not sure or said there were no others. Similar results were found in the May 1987 survey in Britain, France, and West Germany.

The Controversy over Neutron Weapons

The first major controversy over nuclear weapons as NATO entered the new phase of anti-nuclear concern and activism was over the enhanced radiation weapons, the so-called 'neutron bombs', which were a source of great conflict both in 1977–78 while Jimmy Carter was President and again early in President Reagan's term. The neutron weapon, because its low yield would result in more limited blast effects and less long-term radiation and, therefore, less damage to the environment and the civilian areas, was ideally suited to be a precision theatre nuclear weapon; this, in fact, was its only use. When the debate over this weapon became public in the 1977–78 period, it was clearly understood that the purpose for this weapon, if produced, would be its deployment in Western Europe, where it would serve to help in breaking up large-scale Soviet tank attacks. The hope for quiet production and deployment faded as this weapon was attacked as a particularly 'immoral' one which could lower the nuclear threshold. President Carter ultimately decided in March 1978 to defer production, given the widespread public uproar and the uncertainty about whether Western Europeans would ultimately agree to deploy neutron weapons. He was criticised by then West German Chancellor Helmut Schmidt and others, perhaps somewhat 'unfairly' as Kaplan (1988) says, for what they viewed as his weakness.[31] In 1981, when the Reagan Administration took up the issue and decided to proceed with production, the same controversies about the weapon arose. By this time, the West European publics were widely aware of the neutron weapon and opposed to deployment on their soil; in fact, most publics generally opposed even production. Specifically, in an October 1981 survey:

1. large majorities in Britain (65 per cent), France (65 per cent), Italy (64 per cent), the Netherlands (85 per cent), Norway (76 per cent), and West Germany (83 per cent) and a somewhat smaller majority (55 per cent) in Belgium, said they had heard of the neutron weapon;

Table 2.9 Attitudes on the use of nuclear weapons, 1981–87 (per cent)

	Belgium			Britain						Denmark	
	Oct. 1981	Jul. 1982	May 1984	Jul. 1981	Oct. 1981	Apr. 1982	Jul. 1982	May 1984	Feb. 1987	May 1984	Feb. 1987
Under no circumstances	47	51	35	24	31	22	30	24	27	43	44
Only if Soviets use them first	26	28	34	47	41	51	45	51	46	35	36
If Soviet conventional attack threatens to overwhelm NATO forces	16	14	14	19	24	21	19	18	19	7	9
Don't know	10	7	17	10	5	5	6	7	8	15	13
Total	99	100	100	100	101	99	100	100	100	100	

	France					Italy					
	Jul. 1981	Oct. 1981	Apr. 1982	Jul. 1982	Feb. 1987	Jul. 1981	Oct. 1981	Apr. 1982	Jul. 1982	May 1984	Feb. 1987
Under no circumstances	44	39	37	34	26	42	55	39	38	41	44
Only if Soviets use them first	32	32	31	21	36	38	31	42	40	44	36
If Soviet conventional attack threatens to overwhelm NATO forces	17	14	22	14	14	12	10	14	14	9	13

	The Netherlands				Norway		West Germany						
	Jul. 1981	Oct. 1981	Jul. 1982	May 1984	Oct. 1981	May 1984	Jul. 1981	Oct. 1981	Jan. 1982	Apr. 1982	Jul. 1982	May 1984	Feb. 1987
Under no circumstances	36	50	37	36	54	30	29	38	48	34	38	44	45
Only if Soviets use them first	32	31	32	30	31	48	37	28	22	36	33	42	35
If Soviet conventional attack threatens to overwhelm NATO forces	19	11	16	16	11	11	17	16	20	19	16	11	6
Don't know	13	8	15	17	3	10	17	17	10	11	13	2	15
Total	100	100	100	99	99	99	100	99	100	100	100	99	101
Don't know	7	15	10	30	24		7	4	6	8	5	7	
Total	100	100	100	99	100		99	100	101	100	100	99	100

Question: There are different opinions about the use of nuclear weapons. Which one of the following opinions is closest to your own? (HAND CARD)
  – NATO should not use nuclear weapons under any circumstances
  – NATO should only use nuclear weapons if the USSR uses them first in an attack on Western Europe
  – NATO should use nuclear weapons to defend itself only if a Soviet conventional attack threatens to overwhelm NATO forces.

Sources: July 1981 NATO Survey, October 1981 Security Survey, January 1982 West German Security Survey, April 1982 Versailles Economic Summit Survey, July 1982 Security Survey, May–June 1984 Security Survey, February 1987 Security Survey.

2. of those who had heard of neutron weapons, large majorities in six of these countries ranging from 70 to 83 per cent and a large plurality in Britain opposed deployment in their country;
3. of those who had heard of neutron weapons, large majorities in six of the countries and a plurality in Britain opposed US production, even if the weapons were to be stored in the USA.[32]

The Strategic Defense Initiative

Another controversy about nuclear weapons was over the Strategic Defense Initiative (SDI). The Strategic Defense Initiative announced by President Reagan in March 1983 was a research programme 'to study the feasibility of defensive measures against nuclear missiles to maintain the peace rather than relying solely on the threat of retaliation and the fear of mutual destruction' (USIA, 1990, p. 86). SDI played an important part in US–Soviet strategic arms negotiations for the remainder of the Reagan years. European governments were concerned about SDI on a number of scores, including the technological boost it might give the USA, the possibility of a new stage in the nuclear arms race, the sudden US decision to consider a complete change in the successful nuclear deterrence strategy it had followed for more than 20 years, and how this would affect the US defence commitment to its NATO allies (Dean, 1987, pp. 13, 17–18; Kaplan, 1988, pp. 173–4; Hughes, 1990, pp. 33–71).

In May 1984, the British and Italians, but not the Germans, predominantly considered the 'development of a weapon in space which could destroy attacking enemy missiles' a good idea. In February 1985, large pluralities in Belgium, Britain, Italy, and West Germany thought the idea of 'a defence system which could destroy attacking enemy missiles' a good one, while opinion was more divided in Denmark and the Netherlands.[33] As Table 2.10 shows, in December 1985 the British, French, and Italians still predominantly supported continuing SDI research, while opinion was evenly divided in West Germany. However, over the next 14 months, with increasing publicity about SDI, nicknamed 'Star Wars' in the mass media, and its role in complicating a US–USSR arms agreement, opposition to continuing research grew in all four countries. By February 1987, large pluralities in Germany and Italy opposed SDI research, and opinion was divided in Britain and France. Furthermore, as Chapter 6 discusses in more detail, as early as December 1985 the British, Dutch, Germans, and

Italians were predominantly in favour of giving up SDI if necessary to achieve an arms control agreement with the Soviets; a plurality of the French held this view by late 1986.[34]

DEFENCE SPENDING

This chapter has shown the widespread opposition among West European publics to reliance on nuclear weapons for deterrence and for defence as well as the broad opposition to deployment of neutron weapons in their country. Chapter 3 shows that the publics in the five basing countries also generally opposed INF deployment. In sum, the publics do not favour NATO dependence on nuclear weapons. The alternative, of course, is an adequate conventional defence.

What about conventional forces? In May 1984 majorities or large pluralities in Belgium (54 per cent), Denmark (47 per cent), Italy (52 per cent), the Netherlands (53 per cent), Norway (49 per cent), and West Germany (56 per cent) believed NATO's conventional forces adequate rather than in need of strengthening; only between 16 per cent and 33 per cent in these six countries thought that NATO's conventional forces needed to be strengthened. The one exception among the seven countries surveyed was Britain, where 52 per cent wanted NATO's conventional forces strengthened and only 30 per cent considered them adequate at that time. However, on another question in the same survey, a 46 to 35 per cent plurality in Britain, together with a large plurality in West Germany (53 per cent) and a majority in Italy (59 per cent) thought that NATO could stop a conventional attack 'with its present conventional weapons'.[35]

The governments of the United States and its Western European allies, who for decades viewed the Warsaw Pact as having a conventional superiority, nevertheless had great difficulty in achieving agreement on a concrete program for redressing this imbalance. A related issue, raised in the US Congress in the 1960s, 1970s, and 1980s (and, in a somewhat different context, in the 1990s as well) as well as in the US Executive Branch, has been the American belief that the Western European governments are not adequately sharing the defence burden. A big part of the problem has been defining how much each country actually contributes; for example, how does one make defence budgets comparable given different accounting systems or how much does having conscription and a large military reserve count (Golden, 1982, pp. 49–50; Allen and Diehl, 1988, pp. 96–100).

Table 2.10 Attitudes on SDI research, 1985-87 (per cent)

	Britain			France				Italy			
	Dec. 1985	Mar. 1986	Jul. 1986	Feb. 1987	Dec. 1985	Mar. 1986	Jul. 1986	Feb. 1987	Dec. 1985	Mar. 1986	Jul. 1986	Feb. 1987
Favour strongly	18	18	15	15	14	17	13	12	15	14	12	11
Favour somewhat	37	36	24	28	36	33	25	23	36	35	28	29
Subtotal favour	55	54	39	43	50	50	38	35	51	49	40	40
Oppose somewhat	12	16	17	27	15	6	13	20	22	17	24	21
Oppose strongly	15	17	27	18	7	9	13	19	16	16	26	27
Subtotal oppose	37	33	44	45	22	15	26	39	38	33	50	48
Don't know	19	14	17	13	29	35	37	26	11	18	10	12
Total	101	100	100	101	101	100	101	100	100	100	100	100

West Germany

	Dec. 1985	Mar. 1986	Jul. 1986	Feb. 1987
Favour strongly	12	12	9	5
Favour somewhat	24	29	17	17
Subtotal favour	36	41	26	22
Oppose somewhat	16	8	16	21
Oppose strongly	20	18	30	29
Subtotal oppose	36	26	46	50
Don't know	28	33	28	27
Total	100	100	100	99

Question: As you may know, the US has begun research into the possibility of developing an anti-missile defence system – the Strategic Defence Initiative or so-called 'Star Wars'. What is your opinion of the US continuing this research – do you favour this strongly or favour it somewhat, or do you oppose this research strongly or oppose it somewhat?

The December 1985 and March 1986 questions did not include the phrase 'the Strategic Defence Initiative or so-called 'Star Wars''.

In July 1986, there was a split sample, with half asked about 'SDI' and half asked about 'SDI, which some people call 'Star Wars'.

Sources: December 1985 Geneva Summit Survey, March 1986 Tokyo Economic Summit Survey, July 1986 Arms Control Survey, February 1987 Security Survey.

In 1977, after much prodding from President Carter, the NATO members agreed to the '3 per cent solution' under which NATO governments agreed to have annual real increases in defence spending of 3 per cent per year from 1979 until 1983 (Golden, 1982, pp. 47–54). This was seen as a political means to a military objective, since it did not specifically relate to a certain force structure or a specific number of airplanes, tanks, or other weapons. Some NATO members achieved this 3 per cent goal; many, including West Germany, which averaged only a 1 per cent real increase between 1980 and 1985, did not (Allen and Diehl, 1988, p. 99).

In any case, as Table 2.11 shows, throughout the 1980s, nearly all the West European NATO publics have widely opposed increased defence spending. Furthermore, data from the 1960s and 1970s suggest that this has long been true (Table 2.11; Eichenberg, 1982; Everts, 1985, p. 236). The one exception, and then for the late 1970s and early 1980s only, were the British. In the 1980s, support for increased defence spending has been no higher than 14 per cent in Belgium, 14 per cent in Denmark, 16 per cent in France, 18 per cent in Italy, 11 per cent in the Netherlands, 30 per cent in Norway, and 21 per cent in West Germany. In Britain, as many as 48 per cent in 1980 and 44 per cent in 1982 favoured increasing defence spending, but this was not above 31 per cent in surveys between 1984 and 1988. In most countries, the prevailing view in most surveys in the 1980s was for keeping their country's defence spending at its then present level. The major exception throughout the 1980s was Italy, where a plurality consistently favoured decreased defence spending. Sizeable numbers, though never a plurality, also preferred decreases in Belgium and the Netherlands. In West Germany, attitudes changed considerably over the decade; whereas support for continuing defence spending clearly prevailed in the first half of the 1980s, as many favoured decreases (41 per cent) as the present level of defence spending (39 per cent) in July 1988. Undoubtedly, apart from a limited sense of threat, defence spending consistently loses out when pitted in surveys against spending for social programmes. In fact, the priority given to the social welfare state was clearly an important factor in making it difficult for governments in the first half of the 1980s to achieve the defence increases they had agreed upon (Langer, 1986, p. 48). For example, in a March 1981 survey, except in France, about half or more of those saying they favoured increased defence spending, when asked a follow-up question, did not want to spend more for defence if 'social services might decline as a result'.[36]

In addition, all Western European publics believed their country was shouldering at least its fair share of the Western security burden. In fact, no more than 20 per cent in any of the seven countries surveyed in May 1984 felt that their country was not shouldering enough of the Western security burden. Except in West Germany, the prevailing view was that they were doing about the right amount; in West Germany, fully 50 per cent – compared to between 7 per cent and 27 per cent in the other six countries – thought their country was doing too much. When asked about the US share of the burden, large pluralities in Britain, Italy, and West Germany said the USA was doing about the right amount; only between 16 and 20 per cent in these three countries said the United States was sharing too much of the security burden.[37]

CONCLUSIONS

Throughout the 1980s, NATO was widely supported everywhere in West Europe except in Greece and Spain. Neutralism was highly overrated as a problem in the first half of the 1980s; it was never the view of more than a limited minority in Western Europe. Moreover, Western Europeans generally considered the US military presence as important to their security. What, however, did this support for NATO and the security link to the USA mean to Western European publics in terms of concrete commitments to Western defence efforts? Very little, it seems. In fact, Western Europeans were generally against all the major NATO initiatives in the period from the late 1970s to the mid-1980s. Most prominently, these publics predominantly opposed INF deployment, widely opposed increased defence spending, and overwhelmingly opposed the reliance on nuclear weapons which was the key to NATO deterrence strategy. In other words, West European publics did not want to depend on nuclear weapons, but also did not want their country to spend the money for a conventional build-up because they generally believed these forces adequate. Support for NATO does not seem to have varied in a consistent way with the level of East–West tensions, and a variety of analyses done with data from throughout the 1980s shows little, if any, relationship between threat perception and attitudes toward NATO.

Furthermore, knowledge of NATO continues to be limited among the European publics. Even after 30 years of NATO, only 29 per cent of the British could in 1980 correctly say what the initials NATO stand for. A decade later, with NATO at 40, things appeared to have

Table 2.11 Support for defence spending, 1968–88 (per cent)

	Belgium				Britain							Denmark
	May 1984	Jul. 1988	Apr. 1968	Jun. 1972	Mar. 1980	Mar. 1981	Apr. 1982	May 1984	May 1985	Dec. 1985	Jul. 1988	May 1984
Increased	7	14	15	32	48	33	44	23	22	13	31	14
Decreased	37	39	29	20	10	15	16	20	33	28	16	22
Present level	46	43	47	38	33	44	36	52	33	56	44	53
Don't know	10	4	9	10	9	8	4	5	12	3	8	11
Total	100	100	100	100	100	100	100	100	100	100	99	100

	France						
	Apr. 1968	Jun. 1972	Mar. 1980	Mar. 1981	Apr. 1982	Dec. 1985	Jul. 1988
Increased	5	7	15	15	16	12	12
Decreased	38	32	22	24	24	16	25
Present level	47	32	50	49	55	41	53
Don't know	10	10	13	11	5	31	11
Total	100	100	100	99	100	100	101

	Italy					The Netherlands			Norway	
	Mar. 1981	Apr. 1982	May 1984	Dec. 1985	Jul. 1988	Mar. 1981	May 1984	Jul. 1988	Mar. 1981	May 1984
Increased	16	16	18	14	12	11	8	8	21	30

	Apr. 1968	Jun. 1972	Mar. 1980	Mar. 1981	Jan. 1982	Apr. 1982	May 1984	Dec. 1985	Jul. 1988
Decreased	35	27	43	46	42	46	43	36	29
Present level	25	17	36	34	34	33	37	35	49
Don't know	29	40	6	4	7	7	8	17	13
Total	100	100	101	100	101	100	100	99	99

	39	16	21
	45	52	26
	8	11	22
	100	100	99

West Germany

	Apr. 1968	Jun. 1972	Mar. 1980	Mar. 1981	Jan. 1982	Apr. 1982	May 1984	Dec. 1985	Jul. 1988
Increased	10	12	21	15	11	15	7	7	6
Decreased	33	36	13	20	13	26	33	36	41
Present level	50	40	51	50	60	43	58	42	39
Don't know	7	12	15	15	16	16	2	15	14
Total	100	100	100	100	100	100	100	100	100

Questions: April 1968 – In light of the current situation, do you personally feel that the amount of money our country is now putting into defence should be increased, reduced or kept at about the present level?
June 1971 – At the present time, do you think (Survey Country) is spending too little, too much, or about the right amount of money for national defence?
March 1980 – Do you think that the level of (Survey Country's) expenditures for military purposes should be increased, decreased, or left at about their present level?
1981–88 – All things considered, do you think (Survey Country's) defence spending should be increased, decreased, or kept at about its present level?

Sources: USIA surveys in 1968, 1972, and 1979, March 1980
Multiregional Security Survey, March 1981 Security Survey, January 1982 West German Security Survey, April 1982 Versailles Economic Summit Survey, May–June 1984 Security Survey, May 1985 Security Survey, December 1985 Geneva Summit Survey, July 1988 Security Survey.

changed little; in a 1989 survey, majorities in Britain, France, Italy, the Netherlands, and West Germany ranging from 59 to 80 per cent said they knew little or nothing about NATO.[38] All of this does not add up to a very knowledgeable or committed support for NATO. What it does suggest is that support for NATO is a habit, or, at least, that public support for NATO is based largely on the general feeling that it is necessary to maintain a security link with the USA. It does not appear to be based now – nor was it during the 1980s – on support for specific defence initiatives or on a strong sense of threat.

As NATO enters a period of review and re-definition, the continuation of some form of West European security ties to the USA remains on a firm basis among West European publics. They do not necessarily know much about NATO or strongly support it, but they do view ties with the United States as important. Severing this military link in order to become neutral continues to be a minority viewpoint in most of Western Europe. Apart from Greece and Spain, only very small numbers are strongly hostile to US–European security links. As for American troops in Europe, the publics will acquiesce whether these troops are kept, reduced, or withdrawn. The changes in the Alliance's military posture, such as the revision of the flexible response doctrine and the decisions of many governments to cut defence spending, are very easy for the Western European publics to accept, and to accept enthusiastically, since they are in line with the public views expressed throughout the 1980s and even before. In fact, most of the West European publics, with the British and French possible exceptions, would like to go further and eliminate completely Alliance dependence on nuclear weapons. It is in this atmosphere that President Bush announced in September 1991, following the sweeping changes in the Soviet Union, that the USA would withdraw several thousand nuclear weapons from Western Europe.

3 INF Deployment in Western Europe

The deployment of intermediate-range nuclear forces (INF) in Western Europe was a central issue for US policymakers, in US–West European relations, and in US–Soviet relations in the 1980s. The INF issue spans a decade from the first European calls in 1977 for a NATO response to the Soviet deployment of SS–20 missiles targetted on Western Europe to the signing of the INF Treaty by Presidents Reagan and Gorbachev at the December 1987 Washington Summit. INF deployment was the most divisive issue in NATO over the past two decades and split the defence consensus which had existed in Europe over those two decades. In the first half of the 1980s, the two major parties in both Britain and the FRG were more seriously opposed over defence issues than they had been at any time since the 1950s. Even more, as David M. Abshire, US Ambassador to NATO from 1983 to 1987, said, it was 'the final battle of the Cold War', which 'was won in 1983, when NATO stayed together on INF deployment' (Abshire, 1989). The NATO Alliance withstood a major Soviet propaganda campaign which attempted to play on the anti-nuclear sentiments discussed in Chapter 2 to prevent INF deployment.

Unlike most security issues, INF deployment was not one which involved only the experts and government officials. In fact, as the widespread demonstrations and the growth of the anti-nuclear movement in a number of Western European countries showed, this issue generated a strong reaction among a vocal minority of the Western European public. These demonstrations, though they were attended by only a small proportion of Western Europeans, led to a large number of stories in the American and European press which argued that anti-Americanism, neutralism and pacifism were widespread and growing among the general public in Western Europe in the 1980s. Because of the importance of INF deployment and its links to these broader concerns about Western Europe, which many in the Reagan Administration also shared, the US Government put the INF issue at the heart of its public diplomacy and polling efforts in Western Europe in the first half of the 1980s. Other chapters will focus on anti-Americanism and neutralism, while this examines the general public's interest in, information about, and attitudes toward INF deployment and the US–Soviet negotiations on INF. It also looks at the degree of mass participation in demonstrations and other protest activities relating to INF deployment as well as the attitudes and demographic characteristics of the demonstrators.

THE INF ISSUE: 1977–87

In early 1977 the Soviet Union began deploying SS–20 missiles targetted at Western Europe.[1] These missiles represented a substantial upgrading over the SS–4 and SS–5, the earlier generation of Soviet intermediate-range missiles which were, however, not removed by the Soviets even after SS–20 deployment. The SS–20 was a solid fuel, mobile missile with a range of 3100 miles and three independently targetable warheads.[2] In a major speech in October 1977, Chancellor Helmut Schmidt voiced the unease of many West European elites over the ever-growing nuclear imbalance in Europe which was not being dealt with in the US–Soviet SALT II negotiations then in progress; in fact, in September the USA had agreed to exclude the SS–20s from SALT. Schmidt's speech was in part a result of the pressures both his Social Democratic–Free Democratic coalition in West Germany and the Labour Government in Britain felt from their conservative opposition forces for some response to Soviet SS–20 deployment. This speech, and the attendant publicity, was one important factor sparking the discussions within the US Government and NATO leading to NATO's 'dual track' decision in December 1979. Also key was the 1977–78 neutron bomb controversy, which ultimately resulted in President Jimmy Carter's April 1978 decision to defer production – a decision made in the wake of ambiguous signals from European governments and an outcry of public opposition. In any case, Carter's decision, reversing American policy, was seen as a sign of weakness and a betrayal by some West European governments, in particular by Chancellor Schmidt. By mid-1978 US concern over the damage to its leadership in NATO from this controversy and the continuing SS–20 deployment gave new impetus to the consideration of modernising NATO nuclear forces. Furthermore, though NATO had, in response to President Carter's urging, adopted the '3 per cent solution' in 1977 calling for real increases in spending for conventional forces by NATO, it was clear by 1979 that many individual member countries would not honour this commitment and that nuclear deterrence would remain key to NATO strategy.

The 'dual track' decision, agreed to on 12 December 1979, provided for NATO to pursue simultaneously two parallel tracks: INF deployment and arms control negotiations. Preparations for deployment were to start immediately, with actual deployment to begin in about four years. The NATO decision called for the eventual deployment in Belgium, Britain, Italy, the Netherlands, and West Germany of 464 mobile, ground-launched cruise missiles and in the FRG of 108 Pershing II missiles. The ground-launched cruise missiles, which fly like a jet airplane and have a range of 1600 miles, are guided by a computer which adjusts the missile's position at intermediate points along its flight path and which allows it to hug the ground at altitudes of 100–300 feet. The Pershing II is a solid fuel ballistic missile with a single warhead and a range of over 1100 miles which could reach major Soviet cities such as Leningrad and Moscow in about ten minutes.[3] While preparations for deployment went forward, thereby giving teeth to NATO's bargaining position, arms control negotiations with the Soviets would occur, possibly even making deployment unnecessary. Other aspects of the NATO deal were that deployment would occur in countries other than just Britain and West Germany; that the missiles would be land-based, thereby clearly a part of NATO's nuclear deterrence rather than sea-launched; and that they would be under American operation rather than a dual key. Key to the deal, in addition to its arms control aspect, was Italy's firm commitment to deploy cruise missiles on its soil; this was crucial because West Germany had insisted that it not be the only country on the continent to have INF deployment on its soil. Under this definition, Britain's commitment did not count; furthermore, the Belgian and Dutch agreement was lukewarm at best and for deployment at a later time than in Britain, Italy and West Germany.

Within two weeks of the NATO decision, the international political climate changed significantly with the Soviet invasion of Afghanistan and the resulting American efforts for economic sanctions against the Soviets. Preliminary US–Soviet discussions on INF began in October 1980, but the election of Ronald Reagan as President in November 1980, both because his Administration needed time to prepare itself and because of his Administration's distrust of the Soviets, further delayed the start of INF negotiations. Though originally intended as part of the SALT framework, the problems over ratification of the SALT II Treaty, and more generally over strategic arms negotiations, made it necessary for there to be separate negotiations on intermediate-range nuclear forces. The US–Soviet negotiations finally began in Geneva on 30 November 1981, meaning that two years had already passed since the NATO 'dual track' decision. The governments in the basing countries were particularly anxious that the Reagan Administration start these talks. The large demonstrations and other activities of the anti-nuclear movements in Western Europe, to be discussed in the next section of this chapter, had begun in earnest. Interestingly, in a public relations effort to defuse some of the concern of Western European publics about a nuclear war limited to Europe, in October 1981 the US Government changed the general term it used for the cruise missiles and Pershing IIs from Long-Range Theater Nuclear Forces (LRTNF) to Intermediate-Range Nuclear Forces (INF) (Nitze, 1989, pp. 369–70; Nitze, 1990; Talbott, 1984, pp. 78–9).

President Reagan publicly announced the US 'zero option' negotiating position two weeks before the talks started; Reagan said that NATO would agree to forgo all INF deployment if the Soviets would in turn dismantle all their SS–20, SS–4, and SS–5 intermediate range missiles. President Reagan was, in other words, calling for the elimination of an entire class of nuclear weapons. The US 'zero option' was unacceptable to the Soviets, and, for the next two years, the INF negotiations continued with disagreements over a number of key issues: which US and Soviet weapons systems should be included in the negotiations; whether the talks should consider only Soviet INF missiles aimed at Europe or also those aimed at Asia; whether British and French submarine-based nuclear missiles and French land-based nuclear missiles should be counted (something on which the Soviets long insisted); and how to undertake verification (Dean, 1987, pp. 127–9). During the 1981–83 period, a number of proposals were made by both sides, with the first public US offer of an alternative to the zero option the March 1983 interim proposal for equal global levels of US and Soviet INF missile warheads at as low a number as possible. The closest the two came to a deal was the 'walk in the woods' compromise reached by the two chief INF negotiators, Paul Nitze and Yuli Kvitsinsky, in the June–July 1982 period; neither the Soviet nor US Government, however, was willing to accept this compromise.[4] The Soviets, as Chapter 5 discusses, undertook a major propaganda effort to divide NATO and possibly prevent deployment by playing on the anti-nuclear feelings of West European publics. They believed that the pressure of the major demonstrations in Western Europe which occurred during the 1981–83 period and the growing rift between the major parties in Britain and West Germany over defence issues might lead some, or all, NATO governments to renege on deployment. The Soviet goal in the negotiations in the 1981–83 period was to prevent *any* US INF deployment. In other words, as long as the Soviets could hope that internal opposition in Western Europe might kill deployment, they felt no incentive to make substantial concessions in these negotiations. While there was some dissatisfaction among the NATO allies on the American negotiating posture (particularly over the year and a half it took before the USA offered an alternative to what many Western Europeans viewed as the unattainable 'zero option'), there was a substantial degree of solidarity; certainly, the allies agreed that an outcome with no US INF deployment was not acceptable unless the Soviets agreed to the 'zero option'.

The crucial year for deployment was 1983. Parliamentary elections were held in the spring/early summer period in all three countries where deployment was scheduled to begin at the end of the year if no negotiated agreement was achieved. In Italy, the INF issue was a nonstarter in the election campaign despite the efforts of the Communist Party and had virtually no impact on Italian voters (Penniman, 1987). In West Germany, the most vociferous opponents of deployment, the Greens, did win 5.6 per cent of the national vote, thereby becoming the first party since 1961 other than the Christian Democrats (CDU/CSU), Social Democrats (SPD), and Free Democrats (FDP) to win seats in the Bundestag. At the same time, the Christian Democrats, firm supporters of INF deployment and only in power since October 1982, won a major victory with 48.8 per cent of the vote, up more than 4 per cent from the 1980 elections. The evidence, however, suggests that defence issues were of low salience to most German voters and played little role in the election results (Rattinger, 1985, pp. 172–3). In Britain, defence issues were considerably more important than in Italy and West Germany and than in most previous British elections. In 1983, 38 per cent of British voters mentioned defence as one of two issues influencing their vote; in stark contrast, only 2 per cent had named defence during the 1979 election campaign (Crewe, 1985b, pp. 176–80). A large majority of those concerned about defence supported Margaret Thatcher's Conservatives, whose Government had won the Falklands War a year before and strongly supported NATO's two major decisions, INF deployment and 3 per cent annual real increases in defence spending. Many Britons felt uneasy about the Labour Party's defence platform, which was somewhat ambiguous but generally unilateralist (Kellner, 1985, pp. 69–70). In fact, in May 1983,

52 per cent said Britain would be less safe with a Labour government, while only 14 per cent felt the same would be true with a Conservative government (Crewe, 1985b, p. 180). The ability of the Conservatives to win a sizeable parliamentary majority with 42.4 per cent of the vote (down 1.5 per cent from 1979) was due to the Labour Party's huge loss of over 9 per cent which brought its vote to only 27.6 per cent, its lowest national result since 1918. While the INF issue alone may not have swayed many voters one way or the other, general concerns about the Labour Party's defence policies did harm Labour significantly. In sum, the deployment issue had little impact on the voting decisions of most electors in the FRG and Italy, while in Britain the Conservatives benefitted from the Labour Party's overall poor image on defence. In Britain and West Germany, conservative parties firmly committed to deployment won, while in Italy, the five-party coalition which backed deployment remained in power.

While opposition to deployment remained intense, the electoral success of the three pro-deployment governments meant that nothing short of a US–Soviet agreement was likely to stop deployment from occurring on schedule. On 22 November 1983, the Bundestag, with most Social Democrats voting against (though not Helmut Schmidt, who abstained), passed a motion of the Christian Democratic–Free Democratic coalition government to proceed with deployment. Deployment had already begun in Britain, and it began the next day in West Germany. On this day, 23 November, the Soviets also walked out of the INF talks. Part of the Soviet calculation was that deployment, coupled with a breakdown of the negotiations, would intensify opposition in Western Europe and lead to even larger demonstrations. This was a miscalculation. Deployment went forward in Britain, Italy, and West Germany in late 1983/early 1984 as scheduled, and the anti-INF protest movement declined rather than continuing to grow. As the major controversial decision, on the deployment itself, was taken, the story was no longer front-page news, and there was no concrete decision in these three countries to oppose – taking the wind out of the demonstrators' sails.[5]

Negotiations did not begin again until March 1985, and then in an expanded format involving intermediate-range and strategic nuclear arms as well as weapons in space. Just as these negotiations began, a major new development for the chances of an INF agreement occurred as Mikhail Gorbachev became General Secretary of the Soviet Communist Party. Meanwhile, NATO INF deployment continued.

The Belgian government, after vacillating on actual deployment for several years despite having allowed site preparations to go ahead, finally allowed deployment to begin in March 1985. In the Netherlands, the Christian Democrats (CDA), who led all governments in the 1980s but were more divided internally on INF than any other major conservative or Christian Democratic party in the basing countries, wavered on deployment even more than had the Belgian government. It was not until November 1985 that the Dutch government, after winning a narrow 79 to 70 victory in Parliament, agreed to begin site preparations leading to deployment in 1988 (Huygen, 1986, pp. 175–81; Rudig, 1988, p. 34; van Staden, 1989).

Over the two and half years after he came to power, Gorbachev moved the Soviet position closer and closer to the *original* US view, the 'zero option'.[6] Gorbachev adopted a significantly more flexible negotiating posture than the Soviet Union had in the Brezhnev years or even in the short-lived rule of Andropov. Gorbachev, anxious to relieve external pressures as he undertook internal reforms, realized that, given the large arsenal of strategic nuclear weapons, the SS–20s and other Soviet intermediate-range forces were no longer a military necessity. He was willing to give up a larger number of Soviet weapons in exchange for an INF agreement which would have two important results: elimination of the Pershing IIs, which had such a short flight time to major Soviet cities; and the bringing about of further improvement in the general atmosphere of East–West relations (Goldberg, 1990, pp. 111–117). The INF Treaty, signed by Presidents Reagan and Gorbachev at Washington on 8 December 1987, embodied the 'zero option' first proposed by President Reagan six years earlier.[7] This treaty, which came into force on 1 June 1988 shortly after ratification by the US Senate, provided for the removal and destruction within three years of all ground-launched ballistic and cruise missile systems with a range of between 500 and 5500 kilometres (about 300 to 3400 miles). The NATO 'dual track' decision of eight years earlier had finally brought its desired result, primarily because the Alliance had remained firm in undertaking deployment despite the substantial pressures on West European governments from protest movements and opposition parties and had then found a Soviet interlocutor willing to make major changes in his country's policies. Elimination of the INF forces occurred on schedule. On 26 March 1991, the last American INF missles were withdrawn from Europe – seven and a half years after the first were deployed.

THE ANTI-INF PROTEST MOVEMENT

The anti-INF protest movement of the first half of the 1980s, though ultimately unsuccessful, was the most important mass-based challenge to NATO in its entire history. The pressures this movement exerted on West European governments, together with the split in the elite defence consensus in Britain and West Germany, created significant tensions within NATO.[8] For the first time since the late 1950s/early 1960s, mass anti-nuclear protest movements played an active, highly-publicised role in trying to influence policy. The neutron bomb question in 1977–78 was an early stimulus, but it was primarily the INF decision which spurred the movement, with mobilisation picking up substantially in the 1980–81 period and peaking in Fall 1983. The protest movement was not a monolithic group even within each country in terms of individual views on defence issues, the United States, or the Soviet Union. For example, movement activists came from a variety of backgrounds, including long-standing pacifist organizations, religious groups, environmental groups, radical leftist groups, feminist groups, communist parties, and the left-wing of socialist/social democratic/labour parties. The composition of the movement in terms of these various components differed greatly from country to country. However, this movement – both within each country and across all five basing countries – was broadly anti-nuclear in spirit, and the protestors shared one goal in common: preventing INF deployment. In the 1981–83 period, large demonstrations involving altogether several million protestors took place in cities throughout Western Europe in this effort to stop INF deployment. In addition, many other activities, such as the women's camp for over three years at Greenham Common, the site for the first cruise missiles deployed in Britain, also were organized by the anti-INF protest movements.

The large demonstrations took place in all five countries where INF deployment was to occur, but the strength and impact of these anti-nuclear movements varied considerably from one country to another. Among the five basing countries, the protest movement was strongest in Britain, the Netherlands, and West Germany, while it was much weaker in Belgium and Italy. The anti-INF movement in France was also fairly weak. A number of factors help in explaining these national differences. First, in Britain, the Netherlands, and West Germany, much more than in the other three countries, there was a long-standing tradition of militant pacifism and anti-nuclear protest, and there were also well-organized anti-nuclear groups. In Britain, the Campaign for

Nuclear Disarmament, also active in the 1958–64 period and by far the largest anti-nuclear movement in Britain, has long existed and played a key role in organizing British anti-INF protests (Sigal, 1984, pp. 92–5). In the Netherlands, where religious forces played a central role in the anti-nuclear movement, the IKV (Dutch Interchurch Peace Council) has existed since 1966; from 1977, it took an increasingly activist stance (Alting von Geusau, 1985; Huygen, 1986, pp. 170–2; van Staden, 1989, pp. 105–6). In West Germany, the Greens, a mixture primarily of environmentalists and leftists but also of feminist and counter-culture movements, formed as a political party in 1979, first won seats in the Bundestag in 1983, and played a highly visible role in the anti-INF movement (Capra and Spretnak, 1984; Rudig, 1988). Furthermore, the major Socialist parties in Britain (the Labour Party), the Netherlands (the PvdA, or Labour Party), and West Germany (as the SPD became increasingly anti-INF in the 1981–83 period) largely supported the anti-INF views of the protest movement, while the French and Italian Socialists, by contrast, backed INF deployment and the Belgian Socialists waffled. In Italy, the lack of a strong, independent anti-nuclear organization; the political in-fighting between the Radicals and the Communists; and the unwillingness of the Communists, by far the largest leftist party in Italy, to push public demonstrations too far; left the anti-INF movement largely rudderless; the geographic isolation of the cruise missile base, located at Comiso on the island of Sicily, also acted as a damper on the Italian protest movement. In the end, despite the publicity and the political pressure the anti-nuclear movement created in the basing countries, it had little influence on policy and did not stop the decision in each of the five countries to go ahead with deployment.

Having briefly examined the anti-nuclear movement, we will now look at the attitudes of the general public toward it, at how many people actually participated in anti-INF activities, at who the demonstrators were, and at how representative of the public they were. According to surveys during the height of the demonstrations, more of the public was in agreement with than opposed to the anti-nuclear weapons movement and the demonstrations, though this was not the majority view in either Britain or France.[9] In November 1981, a very large majority in the Netherlands (79–17 per cent), a sizeable majority in West Germany (59–38 per cent), and large pluralities in Britain (52–39 per cent) and France (50–34 per cent) said they felt in agreement with the demonstrations. In October 1982, among those who said they heard or read about the anti-nuclear weapons movement (61 per cent in France, about 70 per cent in Britain, Italy, and West Germany, and 89 per cent in the Netherlands), a majority in Italy, large pluralities in the Netherlands and West Germany, and more narrow pluralities in Britain and France favoured rather than opposed the anti-nuclear weapons movement. In Britain, the only country for which trend data are available, large pluralities considered themselves generally in agreement with the demonstrations in October 1981 and February 1983, while in April 1983 opponents slightly outnumbered those in agreement with the demonstrations.

Activism on INF stationing beyond holding an opinion was clearly undertaken by only a minority of Western Europeans. In fact, as Table 3.1 shows, sizeable majorities in all five basing countries said they personally did nothing to show their position on INF stationing. In

Table 3.1 Activities done to show position on INF stationing in their country, June 1983 (per cent)

	Belgium	Britain	Italy	The Netherlands	West Germany
Did nothing	86	65	64	64	71
Tried to persuade others	7	8	16	14	14
Voted for a candidate or party who favours my position	3	23	18	21	14
Wrote to newspaper or magazine to state my position	1	1	1	1	1
Contacted an official or party to tell them my views	1	1	2	1	1
Signed a petition	4	10	6	11	5
Went to meeting or listened to speeches	1	5	7	7	4
Participated in a public demonstration	3	2	3	9	2
Joined an organization	1	2	1	1	1

Question: Are there any things listed on this card (HAND CARD) that you have done to show your position on stationing medium-range nuclear missiles in (Survey Country)? (Multiple responses were permitted.)

Source: June 1983 INF Survey.

three surveys in the April–July period in 1983, between 60 and 70 per cent in Britain, Italy, the Netherlands, and West Germany and more than 80 per cent in Belgium, when given a list of activities which included 'softer' forms of participation such trying to persuade others of their views or voting for a candidate or party who favoured their position as well as forms of participation, like demonstrating, joining an organisation, or signing a petition which involve a greater degree of commitment, said they had done none of the eight activities listed on it.

As Table 3.1 shows, the activities most frequently claimed are 'softer' forms of participation: trying to persuade others to their position (ranging from 7 per cent in Belgium to 16 per cent in Italy) or voting for a candidate or party that favours their position (3 per cent in Belgium, where the last parliamentary election had occurred in 1981; 21 per cent in the Netherlands, where there were parliamentary elections in 1981 and 1982; and between 14 and 23 per cent in Britain, Italy, and West Germany, all of which had elections shortly before the survey was done).[10] About one in twenty in Belgium, Italy, and West Germany and one in ten in Britain and the Netherlands said they had signed a petition relating to INF stationing. Very few (1 to 2 per cent in each country) had written to a newspaper or magazine, contacted a party official, or joined an organisation that works for their position on INF.

The demonstrators, the people actually out in the streets opposing INF deployment, were only a small minority of the adults in the five basing countries. In Belgium, Britain, Italy, and West Germany, only 2 to 3 per cent claimed to have participated in a demonstration. Though the demonstrators in the Netherlands were also only a small minority, participating in a demonstration was by far the most widespread in the Netherlands among the five basing countries; 9 per cent of the Dutch – proportionately three to four times as many as in any of the other basing countries – said they had demonstrated on the INF issue. The question on activism did not ask people whether their activities were for or against deployment, but cross-tabulation with attitudes on INF shows that about 95 per cent of those who said they demonstrated were INF opponents. Among those doing the other activities, opposition was also the predominant view in all but one case. In all five countries, over two-thirds of those writing to a magazine or newspaper, contacting an official, signing a petition, or joining an organisation and a majority of those trying to persuade others were INF opponents. The one exception was in Britain among those saying they voted for a party supporting their views on INF; consistent with the impact of defence issues in the 1983 British election, about 60 per cent of the British saying they did this were INF supporters. In the other countries, majorities of those voting for a party supporting their view on INF were opponents, ranging from slightly over half in West Germany to two-thirds in the Netherlands.

The Anti-INF Demonstrators

Who were the demonstrators?[11] Most demonstrators supported parties of the left. Only a very small proportion (5 per cent or less) voted for the major conservative or Christian Democratic parties in any of the basing countries. Specifically:

1. In West Germany, the demonstrators were about equally split between supporters of the Greens and the Social Democrats.
2. In Britain, most were Labour voters, with a minority supporters of the Alliance, which was the electoral arrangement then in existence between the Liberal Party and the Social Democrats (a group of moderates who had withdrawn from the Labour Party).
3. In Italy, about 90 per cent supported the left, with about 60 per cent Communists and the rest voters of the smaller leftist parties.
4. In the Netherlands, between 80 and 90 per cent of the demonstrators voted for leftist parties, about equally split between PvdA (Labour Party) supporters and voters of the small leftist parties.

The young (aged 18–34) constituted a disproportionate number of the demonstrators in all five basing countries, and this was particularly dramatic in West Germany. Half of the adult demonstrators in Belgium and Italy, two-thirds in Britain and the Netherlands and fully 85 per cent in West Germany were younger than 35. For comparison, between 30 and 40 per cent of the adults in these countries are aged 18–34.

The same pattern holds across these countries in terms of the proportion coming from the 'successor generation', that is, those better-educated and aged 18–34. About 15 to 20 per cent of the Belgian and Italian demonstrators, 25 to 30 per cent of the British and Dutch demonstrators, and fully one-half of the German demonstrators came from this younger, better-educated group. By comparison, in each of these countries, only to 6 to 8 per cent are aged 18–34 and better-educated.

Except in Italy, where roughly two-thirds of the demonstrators were men, there were about equal numbers of men and women among the demonstrators.

How do the views of the demonstrators compare to those of the general public? As one might expect given the overwhelming anti-INF sentiments among demonstrators, three-quarters or more of the demonstrators held attitudes opposed to US positions on most issues related to INF, such as INF's deterrence value, whose interest INF deployment served, and their evaluation of US and Soviet INF negotiating proposals. The demonstrators differed greatly from the publics on these issues.

In all basing countries, the demonstrators, by overwhelming majorities of between 85 and 95 per cent, said they had little or no confidence in the US ability to deal responsibly with world affairs, thought that recent American actions tended more to increase the risk of war than to promote peace, and believed that the USA sought military superiority over the Soviets rather than equality. Two-thirds to three-quarters believed the USA was not making a genuine effort to reach an INF agreement with the Soviets. Depending on the country and the issue, the demonstrators' views on US foreign policy in 1983 ranged from much more negative to somewhat more negative than the views of the general publics.

As to the Soviet Union, majorities of about six in ten among the demonstrators in Belgium, Britain, Italy, and the Netherlands saw recent Soviet policies as having tended more to increase the risk of war than to promote peace, thought the Soviets were seeking military superiority over the USA rather than equality, and said the Soviets were not making a genuine effort for an INF agreement. These views were about the same as those of the general publics in these four countries. By contrast, in West Germany, where opinion of Soviet foreign policy was more mixed than broadly negative, somewhat more among the demonstrators than among the general public viewed Soviet foreign policy in a positive light. In any case, in none of the five basing countries were the demonstrators predominantly favourable to the Soviet Union.

In summary, the demonstrators, who were a small minority of adults in the five basing countries, were overwhelmingly anti-INF in their attitudes and overwhelmingly supporters of leftist parties. They were disproportionately younger and from the 'successor generation'. Very large majorities of the demonstrators – considerably more to somewhat more than among the general publics – held negative views of

US foreign policy, while, in all but West Germany, their views of Soviet foreign policy were about as negative as those of the general public.

PUBLIC CONCERN AND AWARENESS ABOUT INF STATIONING

Despite the publicity about INF and the active anti-INF protest movement, INF was not a central concern to a broad majority of citizens in the basing countries.[12] In April 1983, relatively few picked INF stationing in their country as one of their two greatest concerns from a list of nine important problems facing their country (two in ten in the Netherlands and West Germany and one in ten in Britain and Italy). Many more chose unemployment (64–75 per cent) and crime (32–43 per cent) as the most worrying national problems. INF stationing ranked sixth of nine as a concern in Britain, was tied with four others for third in West Germany, ranked fifth in Italy, and was third in the Netherlands. By December 1983, shortly after deployment had begun in Britain and West Germany and just before it was about to begin in Italy, concern over INF stationing in their country had increased little compared to eight months earlier. In Britain, 20 per cent picked INF stationing, compared to 11 per cent in April; in West Germany and Italy, the numbers were virtually unchanged. In December, it was tied for fourth as a concern in Britain and West Germany and still ranked fifth in Italy. Furthermore, in an open-ended question asked in July–August 1983, only 24 per cent in Britain spontaneously mentioned nuclear weapons or defence, only 21 per cent in West Germany mentioned armaments, disarmament, or stationing, and a minuscule 3 per cent in Italy mentioned stationing. In Italy, no other foreign policy problems were mentioned at all.[13]

Many more said they followed the issue of INF stationing at least fairly closely than considered it of concern. In Britain, 39 per cent in July 1983 and 69 per cent in December 1983 claimed to follow the issue either fairly or very closely.[14] In West Germany, the number saying they followed it at least fairly closely actually dropped a little from 62 per cent in July to 51 per cent in December. In Italy 31 per cent in July and 43 per cent in December did so. However, in all three countries the proportion saying they followed INF stationing *very* closely was small, 5 and 22 per cent in July and December respectively in Britain, 21 and 12 per cent in West Germany, and 5 and 12 per cent in Italy.

Furthermore, in July 1983, three-quarters in each of these countries said that they rarely or never talked about INF stationing in their circle of friends; only 2 per cent in Italy, 6 per cent in Britain, and 8 per cent in West Germany talked about the issue very often.

The publics in the basing countries were generally not well-informed on INF deployment. In mid-1983, most were unaware, when asked in an open-ended question, that deployment was scheduled to begin in Western Europe by the end of the year.[15] In June 1983 only 16 per cent in Belgium and Britain, 21 per cent in Italy, 24 per cent in the Netherlands, and 40 per cent in West Germany correctly said when deployment would begin. Similar levels were found in Britain, Italy, and West Germany in a July–August 1983 survey; this limited knowledge on the deployment schedule was true even though all three countries had recently been through parliamentary elections in which the INF issue, though not decisive for the results, was nevertheless widely discussed during the campaign. Once deployment occurred in these three countries, a majority in each was aware of this; in May 1984, a very large majority in the West Germany (81 per cent) and Britain (70 per cent) but only a bare majority (55 per cent) in Italy said that INF stationing had occurred on their soil.

Awareness that the INF talks were taking place, limited to no more than a half in the publics surveyed shortly after the talks began, grew considerably between early 1982 and mid-1983.[16] In February 1982, about two months after the negotiations began, 52 per cent of the Belgians, 44 per cent of the British, 42 per cent of the French, and 55 per cent of the West Germans said that talks were taking place. In October 1982, actually fewer in Britain (35 per cent), somewhat more in France (52 per cent), and about the same number (52 per cent) in West Germany said they knew of the talks; 59 per cent of Italians and 67 per cent of the Dutch did so.[17] Given the nature of the question, which, by asking about these negotiations, may have implied that they were taking place, the drop in British awareness between February and October suggests that some respondents may have guessed that talks were taking place without really being sure.[18] In any case, awareness of the talks was clearly substantially greater in all but the Netherlands by mid-1983; the magnitude and similar direction of findings leads to the conclusion that real awareness of the talks had grown by mid-1983. In April 1983, 66 per cent of the Dutch and 74 per cent of the Belgians said they knew of the talks. In the three largest basing countries, the number saying correctly that negotiations were taking place reached 64 per cent in Britain, 72 per cent in Italy, and 85 per cent in West

Germany by July 1983. (Of course, some of these undoubtedly were guessing.)

Clearly, even major developments, such as the simple fact of talks occurring or being halted, take a while to penetrate to large segments of the general public. In fact, in December 1983, only a few weeks after the Soviets withdrew from the INF talks, many were not aware that the talks were no longer in progress despite the great amount of coverage in the press; only 29 per cent in Italy and about half in Britain (48 per cent) and West Germany (55 per cent) correctly said that the INF talks were no longer being held.[19]

Tougher questions requiring more detailed information of the respondent and not supplying the information being asked for in the question, showed that many of those with some awareness of the talks or deployment had, in fact, only very limited knowledge of either one. One case of this was the question discussed earlier which asked when deployment would begin. For another example, in September 1987, shortly before the INF Treaty was signed and almost six years after President Reagan's zero-option speech, few – ranging from 15 to 20 per cent in Britain, France, Italy, and West Germany – knew that the United States was the 'country which first proposed eliminating all intermediate-range nuclear missiles'.[20] Somewhat more, ranging from 21 to 35 per cent, thought the Soviet Union had authored this proposal. Strikingly, between 45 and 62 per cent in these four countries said they had not heard or read enough to say. Hans Rattinger (1987) also points out the limited public knowledge about INF in his analysis of a variety of information questions asked in West Germany between Spring 1981 and Fall 1983. In February 1983 only 27 per cent (little different from the September 1987 German result reported above) correctly identified the USA as having proposed the 'zero option'. In three open-ended questions asked in 1981, only 9, 11, and 15 per cent respectively could give what Rattinger calls an 'adequate characterization' of NATO's December 1979 'dual track' decision (Rattinger, 1985, p. 134; Rattinger, 1987, pp. 512–14).

Survey findings from the 1981–83 period, when the INF issue was at its height, suggest that most of the citizens in the five INF basing countries were not greatly concerned over deployment in that it was not highly ranked as one of the most worrisome problems facing their country. They did not pay close attention to the INF issue, did not discuss INF stationing with their friends, and had only limited, shallow knowledge about INF stationing and negotiations. Despite the widespread publicity and the demonstrations, INF was not different from most other foreign policy issues in terms of public interest and information.

TO DEPLOY OR NOT TO DEPLOY?

A wide variety of questions were asked in each of the five basing countries about whether INF deployment should take place in their country. These questions introduced many different factors, with the most common being that the missiles were American, that the Soviets had an INF superiority or monopoly, that deployment was linked to arms control negotiations, and that deployment was the result of a NATO decision. Since, as we have seen, many Western Europeans have only limited information about INF deployment and negotiations, what they are told in the question may have a major impact on their attitude. Clearly, the phrasing of the question will greatly influence the results, meaning that the support for deployment could vary substantially from one question to another. This requires great caution in interpreting the results, but also provides the opportunity to learn how different factors affect attitudes on INF.

The USIA Office of Research asked three major questions on support for INF deployment in their country during the 1981-84 period. These provide the best source of comparable cross-national data. The *first question*, which was the one asked most frequently during the period between March 1981 and April 1983, gave a choice among four options: unconditional opposition; accepting deployment only if the talks had failed; accepting deployment if talks were still going on; and unconditional acceptance. Intepreting this question is complicated both by the nature of the choices (three for acceptance and only one for opposition) and by the fact that, on four occasions, this question was immediately preceded in the questionnaire by another one which told respondents that the Soviets had 450 nuclear warheads on medium-range missiles while NATO had none.[21] While the ranges overlapped over the two year period and opposition fluctuated up and down in all five countries, unconditional opposition was, except in Belgium, at its highest levels when this information was not provided (see Table 3.2). Unconditional opposition was consistently highest in Italy, and only in Belgium and Italy did it reach a majority level in any surveys. In the Netherlands, it was the plurality view in every survey, in most cases ranging between about four in ten and half. In Britain and West Germany, unconditional opposition was

Table 3.2 Support for INF deployment when linked to arms talks, March 1981–April 1983[a]

	Belgium				Britain								
	Oct. 1981	Feb. 1982	Jul. 1982	Apr. 1983	Mar. 1981	Jul. 1981	Oct. 1981	Dec. 1981	Feb. 1982	Apr. 1982	Jul. 1982	Oct. 1982	Apr. 1983
Unconditional opposition	43	38	46	62	31	22	32	36	36	28	38	39	29
Accept only if talks have failed	20	33	25	17	20	27	23	23	17	23	20	18	20
Accept if talks at the same time	11	12	12	11	19	23	22	20	24	30	21	20	29
Accept regardless of talks	7	6	7	7	15	17	15	13	12	12	14	13	16
Don't know	19	11	10	3	15	11	8	8	10	7	7	10	6
Total	100	100	100	100	100	100	100	100	99	100	100	100	100

	Italy							The Netherlands						
	Mar. 1981	Jul. 1981	Oct. 1981	Apr. 1982	Jul. 1982	Oct. 1982	Apr. 1983	Mar. 1981	Jul. 1981	Oct. 1981	Dec. 1981	Jul. 1982	Oct. 1982	Apr. 1983
Unconditional opposition	54	40	50	44	45	59	54	39	38	47	52	44	42	41
Accept only if talks have failed	21	27	25	30	31	19	25	15	20	21	28	20	24	20
Accept if talks at the same time	12	15	13	10	10	9	10	16	22	18	12	15	9	14
Accept regardless of talks	6	10	9	8	9	8	7	8	9	7	5	8	5	5
Don't know	7	8	4	7	4	5	4	21	11	8	3	14	20	19
Total	100	100	101	99	99	100	100	99	100	101	100	101	100	99

West Germany

	Mar. 1981	Jul. 1981	Oct. 1981	Dec. 1981	Jan. 1982	Feb. 1982	Apr. 1982	Jul. 1982	Oct. 1982	Apr. 1983
Unconditional opposition	40	26	32	40	47	39	29	33	42	36
Accept only if talks have failed	27	24	24	27	30	27	34	29	23	29
Accept if talks at the same time	19	21	20	12	15	14	15	17	14	11
Accept regardless of talks	9	12	6	3	6	9	9	7	6	5
Don't know	5	17	18	17	2	12	13	15	15	18
Total	100	100	100	99	100	101	100	101	100	99

[a] In July 1981, April 1982 and July 1982 and in Belgium in February 1982, the question immediately preceding this one mentioned that the Soviets had INF missiles while NATO did not. In October 1981, such a question preceded this on half the questionnaires. No question mentioning the Soviet INF missiles preceded this one in March 1981, December 1981, January 1982, February 1982 (Britain and West Germany), or October 1983. The mention of Soviet INF missiles was included directly in this question in April 1983.

Question: There are many different opinions on how to deal with the issue of stationing in (Survey Country) new nuclear missiles that could reach the Soviet Union. Listed on this card are four opinions about these new nuclear missiles. (SHOW CARD) Which of these opinions is closest to your own? Under no conditions should we agree to station these new nuclear missiles in (Survey Country); We should accept the new nuclear missiles only if arms reduction negotiations with the USSR have failed; We should accept the new nuclear missiles as long as there are arms reduction negotiations going on with the USSR at the same time; We should accept the new nuclear missiles regardless of the current arms reduction negotiations'.

The April 1983 question also contained the following preface: 'At present, the Russians have more than 700 nuclear warheads on medium-range nuclear missiles – the SS-20s – aimed at Western Europe, while the NATO countries have no such missiles aimed at the Soviet Union.

Sources: The following USIA surveys were used in this table: March 1981 Security Survey, July 1981 NATO Survey, October 1981 Security Survey, December 1981 INF Survey, January 1982 West German Security Survey, February 1982 Poland–INF Survey, February 1982 Belgian Security Survey, April 1982 Versailles Economic Summit Survey, July 1982 Security Survey, October 1982 INF Survey, and April 1983 INF Survey.

generally the plurality view in most surveys, and, with a few exceptions, ranged between three and four in ten. Unconditional acceptance was the view of roughly one in ten (slightly higher in Britain). Those in the two middle positions, whose willingness to accept deployment was linked to arms control talks in different ways, numbered 40 to 50 per cent in Britain and West Germany and 30 to 40 per cent in Belgium, Italy, and the Netherlands. Many of these were clearly in the swing group whose attitudes were most likely to be influenced by the question wording, in this case by the linkage to arms control talks, which this question suggests was important in building support for deployment.

A *second question*, which included the preface saying that 'The Russians have about 450 nuclear warheads on new medium-range nuclear missiles (the SS–20s) aimed at Western Europe, while NATO has no such missiles aimed at the Soviet Union.', showed opposition at or near the majority level in most surveys in Belgium, Italy, and the Netherlands, opinion divided or slightly negative in West Germany, and support, which was the majority view the first time the question was asked in July 1981, declining by July 1982 to a slight plurality opposing in Britain (see Table 3.3).

The impact of including the information on Soviet INF capabilities was demonstrated in October 1981, when a split ballot was used; half were asked the question with the preface and half without. As Table 3.4 shows, opposition increased by anywhere from 9 to 17 per cent in the basing countries *without* the information, and support declined between 5 and 10 per cent. With the simple favour-oppose question not including the preface, large majorities in Belgium, Italy, and the Netherlands opposed deployment, while a plurality did so in West Germany; in Britain, opinion was divided.

Finally, a *third question*, the principal one used by USIA in the period between April 1983 and February 1985, was less complicated and more straightforward than the first discussed above. This third question mentioned the 'NATO decision' to deploy in absence of an INF agreement and then asked respondents to choose among four options (strong and weak opposition, strong and weak support).[22] As Table 3.5 shows, a majority in Italy, a majority or large plurality in Belgium, and a large plurality in the Netherlands consistently opposed deployment. In West Germany, opposition grew from a plurality to majority view in the period just after deployment began, but then declined by February 1985, when opinion was close to equally divided. In Britain, a majority or plurality supported deployment in five of six

Table 3.3 Support for INF deployment when information on Soviet missiles included in question, 1981–82 (per cent)

	Belgium			Britain				Italy			
	Oct. 1981	Feb. 1982	Jul. 1982	Jul. 1981	Oct. 1981	Apr. 1982	Jul. 1982	Jul. 1981	Oct. 1981	Apr. 1982	Jul. 1982
Favour	32	37	30	57	49	50	41	45	42	41	38
Oppose	53	52	61	29	35	37	47	48	51	52	53
Don't know	14	11	9	14	15	14	12	8	6	8	8
Total	99	100	100	100	99	101	100	101	99	101	99

	The Netherlands		West Germany			
	Jul. 1981	Oct. 1981	Jul. 1982	Jul. 1981	Oct. 1981	Jan. 1982	Apr. 1982	Jul. 1982
Favour	44	36	30	44	37	32	38	32
Oppose	51	56	50	29	33	41	39	43
Don't know	5	8	20	28	30	27	23	25
Total	100	100	100	101	100	100	100	100

Question: Well, as you may know, the Russians have about 450 nuclear warheads on new medium-range missiles – the SS–20s – aimed at Western Europe, while NATO has no such missiles aimed at the Soviet Union. In view of this, do you favour or oppose having new nuclear missiles that can reach the Soviet Union stationed in (Survey Country)? (Over the year the question was asked, the number of Soviet warheads was increased to keep pace with the actual Soviet total. By July 1982, the question referred to 600 nuclear warheads.)

Sources: The data come from the following USIA surveys: July 1981 NATO Survey, October 1981 Security Survey, January 1982 West German Security Survey, February 1982 Belgian Security Survey, April 1982 Versailles Economic Summit Survey and July 1982 Security Survey.

Table 3.4 Impact on support for INF deployment of information on Soviet INF missiles, October 1981 (per cent)[a]

	Belgium		Britain		Italy		Netherlands		West Germany	
	With	Without	With	Without	With	Without	With	Without	With	Without
Favour	32	23	49	44	42	35	36	26	37	28
Oppose	53	70	35	45	51	60	56	67	33	44
Don't know	14	6	15	11	6	5	8	7	30	28
Total	99	99	99	100	99	100	100	100	100	100

[a] A split ballot technique was used, with half the total sample asked the question with information and half asked the question without information.

Questions: (1) with information – Well, as you may know, the Russians have about 450 nuclear warheads on new medium-range missiles – the SS–20s – aimed at Western Europe, while NATO has no such missiles aimed at the Soviet Union. In view of this, do you favor or oppose having new nuclear missiles that can reach the Soviet Union stationed in (Survey Country)?;
(2) without information – Do you favour or oppose having new nuclear missiles that can reach the Soviet Union stationed in (Survey Country)?

Source: October 1981 Security Survey.

surveys, the exception being in December 1983 shortly after deployment began; support was a majority before this low point and then rebounded again to a large plurality within five months. Separating out the effects of the mention of the 'NATO decision' is not easy, but it appears to have had a much more limited impact on attitudes than the linkage to arms control or the information on Soviet INF capabilites provided in the other two measures.

This question also provides us an opportunity to look at the *intensity* of feelings toward INF deployment. First, there is no consistent growth of more of the public holding intense views, whether in support or opposition, across the two years this question was asked. In West Germany, the number holding intense views peaked around the time of deployment (mid-1983 to mid-1984) and then fell back to earlier levels by 1985. In Britain and the Netherlands, the proportion with intense views was stable in 1983 and dropped somewhat after the initial deployment in the three large countries. In Belgium and Italy, somewhat more held intense feelings from late 1983 on than earlier. In sum, there is certainly no evidence of a growing polarisation of views over time across the five basing countries. Second, in all but Britain, there were consistently more strong opponents than strong supporters of deployment. In Belgium, Italy, and the Netherlands, the number of strong opponents was substantially larger than the number of strong supporters in all surveys. In the three largest countries, the number of strong opponents was at or near its highest level in December 1983, just after deployment began. In Britain and West Germany, the number of strong opponents peaked at the same time as the anti-nuclear movement, and, like the movement's force and activity, dropped over the next year.

None of these three questions was used throughout the 1981–84 period, making it difficult to determine the trend over this entire period. In an effort to sort this out further and to examine other questions used to test for opinion on INF deployment, a more detailed discussion of results in Britain, West Germany, and the Netherlands, including those from the many questions asked for clients other than USIA, will now be undertaken. Attitudes in Belgium and Italy will not be looked at more extensively here for two reasons: (1) much more limited polling on INF deployment was done in these two countries than in the other three basing countries; and (2) in both cases, opposition consistently prevailed (whether at the majority or large plurality level) on the results reported above as well as on the very few others available.

Table 3.5 Support for INF deployment, 1983–85 (per cent)[a]

	Belgium			Britain						Italy			Netherlands			
	Apr. 1983	Jun. 1983	May 1984	Apr. 1983	Jun. 1983	Jul. 1983	Dec. 1983	May 1984	Feb. 1985	Apr. 1983	Jun. 1983	Feb. 1985	Apr. 1983	Jun. 1983	May 1984	Feb. 1985
Strongly support	7	8	7	25	31	26	18	16	17	11	8	6	10	10	15	10
Support	26	17	24	35	35	38	27	37	32	22	25	20	24	23	22	23
Subtotal support	33	25	31	60	66	64	45	53	49	33	33	26	34	33	37	33
Oppose	40	32	25	12	12	16	20	24	20							
Strongly oppose	24	18	34	23	16	18	31	18	22							
Subtotal oppose	64	50	59	35	28	34	51	42	42							
Don't know	3	25	10	6	5	3	3	6	8							
Total	100	100	100	101	99	101	99	101	99							

Oppose Strongly oppose	19 40	22 42	20 39	23 50	21 46	17 54	14 35	13 36	17 32	23 30
Subtotal oppose	59	64	59	73	67	71	49	49	49	53
Don't know	6	2	5	3	3	4	17	17	14	14
Total	98	99	100	101	101	101	100	99	100	100

West Germany

	Apr. 1983	Jun. 1983	Jul. 1983	Dec. 1983	May 1984	Feb. 1985
Strongly support Support	23 13	15 16	27 14	19 10	27 12	24 15
Subtotal support	36	31	41	29	39	39
Oppose Strongly oppose	10 36	12 32	12 38	12 44	16 43	14 29
Subtotal oppose	46	44	50	56	59	43
Don't know	18	24	9	15	2	17
Total	100	99	100	100	100	99

[a] In the April 1983, June 1983, and July 1983 surveys, a preceding question (respectively three before, nine before and six before) mentioned the Soviet INF nuclear warheads and the fact that NATO has none. In the December 1983, May 1984, and February 1985 surveys, no such information was given in any preceding question.

Question: The question was essentially the same one with the same answer categories over the 1983–85 period, but the preface changed a little over this period as deployment actually occurred. In 1983, the preface also differed slightly between Britain, Italy, and West Germany, on the one hand, and Belgium and the Netherlands, where deployment was not scheduled until later.

In April 1983, the question asked in Britain, Italy, and West Germany was: If, by the end of the year, no agreement has been reached between the United States and the Soviet Union to reduce the number of medium-range nuclear missiles in Europe, and (Survey Country's) government, in line with the NATO decision, carries out its pledge to station such nuclear missiles in (Survey Country), which of the following would best describe your reaction? I would strongly support such stationing; I would support such stationing, but I wouldn't feel strongly about it; I would oppose such stationing, but I wouldn't feel strongly about it; I would strongly oppose such stationing.

In December 1983, the preface read: As you may know, no agreement has been reached between the U.S. and the USSR to reduce the number of medium-range nuclear missiles in Europe. As a result of a NATO decision, new medium-range nuclear missiles are now being stationed on (British) (German) (Italian) soil. Which of the following best describes your reaction to the stationing of these missiles in our country? In 1984 and 1985, the preface was: As you probably know, no agreement has been reached between the U.S. and the USSR to reduce the number of medium-range nuclear missiles in Europe. So, in keeping with a NATO decision, some new medium-range nuclear missiles have been stationed in Western Europe. Which of the following best describes your reaction to the stationing of these missiles in Western Europe?

Sources: The data come from the following USIA surveys: April 1983 INF Survey, June 1983 INF Survey, July–August 1983 INF Intensive Survey, December 1983 INF Survey, May–June 1984 Security Survey and February 1985 Arms Control Survey.

In *Britain*, a variety of questions on attitudes toward deployment was asked in the 1981–85 period. As Table 3.6 shows, there was considerable variation in the results between Spring 1981 and early 1983; some of the surveys showed predominant support, others divided opinion, and still others predominant opposition. In fact, four surveys done even in the same month, January 1983, showed this diversity of results. Among the surveys in the Spring 1981–early 1983 period, the greatest support was consistently found when the information on Soviet SS–20s was included in the question, while the greatest opposition was associated with questions which mentioned, or implied, that the missiles were American or American-controlled which Britain was 'allowing' to be based in Britain.[23] In January 1983, opposition predominated on the two questions which mentioned or implied the American factor, opinion was evenly divided on a straightforward question which mentioned no other factors, and support was a plurality when linked to the INF talks reaching no agreement. Taking into account the results reported in Tables 3.2, 3.5, and 3.6, the overall trend appears to have been a growth in opposition in 1982 and then an increase in support in the first half of 1983. From Spring 1983 on, support predominated in Britain, except in the late 1983/early 1984 period right around the time of deployment; the support in May 1984 and after was by a more narrow margin than that in mid-1983.

In *West Germany*, an even wider variety of questions was asked, especially in 1983. In the period between mid-1981 and early 1983, opposition was the plurality view in some surveys, while opinion was close to divided in others; only in July 1981 did support prevail. Support was generally greatest when deployment was linked to the Soviet SS–20s or to the failure of the INF talks. During the period between April and December 1983, the results of questions varied widely, with opposition ranging from 22 to 76 per cent in this period. However, a close analysis suggests that the two questions (out of 13 findings for this period reported in Table 3.7) on which support prevailed were both heavily conditioned by their phrasing to lead to a more positive result. One posed the choice of deployment or leaving NATO, and the other emphasised the need for the West to remain sufficiently strong and deploy in Western Europe if the Soviets did not dismantle their missiles; furthermore, on the latter question opinion was asked on deployment in 'Western Europe' rather than on deployment in West Germany. The two on which opposition was greatest tilted in the other direction by giving the choice (which was

Table 3.6 British views on INF deployment, 1981–84 (per cent)

	Apr. 1981	Jul. 1981	Oct. 1981a	Oct. 1981b	Oct. 1981c	Apr. 1982	Jul. 1982	Oct. 1982	Jan. 1983a	Jan. 1983b	Jan. 1983c
Favour	41	57	49	44	31	50	41	31	36	40	27
Oppose	50	29	35	45	59	37	47	58	54	40	61
Don't know	9	14	15	11	10	14	12	11	10	19	21

	Jan. 1983d	Feb. 1983	Apr. 1983	May 1983	Jun. 1983a	Jun. 1983b	Jul. 1983	Nov. 1983	Dec. 1983	Mar.–Apr. 1984	May 1984
Favour	43	32	60	48	50	66	64	38	45	37	53
Oppose	34	54	35	38	39	28	34	50	51	53	42
Don't know	23	13	5	14	10	5	3	12	3	9	6

Questions and Sources:

April 1981, January 1981c Do you approve or disapprove of the government's decision to allow the Americans to base cruise missiles on British soil? Marplan surveys reported in Crewe (1985a, p. 37).

July 1981, October 1981a, April 1982, July 1982 Well, as you may know, the Russians have about 450 nuclear warheads on new medium-range nuclear missiles – the SS–20s – aimed at Western Europe, while NATO has no such missiles aimed at the Soviet Union. In view of this, do you favour or oppose having new nuclear missiles that can reach the Soviet Union stationed in Britain? USIA surveys: July 1981 NATO Survey, October 1981 Security Survey, April 1982 Versailles Economic Summit Survey, July 1982 Security Survey.

October 1981b Do you favour or oppose having new nuclear missiles that can reach the Soviet Union stationed in Britain? USIA October 1981 Security Survey.

October 1981c, January 1983a I am going to read out some suggestions people have made regarding the defence policies of this country. Please tell me whether, on balance, you think Britain should or should not do each one...Allow cruise missiles to be placed in Britain. MORI surveys reported in Crewe (1985a, p. 37).

October 1982, February 1983 Do you think Britain should or should not allow the new American-controlled cruise missiles to be based here? Gallup surveys reported in Crewe (1985a, p. 37).

January 1983b On balance, to what extent do you support or oppose the siting of Cruise missiles in Britain – strongly support, tend to support, neither support nor oppose, tend to oppose, or strongly oppose? MORI survey on public attitudes toward disarmament (These figures are based on the 77 per cent of the sample who on a previous question said they had heard of cruise missiles; only those having heard of cruise missiles were then asked their opinion on deployment. On the deployment question, those saying neither support nor oppose have been added together with the don't know responses.)

January 1983d If the United States and the Soviet Union cannot agree on limiting nuclear weapons by the end of 1983, should NATO proceed with its plan to deploy Pershing missiles and cruise missiles in Western Europe? Gallup survey of about 500 adults reported in *Newsweek*, 31 January 1983, p. 17.

April 1983, June 1983b, July 1983, December 1983 and May 1984 The preface changed a little as deployment occurred. All preface wordings are reported in Table 3.5.

In April 1983, the question was: If, by the end of the year, no agreement has been reached between the United States and the Soviet Union to reduce the number of medium-range nuclear missiles in Europe, and Britain's government, in line with the NATO decision, carries out its pledge to station such nuclear missiles in Britain, which of the following would best describe your reaction? I would strongly support such stationing; I would support such stationing, but I wouldn't feel strongly about it; I would oppose such stationing, but I wouldn't feel strongly about it; I would strongly oppose such stationing. USIA surveys: April 1983 INF Survey, June 1983 INF Survey, July–August 1983 INF Intensive Survey, December 1983 INF Survey, and May–June 1984 Security Survey.

May 1983 Please say whether you agree or disagree with the following statement: Britain should ban cruise missiles from being stationed in Britain. NOP survey reported in Crewe (1985a, p. 37).

June 1983a Please say whether you think the (following) proposal is a very good idea, a fairly good idea, a fairly bad idea, or a very bad idea: Allowing cruise missiles to be sited in Britain as part of the West's defence? Gallup survey reported in Crewe (1985a, p. 37).

November 1983, March–April 1984 Do you think Britain should or should not allow the new American-controlled nuclear cruise missiles to be based on British soil? Novembr 1983 MORI survey conducted for the Campaign for Nuclear Disarmament, 3–4/84 Gallup survey.

unrealistic beyond late 1983) of continuing negotiations without deploying. Apart from these four, opposition ranged between 40 and 61 per cent, with the trend over this period showing an increase in opposition in the last three months of the year. By late 1983, opposition clearly prevailed – in some cases it was a majority, in others a large plurality – while only about 30 per cent supported deployment.[24] Opposition continued to predominate in May 1984, but by February 1985 opinion was close to divided.

In the *Netherlands*, a wide variety of questions was also asked in the 1981–83 period, but analysis of the results suggests that, once the effects of question wording are factored out, opinion on INF deployment was fairly stable in the Netherlands over these three years, with hard-core opposition remaining in the range of 35 to 40 per cent. In most questions giving little or no information, opposition clearly prevailed at either the majority or large plurality level; as Table 3.3 shows, this was true even when information on the Soviet SS–20s was included in the question. Likewise, when the question provided for deployment as a result of the failure to reach an agreement in the INF talks, a large plurality consistently opposed deployment, according to USIA results reported in Table 3.5 and to a January 1983 survey conducted for *Newsweek*.[25] Support prevailed when deployment was linked to the Netherlands accepting 'its share' following an interim INF agreement (52–40 per cent) or when 'limited' deployment would occur if the Dutch Government and Parliament decided to do so following an interim INF agreement (60–31 per cent).

The question asked most often (nine times) in the period between early 1981 and March 1984 showed remarkable stability of Dutch attitudes toward INF deployment. This question asked 'if, after ample deliberations, the final decision is to install new nuclear missiles under the NATO framework, would you consider that a good decision, regrettable but acceptable, or a mistake that you would remain firmly against?'. It found support for deployment ranging from 52 to 57 per cent and opposition between 36 and 41 per cent. This demonstrates hard-core opposition in the same range as found on USIA questions and suggests, that, if the Dutch Government decided to go along with the NATO allies and accept deployment, then the Dutch public would predominantly support it, though many would view this result with regret. Only 11 to 18 per cent said they would consider this a good decision.[26] To summarize, both USIA and non-USIA results show that in the Netherlands the hard-core opponents numbered about 35 to 40 per cent, the hard-core supporters numbered in the range of 10 to 15 per cent, and the remaining 40 to 50 per cent of the Dutch did not have strong views and could be swayed by the circumstances presented in the question. Underlying opinion appears to have changed little over these three years.

Among the five countries, support for INF deployment was greatest in Britain, especially from early 1983 on; support, in fact, prevailed in most British surveys in mid-1983 and after. The two countries in which majorities or pluralities consistently opposed deployment were Belgium and Italy, interestingly the two basing countries in which the anti-nuclear movement was weakest. In West Germany, opposition increased somewhat between early 1981 and late 1983; for much of this period, there was either plurality opposition or divided opinion, but by the Fall of 1983 opposition clearly prevailed in all surveys. In the Netherlands, opposition prevailed on most questions. The many questions asked in these five countries suggest that factors which could increase support were primarily mention of the Soviet INF capabilities or linkage of support to either continuing or failed arms control negotiations. Mention of the NATO framework or NATO decision might also positively affect opinion, but to a limited degree. By contrast, calling the missiles American or American-controlled, in particular in Britain, generally increased the level of opposition as did presenting deployment as an alternative to continuing negotiations (rather than doing the two simultaneously or the negotiations having failed).

REASONS GIVEN FOR VIEWS ON INF DEPLOYMENT?

In a May 1984 survey in the five basing countries, supporters and opponents of INF deployment were each given a list of eight possible reasons for their views. Both lists were carefully crafted on the basis of a study of which factors in the most extensive of USIA's ten previous surveys on INF related most strongly to views on INF (Crespi, 1984); an analysis, particularly using the many questions asked in the FRG, of how the inclusion of different factors in questions affected the level of support and opposition (Adler, 1983a); previous open-ended questions; and press and academic commentary on INF. While it is difficult for such a list to capture the major reasons accurately and for respondents, many of whom have not thought intensively about the question, to explain the reasons for their own views, these two lists

Table 3.7 West German views on INF deployment, 1983 (per cent)

	Jan. 1983	Apr. 1983	Jun. 1983	Jul. 1983a	Jul. 1983b	Aug. 1983a	Aug. 1983b	Aug. 1983c	Aug. 1983d	Sep. 1983a	Sep. 1983b	Sep. 1983c	Sep.–Oct. 1983	Dec. 1983
Favour	37	36	31	41	23	46	37	31	19	28	34	58	31	29
Oppose	35	46	44	50	76	22	40	48	61	53	65	39	46	56
Don't know	28	18	24	9	1	32	23	21	20	19	1	13	23	15

Questions and Sources:

January 1983 If the United States and the Soviet Union cannot agree on limiting nuclear weapons by the end of 1983, should NATO proceed with its plan to deploy Pershing missiles and cruise missiles in Western Europe? Survey of 723 adults reported in *Newsweek*, 31 January 1983, p. 17.

April 1983, June 1983, July 1983a, and December 1983 The preface changed a little as deployment occurred. All preface wordings are reported in Table 3.5. In April 1983, the question was: If, by the end of the year, no agreement has been reached between the United States and the Soviet Union to reduce the number of medium-range nuclear missiles in Europe, and West Germany's government, in line with the NATO decision, carries out its pledge to station such nuclear missiles in West Germany, which of the following would best describe your reaction? I would strongly support such stationing; I would support such stationing, but I wouldn't feel strongly about it; I would oppose such stationing, but I wouldn't feel strongly about it; I would strongly oppose such stationing. USIA surveys: April 1983 INF Survey, June 1983 INF Survey, July-August 1983 INF Intensive Survey, and December 1983 INF Survey.

July 1983b, September 1983b If the Geneva talks fail to yield an agreement by Fall, what should be done?: Continue negotiations concerning disarmament and do not deploy new missiles in the Federal Republic; Continue negotiations concerning disarmament but deploy new missiles at the same time; Break off the disarmament talks and deploy new missiles in the FRG. (Only 3 per cent picked the third option in either survey, and they have been added together with those taking option two as favouring deployment.) Forschungsgruppe Wahlen survey reported in Adler (1983b, p. 1).

August 1983a   Assuming we can only choose between leaving NATO or deploying the new American missiles in the FRG, what should we do? - Survey reported in Rattinger (1987, p. 510).

August 1983b, September–October 1983   If Geneva yields no agreement and the Soviet Union keeps its SS–20 missiles targetted on Europe: should the new Pershing II and cruise missiles then be deployed in the Federal Republic, as provided in the NATO dual track decision, or should they in your opinion not be deployed?   Allensbach surveys reported in Adler (1983a, p. 3).

August 1983c   Which of the following views is closer to your own:

I favour stationing the Pershing II missiles because more modern weapons mean greater security; Still more powerful weapons means greater danger. I am therefore against stationing the Pershing IIs.   Allensbach survey reported in Adler (1983b, p. 2).

August 1983d   In the event that the negotiations between the United States and the Soviet Union should not bring any results, new missiles are then supposed to be deployed here in the Federal Republic as well. Are you in favour of or opposed to the deployment of new missiles?   Emnid survey reported in Adler (1983b, p. 3).

September 1983a   Suppose the two superpowers, the USA and the USSR, do not agree in Geneva by this Fall concerning the medium-range missiles. What in your opinion should be done? (a) New medium-range missiles should then be stationed in the Federal Republic, as provided in the NATO double-track decision; (b) There should be a partial stationing, but the negotiations in Geneva should nonetheless continue; (c) There should be no stationing for the present, and the negotiations in Geneva should continue; (d) One should entirely forego stationing of new missiles in the Federal Republic.   INFAS survey reported in Adler (1983b, p. 2).

September 1983c   Here is a list of statements. For each one, please tell me whether you tend to agree or to disagree with it: The West must remain sufficiently strong with regard to the Soviet Union. It is, therefore, necessary to deploy modern nuclear weapons in Western Europe if the Soviet Union does not dismantle its new intermediate-range weapons.   Emnid survey reported in Adler (1983b, p. 1).

provide very useful insights into the reasons that many Western Europeans supported or opposed INF deployment.

The belief that INF deployment will help prevent an attack/will make a war less likely was by far most frequently picked from a list as the reason *supporters* gave to explain their support for deployment. As Table 3.8 shows, far more of the supporters picked this than any other factor on the list as the most important reason or as one of their reasons for their support. Half or nearly half in all five basing countries chose this as most important and roughly seven-in-ten picked it as one of the reasons. No more than 19 per cent in any country chose any other single reason as the most important. Apart from the deterrence value of INF, other reasons picked by anywhere from a quarter to a half in these countries included the defensive value of INF, the need to match Soviet missiles, preventing the Soviets from taking advantage of Western weakness, and forcing the Soviets to negotiate reductions. This latter reason, key to the 'dual track' decision, was one of the reasons for supporting INF named by 48 per cent in Belgium, 41 per cent in Italy, 35 per cent in the Netherlands, 32 per cent in West Germany, and 28 per cent in Britain.

Among *opponents*, as Table 3.9 demonstrates, generalised antinuclear feelings were clearly the single greatest source of opposition to INF deployment. In fact, majorities of the opponents in Italy (71 per cent), Belgium (63 per cent), the Netherlands (59 per cent), and West Germany (57 per cent) and a sizeable plurality in Britain (38 per cent) chose the reason 'all nuclear weapons should be abolished' from among the list of eight given as the most important explaining their views on INF. An additional 15 per cent in Britain, 14 per cent in the Netherlands, 13 per cent in Belgium, 11 per cent in West Germany, and 9 per cent in Italy picked the statement 'there are already too many nuclear weapons in the world – no new ones are needed'. Sizeable numbers in each country picked concerns about INF deployment escalating the US–Soviet arms race (62 per cent in West Germany, 52 per cent in Italy, and 49 per cent in the Netherlands chose this one of their four reasons, though no more than one in ten called it the most important). They also picked involving their country in a US–Soviet war, or leading to a limited nuclear war confined to Europe. Clearly, however, more than any specific fears or, as explained below, than the fact that these were American missiles, *general* opposition to all nuclear weapons was the key to the views of the largest number of INF opponents. The core of INF opposition comes from the 'nuclear pacifists', those who oppose the use of nuclear

Table 3.8 Why INF supporters favour deployment, May 1984[a] (per cent choosing each reason as most important and per cent altogether picking each reason)

	Belgium		Britain		Italy		The Netherlands		West Germany	
	Most	Total	Most	Total	Most	Total	Most	Total	Most	Total
Prevent war	46	71	43	68	48	71	45	68	48	72
Defend West Europe	15	52	13	35	11	42	19	57	14	52
Match Soviet missiles	15	44	9	26	19	50	10	41	16	46
Force USSR to negotiate	8	48	7	28	11	41	8	35	5	32
Share defence responsibility	1	16	3	19	3	14	2	12	2	20
Avoid Soviets taking advantage of us	8	49	14	43	7	34	10	43	10	43
Honour NATO commitment	2	15	5	17	2	14	5	25	3	23
Demonstrate NATO strength	3	21	4	15	1	7	N/A	N/A	N/A	N/A

[a] This question was asked only of those who supported INF deployment in the preceding question in the survey: 320 in Belgium, 589 in Britain, 323 in Italy, 451 in the Netherlands, and 399 in West Germany.

Question: Here are a number of reasons why some people support stationing of these missiles (HAND CARD). Which one of these reasons is for you the most important? Which of the other reasons are important for you?: To help prevent/ deter an attack/to make war less likely; To defend/protect Western Europe in case of an attack by the East; To balance/match the medium-range nuclear missiles the Soviets have aimed at Western Europe; To force the Soviets to negotiate reductions in medium-range nuclear missiles; To share greater responsibility for West Europe's defence; To avoid having the Soviet Union take advantage of our weakness; To honor the commitment of all NATO countries to deploy these missiles in Western Europe if arms control negotiations with the USSR fail; To demonstrate NATO's strength and determination. (Up to four answers allowed.) The last item was not included in the Netherlands and West Germany.

Source: May–June 1984 Security Survey.

Table 3.9 Why INF opponents oppose deployment, May 1984[a] (per cent choosing each reason as most important and per cent altogether picking each reason)

	Belgium		Britain		Italy		The Netherlands		West Germany	
	Most	Total	Most	Total	Most	Total	Most	Total	Most	Total
Abolish all nuclear weapons	63	82	38	51	71	84	59	76	57	72
No new nuclear weapons needed	13	57	15	43	9	40	14	58	11	47
US weapons we can't control	4	28	14	35	1	14	2	24	2	22
May provoke Soviet attack	5	34	9	25	1	15	2	17	2	25
Likely to involve us in US–USSR war	4	28	10	32	5	30	6	34	4	39
Could lead to nuclear war just in Europe	5	36	6	24	2	16	4	28	9	43
US–USSR balance exists	2	16	4	10	1	8	2	15	1	17
Will escalate arms race	5	38	4	25	9	52	10	49	12	62

[a] This question was asked only of those who opposed INF deployment in the preceding question in the survey: 593 in Belgium, 477 in Britain, 688 in Italy, 597 in the Netherlands, and 612 in West Germany.

Question: Here are a number of reasons why some people say they are opposed to stationing these missiles (HAND CARD). Which one of these reasons is for you the most important? Which of the other reasons are important for you?: All nuclear weapons should be abolished; There are already too many nuclear weapons in the world – no new ones are needed; They are American weapons over which we would have no control; These missiles may provoke a Soviet attack; These missiles are likely to involve us in a US–Soviet war; These missiles could lead to a nuclear war confined to Europe; A nuclear balance between the US and the Soviet Union already exists in Europe, and no new weapons are needed; The missiles will escalate the US–Soviet arms race. (Up to four answers allowed.)

Source: May–June 1984 Security Survey.

weapons under any circumstances and are discussed in more detail in Chapter 2; in surveys during the 1980s, these 'nuclear pacifists', the overwhelming majority of whom are INF opponents according to cross-tabular analysis, ranged from 35 to 51 per cent of the Belgians, from 22 to 31 per cent of the British, from 36 to 50 per cent of the Dutch, from 29 to 48 per cent of the Germans, and from 39 to 55 per cent of the Italians.

Many press accounts clearly exaggerated in arguing that the primary reason for the opposition to INF deployment was a perception that these weapons were being forced on the Europeans by the USA. While it undoubtedly had some impact, as the results earlier reported from Britain showed, the fact that these were 'American weapons over which we would have no control' was chosen as the most important reason for their opposition by 14 per cent of opponents in Britain and only a handful (1 to 4 per cent) in the other four countries. Altogether only 14 per cent in Italy, a quarter in Belgium, the Netherlands, and West Germany, and a third in Britain picked this factor as one of the up to four reasons explaining their INF opposition. Furthermore, in a mid-1983 survey in the three largest basing countries, while a substantial number of the entire public (25 per cent in Britain, 32 per cent in Italy, and 37 per cent in West Germany) said that INF deployment was mainly in American rather than West European interest, this was the minority view. Instead, pluralities (50 per cent in Britain, 39 per cent in Italy, and 43 per cent in West Germany) thought it to be equally in the interest of both. Smaller numbers (15 to 18 per cent) considered deployment as mainly in Western European interest.[27]

PERCEPTIONS OF US AND SOVIET ARMS CONTROL EFFORTS

As discussed earlier, as late as October 1982 only half or less in the basing countries were even aware of the INF talks. In 1983 this reached two-thirds or more, but no more than about half knew in December 1983 that the talks had broken down. Many fewer, of course, had detailed knowledge of specific proposals. Therefore, to a large extent the opinions of many of the citizens in the basing countries about US and Soviet efforts for an arms control agreement were based more on general moods about the countries, their leaders, and their foreign and defence policies.

United States efforts for an arms agreement received varying evaluations in the five basing countries. Only in West Germany was opinion of US arms control sincerity consistently positive between mid-1981 and mid-1986 (opinion was divided in one survey). In Belgium, a large plurality in April 1983 said the USA was not making a sincere effort, while opinion was divided in June 1983, May 1984, and February 1985. In Britain, the USA was, in most surveys in 1982 and 1983, seen by a plurality as making a sincere effort, but from late 1983 until mid-1986 opinion varied up and down. In Italy, except for negative majorities in October 1982 and July 1986, opinion generally fluctuated back and forth between slightly positive and slightly negative readings. In the Netherlands, opinion of US efforts was predominantly positive in three of four surveys in the period from mid-1981 to mid-1983 and then was only slightly positive in surveys between June 1983 and June 1985.

In the 1981–85 period, Western Europeans generally believed that the Soviet Union was not making a genuine effort for an arms control agreement with the US. In *Belgium, Britain, and Italy*, this negative image of Soviet arms control efforts was the majority view in most surveys until late 1985. After that, following the Geneva Summit in November 1985, a plurality in Britain viewed Soviet efforts favourably, while opinion was either close to divided or only slightly negative in Italy; no post-Geneva data are available for Belgium. In *West Germany*, a plurality in ten of 14 surveys between July 1981 and September 1985 viewed the Soviet Union as not making a genuine effort for an arms control agreement; in the other four surveys in that period, opinion was divided or close to it. In the period between late 1985 and mid-1986 opinion was divided in three successive surveys. In *the Netherlands*, predominantly positive opinion in 1981 changed to predominantly negative opinion in the period between October 1982 and June 1985.

Overall, the USA came out better than the Soviet Union for the period between mid-1981 and Fall 1985, though opinion of US arms control efforts was mixed across the five basing countries. When a direct comparison of the arms control commitment of the two was asked for in the same question, the USA usually did somewhat better than the Soviets, but the largest number generally tarred both with the same brush. For example, in October 1981, considerably more called the United States the more sincere (between 18 and 31 per cent said this while only 4 to 8 per cent said the Soviets were more sincere), but between half and two-thirds in each country lumped the two together:

specifically, 25 to 44 per cent in the basing countries said *neither* was making sincere efforts to enter into arms control negotiations, and between 13 and 31 per cent said *both* were. In October 1982, both superpowers were predominantly seen by the publics in Britain, Italy, the Netherlands, and West Germany as being rigid rather than flexible in nuclear arms negotiations, with majorities saying this of the Soviets and pluralities doing so for the USA. In December 1983, shortly after the Soviets had walked out of the INF talks, about half in Britain, Italy, and West Germany said both would be equally responsible if no agreement resulted from the INF talks. About three in ten said they would blame the Soviets more, and between 6 and 18 per cent the United States more.[28]

At the same time, the United States proposals were consistently preferred, usually by majorities, sometimes by large pluralities, on the more specific questions in the 1982–83 period comparing Reagan and Brezhnev proposals or Reagan and Andropov proposals. However, by 1987, the Gorbachev effect had made an impact, with Gorbachev rating considerably ahead of Reagan on efforts for an arms control agreement in three telephone surveys between May and November in that year. In these surveys, majorities of about six in ten in Britain and West Germany and pluralities of about four in ten in France gave Gorbachev more credit for the progress on arms control then occurring, while no more than about two in ten in any of these countries thought that Reagan deserved more credit. In comparisons between the efforts of the two countries – rather than the leaders – in a September 1987 survey, just three months before the INF Treaty was signed, a large plurality in Britain gave the Soviets (40 per cent) more credit than the USA (21 per cent), while a somewhat smaller plurality (38–27 per cent) did so in West Germany; opinion was close to evenly divided in Italy (31 per cent naming the USA, 26 per cent the Soviets). However, in all three cases, between 35 and 44 per cent did not pick either one as making the greater effort.[29]

THE INF TREATY

Huge majorities in the five INF basing countries plus France supported the INF Treaty both before and after the signing at the Washington Summit.[30] In a September 1987 survey prior to the signing, 79 per cent in Britain, 66 per cent in France, 93 per cent in Italy, and 75 per cent in West Germany supported the INF Treaty.

Furthermore, many of these supporters said they strongly favoured it (58 per cent in Britain, 39 per cent in France, 75 per cent in Italy, and 52 per cent in West Germany). No more than 12 per cent in any country opposed. In a December 1987 survey conducted less than a week after the signing of the treaty, between 78 and 97 per cent in the five basing countries plus France supported the Treaty; no more than 14 per cent in any country opposed it. Strong support numbered 65 per cent in Britain, 79 per cent in Italy, 76 per cent in the Netherlands, and 77 per cent in West Germany, though considerably less in Belgium (26%) and France (34%). In March 1988, total support for the Treaty was little changed. This level of support, and, even more, this level of strong support, is found on only a very limited number of questions, most of which usually deal with pie-in-the-sky proposals. This underlines the unprecedented nature of the INF Treaty, the first US–Soviet nuclear arms agreement to bring about actual reductions rather than simply limiting increases, as well as the Western European public's satisfaction that American–Soviet relations had greatly improved compared to the early 1980s.

While there may have been some reservations at the time of the signing among some Western European elites, particularly from conservative groups (Hunter, 1988), these reservations were certainly not shared by the West European publics and were shared by only a limited number of West European newspapers. Almost all newspapers (93 out of 101) from 15 countries whose editorials or staff commentaries were analyzed either fully supported the INF Treaty or supported it with limited reservations (Ederma, 1988a). Of the 93 newspapers supporting it, only 28 expressed some reservations. Among those with reservations, the conservative and moderate papers were concerned about 'decoupling' of US–European defence links, about Warsaw Pact conventional superiority, and about the impact on NATO's deterrence strategy and the credibility of 'flexible response',[31] while those of the left and center-left were concerned that it ultimately might not change much in the security policies of the Alliance. In any case, almost all the papers said they supported the Treaty because of its political importance and the hope that it would lead to further agreements.

4 The American Image

In the postwar period, with the United States emerging as a global power, in fact, *the* global power, and with the rapid development of worldwide means of communication, the American image among foreign peoples, especially in Western Europe, East Asia, and parts of the Third World, has become an important concern of the American government and news media and, to a lesser extent, the American public. In other words, American fears of anti-Americanism have been with us for almost four decades.

In fact, most foreigners have attitudes about the United States (whether positive or negative) because of: (1) the vast amount of information about the USA in the mass media in much of the world and particularly in the industrialised, media-rich societies of Western Europe; and (2) the penetration throughout the world of American commercial products, American fads and habits, such as blue jeans or fast food, and American mass culture, such as television shows, movies, and pop music. For example, many of the most popular American TV series are broadcast almost everywhere in Western Europe; today about 30 per cent of television programming in Western Europe is American.[1] Because the United States is a global power with a global image, it is much more salient to Europeans and other peoples in the world than is Western Europe or other world regions to the average American. This is not to say that attitudes are well grounded in fact or reality, but simply that nearly all in Western Europe and in many other areas of the world have formed attitudes about the United States.

The term anti-Americanism has been widely used by the American media, but it has, at the same time, been overused and often misused by the media. Despite this imprecision and misuse, surprisingly little effort has been made by journalists or scholars to define the concept of anti-Americanism. What then is anti-Americanism? This term has often been used, and this was particularly true in the 1980s, in the mass media or even by US Government policymakers to refer to the opposition to current American policies, or even to nuclear weapons. This is not anti-Americanism. As former West German Chancellor Willy Brandt (1983) wrote: 'It would be wrong, and a political mistake, if people in the United States took the European anti-missiles attitude for anti-Americanism, or if the two were confused'. Not all criticism of the United States is anti-Americanism. Instead, anti-Americanism connotes a much deeper, more fundamental resentment toward or opposition to American society, culture, values, and people.[2] The roots of anti-Americanism are many – nationalism, longstanding intellectual trends, resentment at the richest and most powerful country in the world, anti-capitalism, distaste for American mass culture and its impact on the rest of the world (fear of 'Americanisation'), dislike of American military presence, the feeling that the USA dominates and/ or interferes in their country and does not respect or consider its views, and the failure of America to live up to the high standards set for it – and may vary considerably from one country to another.

In sum, anti-Americanism means much more than simply being opposed to the current foreign policies or leaders of the USA. Survey data demonstrate this very clearly. In the early 1970s during the height of the anti-Vietnam War protests, US policies in Vietnam were broadly opposed in Britain, France, the FRG, and Italy, but large majorities in these countries continued to have favourable overall opinions of the United States (Crespi, 1982a). Similarly, even among those opposing INF deployment in their country in the early 1980s, a majority, or in some countries a sizeable minority, of these INF opponents at the same time expressed a positive overall opinion of the United States.[3] Just as opposition to major US policies does not equal anti-Americanism, an overall favourable image of the USA does not necessarily mean that there will be broad support for US foreign policy goals or for specific US policies.

The image West Europeans have of the USA is largely independent of their image of the Soviet Union. Anti-Americanism is in most cases not the result of attraction to the Soviet model, which attracts very, very few Western Europeans. Throughout the postwar period, countless surveys have shown very few with positive views on Soviet society and political institutions. As Chapter 5 demonstrates, even as attitudes toward Soviet leaders, foreign policies, and the Soviet Union overall began to change in the second half of the 1980s, more fundamental attitudes toward Soviet values, society and institutions were slower to change and remained widely negative.

Some view anti-Americanism, which has deep cultural, historical underpinnings in Western Europe, as exclusively or primarily an 'elitist phenomenon' among intellectuals (Haseler, 1987, pp. 36–8). However, many others, including the American media and policymakers, have been more, or at least as, concerned about its manifestations among the mass public. Anti-Americanism is viewed in this chapter as something which can exist among both elites and mass publics; public opinion surveys will be used here to examine mass-level anti-Americanism.

This chapter will look at anti-Americanism, but it is about the American image much more broadly. The American image is composed of many different levels and types of opinions; individuals can have some positive attitudes about the USA mixed together with some negative ones. However, it is only the most fundamental attitudes relating to overall opinion of the United States and its society, institutions, values, and culture which speak directly to the question of anti-Americanism. Nevertheless, opinions of US foreign policy, specific US actions, or individual US leaders are part of the American image and will be examined here together with more underlying attitudes toward the United States.

ANTI-AMERICANISM IN WESTERN EUROPE

American fears of anti-Americanism are not new. American concerns about anti-Americanism in Western Europe specifically have reached their height at three times: in the late 1950s and early 1960s when the Ban the Bomb movement was active, in the late 1960s and early 1970s during the Vietnam War, and in the first half of the 1980s with the anti-INF demonstrations. In the 1980s, both the Reagan Administration and the American media, for example, cover stories in both *Newsweek* and *US News and World Report*, raised the spectre of anti-Americanism in looking at the anti-INF movement in Western Europe. Concern in the 1980s was greatest about the younger, better-educated individuals, dubbed the 'successor generation', and about Britain, the Netherlands, and West Germany, the countries with the most active movements against nuclear weapons.[4]

What then was the extent of anti-Americanism in Western Europe in the 1980s? Three different questions were used in the 1980s to measure overall opinion of the United States and, thereby, give some gauge of the level of anti-Americanism (or at least the maximum number who could be considered anti-American). These asked about pro- or anti-American feelings; good or bad opinion; or favourable or unfavourable opinion. Of course, there is no perfect measure: an overall opinion of the USA is a composite of attitudes about a wide variety of aspects of the United States, and it is defined by each individual in his or her own way. In addition, anti-American, unfavourable, and bad opinion are not exactly the same thing, and these terms may elicit somewhat different reactions from different respondents.

Nevertheless, the three measures described here are the best available and do provide at least an approximate idea of the extent and depth of anti-American feelings as well as of the trends in the 1980s. Furthermore, they do appear largely comparable. This is even true of the more direct, possibly more intimidating question, never used before the 1980s, asking one to describe himself as pro- or anti-American. As the analysis in this chapter will show, the three questions yielded very similar results. More direct evidence of this comparability comes from the September–October 1987 American Image Survey, when two of these questions (pro-/anti-American and favourable/ unfavourable opinion) were asked in the same survey; cross-tabulation of the results of the two questions shows only a small minority expressing positive feelings toward the USA on one and negative feelings on the other.[5]

One factor which creates some differences in the total number of positive and negative responses (though not in whether positive or negative feelings prevail) is how the 'neither' option is treated, that is, whether it is included directly in the question, is a volunteered response but printed on the questionnaire, or is not permitted as a response. When neither is included directly, it may draw 40 per cent or more of the responses in some countries; even when it is a volunteered response printed on the questionnaire but not included in the question as many as a quarter or more in some countries will pick this option.[6]

Among the nine Western European publics asked in the 1982–88 period whether they would describe their feelings toward the USA as either pro- or anti-American, anti-American feelings were held by roughly 15 to 25 per cent in Belgium, France, Italy, the Netherlands, Portugal, and West Germany, by a quarter to a third in Britain, by about 40 per cent in Spain, and close to half in Greece (see Table 4.1). The proportion calling themselves anti-American changed only minimally throughout the 1982–88 period in the four countries (Britain, France, Italy, and West Germany) where the question was asked most often. Not only were anti-American feelings the view of a limited minority in most countries, but, with the exception of Greece and Spain, very few (no more than 10 per cent) called themselves *strongly* anti-American. In fact, most Europeans did not hold extreme feelings toward the USA: in no country did more than 12 per cent call themselves *strongly* pro-American. In most cases, about a quarter or more volunteered a neither pro- nor anti-American response.

Pro-American feelings were the prevailing view in most or all surveys in five of the nine countries: Britain, France, Italy, the Netherlands, and West Germany. In Belgium and Portugal considerably more were pro- than anti-American, but the largest number volunteered 'neither pro- nor anti-American'. Anti-American feelings predominated, in both cases by a large plurality, in only two countries: Greece (in 1982 and 1984) and Spain (in 1986 and 1987). In Greece, the anti-Americanism can be explained largely by perceptions of American support for Turkey on the Cyprus question, while in Spain opposition to the American military presence as well as the residue of perceptions that the USA allied itself with Spanish dictator Francisco Franco are major factors.

Voters of the large leftwing parties are, depending on the country, about two to three times as likely as the voters of large centrist or conservative parties to consider themselves anti-American.[7] Differences by age, sex, or level of education are considerably smaller than those by political leaning, with those aged 25–34 and the better-educated somewhat more likely to be anti-American. Among those with anti-American feelings, the majority are leftwing, whether measured by self-placement on a left-right scale or by party preference, but a number of those calling themselves anti-American do vote for centrist or conservative parties. This minority ranges from the one in six in France who vote for the UDF, RPR, or National Front to the one in three in Britain who vote for the Conservative Party (45 per cent if those voting Liberal are also counted).

A second measure frequently asked in the 1980s gives results similar to those found through the pro-/anti-American question. When forced to choose between a favourable and unfavourable overall opinion of the United States (and not allowed to say neither), half or more in Britain and France and two-thirds or more in Italy and West Germany indicated a favourable opinion of the USA throughout the 1980s (see Table 4.2). Unfavourable opinion was at the same levels as found in the anti-Americanism question, varying between 26 and 36 per cent in Britain, 14 and 30 per cent in France, 16 and 29 per cent in Italy, and 14 and 26 per cent in West Germany.

Eight years of Ronald Reagan as US President did not cause a deterioration in the overall US image in Western Europe. In fact, in the four largest countries, favourable opinion was greater in the second

Table 4.1 Anti-Americanism in Western Europe, 1982–88 (per cent)[a]

	Belgium	Britain							
	Jul. 1988	Apr. 1982	Jul. 1982	Dec. 1983	Feb. 1984	Oct. 1984	Jun. 1986	Sep. 1987	Jul. 1988
Anti-American	15	33	23	35	32	32	36	27	26
Pro-American	35	42	52	51	55	45	38	61	47
Neither[a]	47	18	20	—	—	21	23	10	23

	France				Italy					Greece				The Netherlands		Portugal
	Apr. 1982	Jul. 1982	Oct. 1984	Jun. 1986	Jul. 1983	Dec. 1983	Feb. 1984	Sep. 1987	Jul. 1988	Apr. 1982	Jun. 1986	Oct. 1984	Jul. 1988	Jul. 1982	Jul. 1988	Jun. 1986
Anti-American	25	20	18	16	18	23	20	15	18	49	22	47	20	25	20	15
Pro-American	41	48	43	48	51	43	44	44	40	11	49	23	46	58	68	37
Neither[a]	17	32	36	33	27	30	32	39	34	24	26	22	30	—	—	48

	Spain		West Germany								
	Jun. 1986	Sep. 1987	Apr. 1982	Jul. 1982	Jul. 1983	Dec. 1983	Feb. 1984	Oct. 1984	Jun. 1986	Sep. 1987	Jul. 1988
Anti-American	40	37	18	14	28	24	22	20	14	19	18
Pro-American	14	25	38	38	66	56	56	51	30	53	47
Neither[a]	38	24	37	48	–	–	–	27	41	25	23

[a] 'Neither pro- nor anti-American' was a volunteered response. In some surveys in Britain, The Netherlands and West Germany, this response was not accepted by interviewers. Though they are clearly not fully comparable to the others in this table, these results are included in the table to give an indication of the level of anti-Americanism even without the 'neither' option.

Question: How would you describe your feelings toward the US – as strongly anti-American, somewhat anti-American, somewhat pro-American, or strongly pro-American?
In April 1982 and July 1982, the question also included the following preface: Recently, there have been some expressions of anti-American feelings among West Europeans. (Totals do not add to 100 per cent because don't know responses are not included in the Table.)

Sources: The following USIA surveys were used: April 1982 Versailles Economic Summit Survey, July 1982 Security Survey, July–August 1983 INF Intensive Survey, December 1983 INF Survey, February 1984 Middle East Issues Survey, October–November 1984 Eurobarometer, June 1986 Terrorism Survey, September–October 1987 American Image Survey and July 1988 Security Survey.

Table 4.2 Favourable opinion of the USA, 1981–89 (per cent having a favourable opinion)

	Oct. 1981	Apr. 1982	Jul. 1982	Dec. 1982	Jun. 1985	Sep. 1987	Oct. 1987	Apr. 1988	Mar. 1989	May 1989	Oct. 1989
Britain	52	60	63	56	64	59	72	70	66	63	72
France	56	59	52	48	70	60	77	68	71	66	69
Italy	67	65	66	66	80	70	76	72	—	77	78
West Germany	65	67	67	60	69	66	79	65	62	65	79

Question: And what is your overall opinion of the United States – do you have a very favourable, somewhat favourable, somewhat unfavourable, or very unfavourable opinion of the United States?

Sources: October 1981 Security Survey, April 1982 Versailles Economic Summit Survey, July 1982 Security Survey, December 1982 Correlation of Forces Survey, June–July 1985 Baseline Survey, September–October 1987 American Image Survey, October 1987 Eurobarometer, April 1988 Toronto Economic Summit Survey, March 1989 Security Survey, and May 1989 Paris Economic Summit Survey. The October 1989 data are reported in *Eurobarometer*, no. 32 (December 1989), p. A38.

Table 4.3 Favourable opinion of the USA in Western Europe, late 1980s (per cent)

	Belgium	Britain	Denmark	Finland	France	Greece	Ireland
Very favourable	12	18	13	6	9	18	21
Somewhat favourable	59	54	64	60	60	40	52
Subtotal	71	72	77	66	69	58	73
Somewhat unfavourable	21	18	18	20	20	21	12
Very unfavourable	4	6	2	2	3	9	6
Subtotal	25	24	20	22	23	30	18
Don't know	5	6	2	12	3	12	10
Total	101	101	100	100	99	100	101

	Italy	Netherlands	Norway	Portugal	Spain	Sweden	West Germany
Very favourable	21	9	10	18	10	4	20
Somewhat favourable	57	63	53	48	37	57	59
Subtotal	78	72	63	66	47	61	79
Somewhat unfavourable	13	20	23	8	25	25	13
Very unfavourable	3	2	4	1	12	2	1
Subtotal	16	22	27	9	37	27	14
Don't know	6	6	10	25	15	10	5
Total	100	100	100	100	99	98	100

Question: And what is your overall opinion of the United States – do you have a very favourable, somewhat favourable, somewhat unfavourable, or very unfavourable opinion of the United States?

Sources: Data for Finland, Norway, and Sweden are from the October 1987 Scandinavian Survey. Data for the other 11 countries are from the October 1989 Eurobarometer reported in *Eurobarometer*, no. 32 (December 1989), p. A38.

half of the 1980s than in the first half. Most pronounced was the improvement in France, where favourable opinion averaged 54 per cent in four surveys in the 1981–82 period and 69 per cent in six surveys in the 1987–89 period. In Britain, the averages for the 1981–82 and 1987–89 periods were 58 per cent and 67 per cent respectively, in Italy 66 and 75 per cent, and in West Germany 65 and 69 per cent. Furthermore, as Table 4.3 demonstrates, the most recent results from 14 West European countries show that by the late 1980s favourable opinion of the USA predominated in all 14 countries, including even Greece and Spain, where more negative views of the USA prevailed earlier in the decade. In 13 of the 14 countries, a majority held a favourable opinion of the United States by the late 1980s, while a 47–37 per cent plurality felt this way in Spain. In these 14 countries, the number with an unfavourable opinion ranged from nine per cent in Portugal to 37 per cent in Spain. Only a handful (2–6 per cent) in 12 of the countries and slightly more in Greece (9 per cent) and Spain (12 per cent) said they had a *very* unfavourable opinion.

Finally, a third measure shows good opinion of the USA prevailing over bad opinion in Fall 1987 in all 12 EC countries, though this was by a narrow margin in Greece and Spain.[8] In Greece, the picture was considerably improved in 1987, when 34 per cent had a good opinion of the USA and 29 per cent a bad opinion, from the predominantly bad opinion in October 1985. In most countries, good opinion of the USA prevailed by a wide margin in all three surveys in the 1985–87 period. As with the other two measures, few expressed strong overall views about the United States: very bad opinion totalled only about 5 per cent for the EC as whole in these three surveys and very good opinion only about 9 per cent. Almost one in four in the EC volunteered neither, which was printed on the questionnaire but not included in the question, in these three surveys.

This question was used by the United States Information Agency in surveys beginning in 1954, with an October–November 1984 survey the last time it was asked in the pure trend form used since 1954, that is, with the 'neither good nor bad' option directly included in the question wording. Looking only at this pure trend allows us to compare attitudes toward the USA in Britain, France, the Italy, and West Germany from the 1950s, 1960s, and 1970s with those in the mid-1980s (see Table 4.4). Throughout the 30 years covered by these surveys, good opinion of the USA generally predominated over bad opinion. However, except in France, the margin of good over bad opinion was substantially smaller in 1984 than in the 1950s, 1960s, and early 1970s;

this was primarily because the number of those with a good opinion dropped, while a considerably larger number chose the 'neither good nor bad' option. At the same, the proportion with bad opinion was only a little higher in Britain, Italy, and West Germany, but not France, compared to the 1950s and 1960s. Those with a bad opinion of the United States numbered only 15 per cent in Italy and West Germany, 17 per cent in France, and 21 per cent in Britain in October 1984. In sum, while substantially fewer than in earlier postwar decades were willing to express a good opinion of the USA and more had a non-committal attitude, there was no broad increase in anti-Americanism in the 1980s compared to earlier postwar decades.

Looking at the results from the three different measures together, the data show that pro-American/favourable/good opinion *consistently* prevailed over anti-American/unfavourable/bad opinion throughout the 1980s in all but two (Greece and Spain) of the 15 countries in which one or more of these three questions was asked. Furthermore by the end of the 1980s positive overall opinion of the USA predominated in Greece and Spain as well. In Western Europe as a whole, even during the height of the anti-INF demonstrations in the 1981–83 period, the proportion with a negative overall opinion of the USA was not markedly greater than in the rest of the 1980s. While opinions are generally positive, most Europeans do not have strong overall feelings about the USA one way or the other: few expressed an opinion which was strongly anti-American, very unfavourable, or very bad, but almost as few thought their opinion strongly pro-American, very favourable or very good. In addition, substantially more today than in the 1950s or 1960s choose the 'neither good nor bad' option, a non-committal view, when it is included in the question.

In sum, anti-Americanism has been the view of only a limited minority in most Western European countries throughout the postwar period and was only slightly higher in the 1980s than in the 1950s and 1960s. American preoccupation with widespread West European anti-Americanism at the time of the anti-INF demonstrations was more in the imagination of American leaders and mass media than in the reality of Western Europe. Even if many of the demonstrators were anti-American, the anti-INF demonstrations (which, as Chapter 3 showed, involved no more than two or three per cent of the population in most societies) do not equal public opinion. Clearly the term anti-Americanism was overused and misused greatly by American policymakers and mass media in describing the feelings of the West European public about the USA in the 1980s.

Table 4.4 Good/bad opinion of the USA, 1954–84 (per cent)

Britain	Average 1954–59 (15 surveys)	Average 1960–69 (8 surveys)	Jul. 1971	Mar. 1972	Jul. 1976	Oct. 1978	May 1984	Oct. 1984
Good	56	61	50	60	34	42	40	39
Bad	7	9	13	11	10	11	20	21
Neither	27	22	27	28	49	41	39	38
Don't know	10	8	10	1	7	6	1	3

France	Average 1954–59 (15 surveys)	Average 1960–69 (8 surveys)	Jul. 1971	Mar. 1972	Jul. 1976	Oct. 1984
Good	29	45	45	50	38	27
Bad	17	10	13	12	10	17
Neither	34	34	30	37	42	51
Don't know	20	11	14	1	10	5

Italy

	Average 1954–59 (15 surveys)	Average 1960–69 (8 surveys)	Mar 1972	Apr 1973	Jul 1976	Mar 1981	May 1984	Oct 1984
Good	69	65	68	66	41	52	44	39
Bad	8	5	8	9	16	9	11	15
Neither	14	15	21	20	35	38	44	43
Don't know	9	15	3	5	9	1	1	3

West Germany

	Average 1954–59 (15 surveys)	Average 1960–69 1971	Jul 1972	Mar 1973	Apr 1976	Jul 1984	May 1984	Oct 1984
Good	63	73	59	57	53	57	40	34
Bad	4	3	8	11	8	7	16	15
Neither	22	17	26	30	35	33	44	49
Don't know	11	7	8	2	4	3	—	2

Question: Please use this card to tell me your feelings about the U.S. (HAND CARD.) Do you have a very good, good, neither good nor bad, bad, or very bad opinion of the U.S.? Totals for good are both very good and good responses; totals for bad are both bad and very bad responses.

Sources: USIA Office of Research Reports M-31-72, M-34-72, M-36-72, M-37-72 and R-20-76 as well as the following USIA surveys: March 1931 Security Survey, May–June 1984 Security Survey, and USIA portion of the October–November 1984 Eurobarometer.

PERCEPTIONS OF US VALUES, SOCIETY, PEOPLE, CULTURE, AND TECHNOLOGY

This section will deal with fundamental Western European attitudes about the United States: how American values compare to their own, the American influence on their way of life, and evaluations of American society, American cultural and technological achievements, and the characteristics of American people.

Western Europeans widely believe that the USA, far more than any other country, has a great deal of influence on their way of life, though opinion is mixed on whether this influence is good or bad. In 1985, in an open-ended question, sizeable majorities in six countries and a large plurality in the seventh country surveyed named the USA as the country which 'exercises the greatest influence on the way we live today in our country'. Results were: 56 per cent in France, 65 per cent in the Netherlands and in Norway, 67 per cent in West Germany, 70 per cent in Italy, 72 per cent in Britain, and 43 per cent in Denmark. Furthermore, in all cases, the USA was named most often by a very large margin: when allowed only a single choice, no more than 5 per cent in any of these countries named any other single country as having the greatest influence.[9] In a follow-up question, opinion was roughly divided in these countries on whether this US influence was good or bad. A 1983 survey in Britain, France, and West Germany suggests that West Europeans believe there is a great deal of American influence on pop music, movies and TV and on business in their country, a fair amount of American influence on the sciences and on government policy, and very little American influence on fine arts. On fashion and style, West Germans see a fair amount of American influence, while the British and French are less likely to see substantial American influence.[10]

Opinion varies among West European publics on whether Americans and the people in their own country value similar or different things in life. As Table 4.5 shows, in 1985 a majority in France and large pluralities in Denmark and the Netherlands said they value different things, opinion was divided in West Germany, and majorities in Britain, Italy, and Norway said they do value similar things. Relatively few saw the values as either very similar (between 2 and 15 per cent) or very different (between 5 and 20 per cent). Compared to 1968 and 1982 findings, British and German opinion has not changed greatly. In France, the 1985 majority considering French and American values as different was almost exactly the same as in 1968 but a

Table 4.5 Perception of whether American values are similar to or different from their own, June 1985 (per cent)

	Britain	Denmark	France	Italy	Netherlands	Norway	West Germany
Values are:							
Very similar	15	4	2	7	6	12	11
Somewhat similar	45	38	23	47	36	63	35
Subtotal	60	42	25	54	42	75	46
Somewhat different	24	34	40	30	39	16	29
Very different	14	18	20	12	10	5	14
Subtotal	38	52	60	42	49	21	43
Don't know	2	6	16	4	9	3	10
Total	100	100	101	100	100	99	99

Question: As you know, what people value in life may vary from country to country. All things considered, do you think that what the (survey country) people and the Americans value in life are very similar, somewhat similar, somewhat different or very different?

Source: June–July 1985 Baseline Survey.

switch from 1982, when a plurality saw the values as similar. In Italy somewhat fewer than in 1982 but many more than in 1968 saw the values as similar.

On many aspects of American society – providing a chance to get ahead economically, ensuring equal justice under law, providing an adequate standard of living, guaranteeing individual political rights, ensuring religious freedom, and encouraging artistic diversity and freedom – the USA was generally rated as performing well by the publics in all four major Western European countries in both 1982 and 1987 surveys (see Table 4.6 for 1987 results). On providing jobs to its people, the USA was generally seen by the British and Italians as doing well, but opinion was mixed in France and West Germany. US ratings were lowest in two areas, taking care of its sick and elderly and assuring ethnic and racial minority rights. Studies of the university-educated in Italy and West Germany also suggest that, in addition to concerns about the American social welfare system and racial discrimination, many Europeans criticise American society as overemphasising materialism.[11] In Spain, pluralities ranging from 31 to 46 per cent (except on the issue of minority rights) saw the USA as doing well. However, the proportion with no response was considerably higher in Spain than in Britain, France, Italy, and West Germany.

Among the four largest countries, where these questions were asked in both 1982 and 1987, the biggest change in attitudes was in Britain, where opinion of US performance declined substantially on more than half the items. In France, Italy, and West Germany, attitudes did not change greatly on most items. The item on which the rating of US performance dropped the most across all four countries between 1982 and 1987 was on taking care of its sick and elderly. This was very likely in reaction to perceptions of Reagan Administration cutbacks in social welfare programs. In addition, despite the relatively low rating in 1982 of US performance on the rights of ethnic and racial minorities, there was no improvement, and in two of the four countries actually a decline, by 1987 in the ratings given the USA; clearly, Reagan Administration policies were not seen as furthering minority rights in the USA.

At the end of this battery of items, the publics were asked to provide a kind of summary judgment of American society, that is, whether it provides 'a desirable model for other countries'. As Table 4.6 shows, in 1987 a majority of Italians and a large plurality of French thought the USA does provide a desirable model. In West Germany, many more saw the USA as doing a good than a poor job as a model, but large numbers also thought the United States was doing only fairly as a model. The British and Spanish were least likely to see the USA as a good model, with opinion fragmented among those calling the USA a good, fair, or poor model. In Italy and West Germany, opinion changed little between 1982 and 1987; in France the proportion considering US performance good declined from 65 to 49 per cent, but the number saying poor remained less than 10 per cent. However, the largest change by far was once again in Britain, where a 40 per cent margin of good (52 per cent) over poor (12 per cent) dropped to only a 5 per cent margin (31–26 per cent).

American achievements in music, film, and sports were all rated as good by large majorities in Britain, France, Italy, Spain, and West Germany in a Fall 1987 survey. In fact, these achievements were seen as *very* good by between 19 and 36 per cent in the case of music, by between 21 and 56 per cent in the case of film, and by between 35 and 61 per cent in the case of sports.[12] The majority of those with an opinion on American literature and American magazines rated them as good in all five countries, but many had no opinion, ranging from 24 to 59 per cent in the case of literature and from 32 to 66 per cent in the case of magazines. Among the six aspects of American cultural life tested, only on American television, to which most Europeans are widely exposed through the many American programmes broadcast on stations in every West European country, was opinion mixed. Sizeable majorities in Italy (64–13 per cent) and Spain (56–7 per cent) and a plurality in West Germany (45–33 per cent) saw US television as good rather than poor. However, opinion was evenly divided in France (40–39 per cent), and a plurality of the British (50–42 per cent) thought American television poor rather than good.

American technology and management techniques receive very high marks among West European publics. In all five countries where this question was asked in Fall 1987 (Britain, France, Italy, Spain, and West Germany) large majorities rated American achievements in medical research, space technology, business management techniques, telecommunications, and information processing as good.[13] In fact, many rated American achievements as *very* good: between 60 and 73 per cent for medical research; between 58 and 80 per cent for space technology; between 27 and 50 per cent for management techniques; between 34 and 63 per cent for telecommunications; and between 43 and 65 per cent for information processing.

Western Europeans generally hold favourable opinions of the American people. In a Fall 1987 survey, large majorities of two-thirds

Table 4.6 Attitudes on US society, September–October 1987 (per cent)

	Britain	France	Italy	Spain	West Germany
US performance on:					
Providing its people a chance to get ahead economically					
Good	65	50	72	76	49
Fair	21	28	20	16	37
Poor	9	7	4	6	9
Maintaining law and order					
Good	32	50	53	36	55
Fair	34	29	31	23	32
Poor	25	8	12	13	9
Ensuring equal justice under law					
Good	39	38	43	31	46
Fair	31	29	31	18	34
Poor	21	17	19	20	13
Providing an adequate standard of living for its people					
Good	38	41	53	37	45
Fair	33	35	29	21	36
Poor	24	13	11	10	15
Guaranteeing individual political rights					
Good	46	48	47	31	51
Fair	27	26	28	19	30
Poor	15	9	14	15	11
Taking care of its sick and elderly					
Good	23	26	37	32	19
Fair	24	16	27	17	26
Poor	32	21	15	11	43
Ensuring religious freedom					
Good	63	60	64	45	67
Fair	19	13	22	14	20
Poor	8	5	6	8	5
Providing jobs for its people					
Good	35	22	50	33	26
Fair	39	39	29	20	40
Poor	15	20	14	14	25
Assuring ethnic and racial minority rights					
Good	26	22	28	18	26
Fair	30	26	21	14	36
Poor	31	32	40	37	30

	Britain	France	Italy	Spain	West Germany
Encouraging artistic diversity and freedom					
Good	55	69	54	44	65
Fair	25	9	24	13	18
Poor	6	2	4	6	5
Providing a desirable model for other countries					
Good	31	49	62	24	37
Fair	36	28	20	20	37
Poor	26	8	9	21	16

Question: Now, please give me your impression of U.S. performance in each of the following areas. Is it very good, good, fair, poor, or very poor?

Source: September–October 1987 American Image Survey.

or more in Britain, France, the FRG, and Italy thought that Americans appreciate the history and culture of each of their own countries; similarly large majorities in these four countries said that Americans are 'generous, friendly people'.[14] In Spain, pluralities held these favourable opinions.

On the question of trustworthiness of the American people, majorities in eight of the 12 EC countries and pluralities in two others believe Americans to be at least fairly trustworthy (see Table 4.7). In two others, Greece and Spain, where overall opinion of the United States has not been consistently favourable in the 1980s, pluralities said the Americans were not very or not at all trustworthy. In the 10 countries where this was asked in 1980 and 1982 as well, there was overall little change in the degree of trust in Americans. Among the six founding EC members (Belgium, France, Italy, Luxembourg, the Netherlands, and West Germany), the weighted average of trust in Americans was slightly lower in 1986 than the first time this question was asked in 1970, but virtually unchanged since the second time it was asked in 1976.[15] The question of trust in other peoples was also asked about all 12 EC peoples, including their own, and five other non-EC peoples in each EC country. Looking at the weighted average for the 12 EC publics together in the 1986 survey, the American people rated a little below four of the EC peoples (the Belgians, Danish, Dutch, and Luxembourgers), about the same as the Germans, a little above the

Table 4.7 Trust in Americans, March–April 1986

	Belgium	Britain	Denmark	France	Greece	Ireland
Americans are:						
Very/fairly trustworthy	55	59	47	65	31	58
Not very/not at all trustworthy	27	22	19	25	40	15
Don't know	18	19	34	10	29	28
Total	100	100	100	100	100	101

	Italy	Luxembourg	The Netherlands	Portugal	Spain	West Germany
Americans are:						
Very/fairly trustworthy	55	61	59	44	26	61
Not very/not at all trustworthy	34	21	24	21	37	31
Don't know	11	18	17	35	37	8
Total	100	100	100	100	100	100

Question: Now I would like to ask about how much you would trust people from different countries. For each country please say whether in your opinion they are in general very trustworthy, fairly trustworthy, not particularly trustworthy, or not at all trustworthy. The Americans? (Eighteen countries, including their own, were included in the list.)

Source: March–April 1986 Eurobarometer reported in *Eurobarometer, Public Opinion in the European Community*, no. 25 (June 1986), p. 41.

British, French, and Irish, and further above the four southern European peoples in the EC, the Greeks, Italians, Portuguese, and Spanish (see Table 4.8). Among the non-EC peoples, the Americans rated below the Swiss in trustworthiness, slightly above the Japanese, further above the Chinese, and far ahead of the Russians and Turks. (Changes in overall attitudes toward the Soviet Union in the late 1980s suggest that this very low rating of the Russian people would be improved by now.)

Most Western Europeans who have had contacts with Americans, have considered these contacts positive experiences, whether through American friends or acquaintances in their own country or through travel to or living in the US. In a Fall 1987 survey, about half of the British and Italians, a quarter of the French and West Germans, and 15 per cent of the Spanish reported having had such contacts with Americans; among those having contacts with Americans, between 80 and 90 per cent in each of these countries considered them positive experiences.[16]

America, far more than any other country, is seen as exerting great influence on their country's culture, though opinion is mixed on whether this influence is good or bad; there is no consensus among Western Europeans on whether American values are similar to those of their own country. Most, though not all, aspects of American society are generally viewed positively, with criticisms related to an inadequate social welfare system, racial discrimination, and materialism the most common. A majority in Italy and pluralities in France and West Germany see the USA as providing a desirable model, but opinion is divided on this in Britain and Spain. Most West European publics think human rights are well protected in the USA. American achievements in sports, music, film, and technology are highly admired, while American television is rated positively in some, but not all, European countries; and Western Europeans generally like the American people.

BILATERAL RELATIONS BETWEEN THE USA AND WEST EUROPEAN COUNTRIES

Most Western Europeans think that their country has good bilateral relations with the United States, and this has been consistently true throughout the 1984–89 period in which the question was asked despite disputes over economic issues and policies toward the Soviets. When last asked in the 1987–89 period, majorities in nine of

Table 4.8 Trust of Western Europeans in 18 different peoples, March–April 1986 (EC-wide weighted average[a])

	Very/fairly trustworthy	Not very/not at all trustworthy	Net[b]
Swiss	65	12	+53
Dutch	56	15	+41
Danes	52	14	+38
Luxembourgers	50	14	+36
Belgians	52	18	+34
West Germans	55	26	+29
Americans	54	29	+25
Japanese	50	27	+23
French	49	32	+17
British	49	34	+15
Irish	42	27	+15
Spanish	45	35	+10
Greeks	39	31	+8
Portuguese	38	31	+7
Chinese	40	34	+6
Italians	42	38	+4
Russians	29	49	−20
Turks	22	47	−25

[a] The EC-wide weighted average is the average for all 12 European Community member countries taking into account the adult population of each.

[b] The net is the total of those saying very/fairly trustworthy minus the total of those saying nor very/not at all trustworthy. Don't know responses are excluded from the table. The peoples are listed in descending order of trustworthiness.

Question: Now I would like to ask about how much you would trust people from different countries. For each country please say whether in your opinion they are in general very trustworthy, fairly trustworthy, not particularly trustworthy, or not at all trustworthy'. (Eighteen countries, including their own, were included in the list.)

Source: March-April 1986 Eurobarometer reported in *Eurobarometer, Public Opinion in the European Community*, no. 25 (June 1986), pp. 28, 41, and 43.

eleven countries considered their country's relations with the USA as good; in a twelfth country, Norway, an overwhelming majority saw relations as good when last asked in 1985.[17] The two exceptions among these 12 countries were Spain, where a large plurality, however, did view relations as good, and Greece, where opinion was divided. In other words, in no West European country were bilateral relations with the USA predominantly viewed as bad when most recently asked. Furthermore, except for Greece and Spain, no more than one in ten in any country saw relations with the USA as bad. At the same time, in most countries, no more than about one in ten saw relations as *very* good; exceptions were Britain (39 per cent), Ireland (43 per cent), and Italy (26 per cent). In the four largest countries, where the question was asked several times in the 1987–89 period, very large majorities considered relations with the USA good, ranging from 88 to 95 per cent in Britain, from 70 to 87 per cent in France, from 77 to 94 per cent in Italy, and from 72 to 89 per cent in West Germany. In 1985, the publics in 11 of the 12 countries predominantly saw relations as good; only Greece, where more saw them as bad than good, was an exception. In 1984, when the 'neither good nor bad' option was directly included in the question, results were generally the same, though in three countries (Belgium, France, and Spain) the number saying 'neither' equalled the number saying 'good'.[18]

Furthermore, the publics in the four largest countries saw the basic interests of the United States and their own country as in agreement even during the period of most intense anti-INF activity. In December 1982, large majorities in Britain (79–19 per cent), the FRG (70–17 per cent), and Italy (78–19 per cent) and a large plurality in France (52–37 per cent) considered the basic interests of the USA and their country to agree. This question was asked roughly twenty times in the four largest West European countries in the period between 1956 and 1976. Compared to these trend results, the 1982 findings represented an all-time high in Italy and the third or fourth highest levels in the other three countries.[19]

Nevertheless, many Western Europeans see their country's foreign policy as too closely linked to US foreign policy rather than as independent. In July 1988, this was the view of a majority in Italy, a large plurality in West Germany, and a bare plurality in the Netherlands, while in Belgium equal numbers said their foreign policy was too closely tied or that they were not sure. In Britain, opinion was evenly divided over whether their foreign policy was too closely tied or was independent but with many of the same goals. Only the French among these six publics predominantly, by a large plurality, saw their foreign policy as independent.[20]

Many Western Europeans also think the USA is not sensitive to their country's interests or views. Specifically, Europeans generally believe that the USA expects their country to give in to its wishes on matters of mutual concern and that the USA takes their country's view into account only a little at most on decisions affecting their own country's security or Western Europe's economy. In Fall 1987, eight in ten in Britain and West Germany, two-thirds in France and Spain, and 55 per cent in Italy thought that 'America expects us to give in to its wishes in matters that concern both countries'. Furthermore, in Fall 1987 majorities in Britain (64 per cent), France (59 per cent), and Spain (56 per cent) and a near majority in Italy (53 per cent) agreed with the statement 'America does not try to understand our country's problems'. Opinion was evenly divided between agreement and disagreement in West Germany.[21] In 1982, majorities in Britain, France, and Italy and a large plurality in West Germany said the USA considers their country's views on security issues only a little rather than a fair amount or a great deal, while in 1984 and 1985 large majorities in all four countries had the same negative feelings about how much the USA takes into account their country's views on decisions affecting Western Europe's economy.[22]

Many West Europeans are also sceptical that the USA will protect their country's interests in US–Soviet arms control negotiations. In a number of surveys in the 1984–88 period, about 40 to 50 per cent in Britain, France, Italy, and West Germany had little or no confidence that the USA would protect their country's interests on arms control issues key to their own national security.[23] In these four countries, this lack of confidence either prevailed by a small margin or opinion was close to divided (the only exception was the first time this was asked, when a 56 to 40 per cent majority in Britain in May 1984 had at least a fair amount of confidence in the USA). In three smaller NATO countries (including the two smaller INF basing countries) surveyed in 1985, a majority in the Netherlands and large pluralities in Belgium and Denmark had little or no confidence in the USA to protect their interests.

Despite these broadly negative feelings that America does not consider their country's wishes very seriously in making foreign, economic, and security policy decisions, large majorities in Britain (64 per cent), France (71 per cent), Italy (62 per cent), and West Germany (66 per cent) in Fall 1987 thought that 'America treats our country with dignity and respect'. In Spain, opinion was evenly divided between agreement and disagreement.[24] Furthermore, in surveys during the 1980s, most Western Europeans opposed weakening their country's ties with the United States. When asked in 1985 and/or 1987 whether it would be best for the long run to strengthen its ties, to continue relations as they were, or to lessen ties with the USA, the prevailing opinion, of a majority or large plurality, in ten of the 12 Western European countries favoured keeping relations about the same. In no country did the view that ties should be weakened predominate; in fact in 1987 the proportion wanting to weaken ties to the USA numbered one in five or more only in four countries: the Netherlands (19 per cent), Britain (22 per cent), Greece (28 per cent), and Spain (29 per cent).[25]

Western Europeans, in sum, widely think their relations with the USA are good. However, they are far from satisfied with the way these relations work and see them as unequal. In particular, Western Europeans do not think that their country's views are seriously considered on most economic and security issues, and they believe that the USA expects their country to give into its wishes on matters of mutual concern. Many are also concerned about whether the USA will protect their country's interests in arms control negotiations. Nevertheless, the bottom line is that most Western Europeans do not favour weakening their ties with the United States.

WEST EUROPEAN VIEWS ON US FOREIGN POLICY

This section will examine West European views on American foreign policy during the Reagan years. Because opinion about US foreign policy is considerably more sensitive to events of the moment than most of the other attitudes about the USA examined in this chapter, we will use data only from the four largest countries for much of this section. It is only for these four countries that the two major measures of attitudes toward American foreign policy – about confidence in the USA to deal responsibly with world affairs and about whether US policies in the previous year have done more to promote peace or to increase the risk of war – were asked more than sporadically in the 1980s.

Confidence in the ability of the United States to deal responsibly with world affairs has often varied considerably, sometimes even from one month to the next, in each of the four major West European countries during the 1980s, as it did in the 1960s and 1970s. At some times in the 1980s, however, the fluctuation was more limited. In any case in Britain and West Germany in particular, and in Italy to a lesser extent, the overall trend in confidence in US foreign policy was downward; positive opinion prevailed much less often in the 1980s than in the 1960s and 1970s, the high points were not as high as in the earlier decades, and the low points were lower. In France, by contrast, confidence in US foreign policy was a little greater in the 1980s than in earlier decades. In all four countries, the confidence in US foreign policy rose considerably in the first year of President Bush. (See Table 4.9 for a summary of results; full data for the 1960–89 period is in Table A.1 in Appendix 3.)

The decline in the level of confidence in US foreign policy in Britain, Italy, and West Germany during the Reagan years was very likely the result of the more confrontational American polices toward the Soviet Union in the first half of the decade. These policies, as well as American rhetoric, for example President Reagan's March 1983 'evil empire' speech, raised concerns among many Western Europeans about being involved in an East–West conflict. Furthermore, crosstabulation of questions on confidence in US foreign policy and confidence in Soviet foreign policy shows that lack of confidence in one does not necessarily mean having confidence in the other.[26] In other words, the strong criticism of Soviet foreign policy by the Reagan Administration did not increase confidence in US foreign policy and probably lowered it.

In West Germany, between early 1981 and early 1989, little or no confidence in US foreign policy prevailed in 14 of 21 surveys. This was in direct contrast to the 1960–75 period, when the West Germans predominantly had at least a fair amount of confidence in 10 of 15 surveys. Moreover, on six occasions between 1960 and 1975, the net measure of confidence, that is the proportion having a great deal or fair amount of confidence minus the proportion with little or no confidence, reached +50 or more. In the Reagan years, this margin was never higher than +19; in President Reagan's second term, it was never higher than +8. In the 1960–75 period, the net never went below −3, while in the 1980s it reached −24 and was at −11 or lower in half of the surveys.

In Britain, the 1980s also registered overall lower confidence in US foreign policy than in the 1960–75 period. In the 1980s opinion of US foreign policy varied greatly, predominantly negative seven times, divided six times, and predominantly positive six times. By contrast

Table 4.9 Confidence in US foreign policy, 1960–89 (net confidence – per cent with great deal or fair amount of confidence minus per cent with little or no confidence)

	Britain			France		
	Average	Range	No. of surveys	Average	Range	No. of surveys
1960–75	+20	−16 to +50	15	−2	−22 to +30	16
1981–82	+5	−9 to +14	6	+8	+3 to +17	3
1983–84	−3	−32 to +13	5	—	—	none
1985–86	−12	−23 to −3	5	+8	+4 to +16	3
1987–88	−10	−24 to +4	2	+7	+1 to +13	2
1989	+20	+19 to +21	2	+22	+17 to +27	2

	Italy			West Germany		
	Average	Range	No. of surveys	Average	Range	No. of surveys
1960–75	+37	+17 to +49	11	+33	−5 to +68	15
1981–82	+34	+24 to +45	5	+1	−14 to +19	7
1983–84	+17	+4 to +30	6	−18	−24 to −11	6
1985–86	+18	+7 to +23	5	−7	−18 to 0	5
1987–88	+20	+10 to +29	2	−4	−15 to +8	2
1989	+43	both +43	2	+20	+2 to +49	2

Question: How much confidence do you have in the ability of the United States to deal responsibly with world problems – a great deal, a fair amount, not very much, or none at all? The question wording varied slightly from this in some earlier surveys in the 1960–75 period, but not enough to affect comparability.

Sources: See Table A.1 in Appendix 3.

in the 1960–75 period positive opinion prevailed 11 of 15 times. During the Reagan years, the margin of positive over negative opinion never got higher than 14 per cent; in the 1960–75 period, it was 25 per cent or more in about half the surveys. Furthermore, the trend was downward during the Reagan years themselves; in his second term the net never rose above +4, and negative opinion prevailed in 5 of 7 surveys.

In Italy, this question on confidence in US foreign policy has never registered negative readings in the 1960s, 1970s, or 1980s, although the margin of positive over negative views was more narrow in several surveys in the 1980s than in any survey in the 1960s or 1970s. Specifically, in four surveys in the 1980s, positive views prevailed by only 4, 9, 7, and 10 per cent; by contrast in the 1960–75 period, except for one survey in which confidence predominated by only 17 per cent, the lowest net was +28. Net confidence, though still overall quite positive in the 1980s, averaged 15 points less in the Reagan years (+22) than in the 1960–73 period (+37). In France, the general trend is opposite to that in the other three countries. In the 1980s French confidence in US foreign policy was *never* predominantly negative; in the 1960s and 1970s it was frequently so. In the 1980s French opinion was either divided (five times) or generally positive (four times).

The second major measure of attitudes toward US foreign policies asks whether 'US policies and actions during the past year have done more to promote peace or done more to increase the risk of war'. Attitudes toward US foreign policy as measured by this question also often vary considerably from survey to survey, and it is, in fact, even more directly sensitive to events than the confidence question (see Table 4.10 for the net of promotes peace minus risks war and Table A.2 in Appendix 3 for the full results). On this peace–war question, which appears to reflect more immediate fears and concerns, the West German public's evaluation varied greatly during the Reagan years: six times generally viewing US policies as promoting peace, six times being divided or close to divided, and four times predominantly seeing US policies as risking war. The British were the most consistently negative about US policies; in 11 of 16 surveys in Britain during the Reagan Administration, majorities or large pluralities saw US policies as tending more to risk war. In Italy, in contrast with the confidence question on which negative views never prevailed, the public saw US policies as tending more to risk war in 6 of 16 surveys; Italian opinion was divided in six surveys. France, where the question was only asked half as often as in the other three countries, was the exception in that opinion changed relatively little, with pluralities in six of nine

Table 4.10 Effects of US policies, 1982–89 (net – per cent saying US policies have done more to promote peace minus per cent saying they have done more increase the risk of war)

	Apr. 1982	Jul. 1982	Apr. 1983	Jul. 1983	Dec. 1983	Feb. 1984	May 1984	Feb. 1985	May 1985
Britain	0	+ 8	− 33	− 18	− 54	− 47	− 23	− 14	− 32
France	− 4	+ 10	—	—	—	—	—	—	—
Italy	− 1	+ 8	− 15	− 10	− 26	− 20	+ 1	− 2	− 4
West Germany	+ 13	− 1	− 7	− 21	− 15	− 21	− 7	+ 11	+ 6

	Jun. 1985	Sep. 1985	Dec. 1985	Mar. 1986	Jun. 1986	Jul. 1986	Nov. 1987	Mar. 1989
Britain	− 15	− 26	+ 17	+ 1	− 48	− 47	0	+ 30
France	+ 25	+ 8	+ 28	+ 39	− 6	+ 14	+ 8	+ 42
Italy	+ 27	− 5	+ 13	+ 11	− 27	− 29	− 1	−
West Germany	+ 12	0	+ 21	+ 24	− 24	− 3	+ 22	+ 49

Question: On balance, do you think that US policies and actions during the past year have done more to promote peace or more to increase the risk of war?

Sources: All surveys are listed in Table A.2 in Appendix 3, where full results are given.

surveys and a majority in another seeing US policies as tending more to promote peace.

Looking at the results of this peace–war question in Britain, Italy, and West Germany over the 1982–88 period, opinion of US foreign policy was most consistently negative in 1983. This was the low point of US–Soviet relations in the 1980s marked by President Reagan's 'evil empire' speech in March 1983, his announcement, also in March, of the Strategic Defense Initiative, the Soviet shootdown of the Korean airliner in September 1983, the US intervention in Grenada in October 1983, the Soviet walkout from the INF negotiations in Geneva in November 1983, and INF deployment in Britain, West Germany, and Italy beginning in late 1983. Approval of US foreign policy rebounded considerably by late 1985 immediately following the first Reagan–Gorbachev Summit, but then dropped substantially once again by mid-1986. In fact, between March 1986 and June 1986, the net opinion (the proportion saying US policies tended more to promote peace minus the proportion saying they tended more to increase the risk of war) fell from $+24$ to -24 in West Germany, from $+11$ to -27 in Italy, and from $+1$ to -48 in Britain. This quick drop undoubtedly was the result of the US bombing raid on Libya in April 1986, which was widely disapproved of by the British, German, and Italian publics. A month later, in July, opinion was still highly negative in Britain and Italy, but had partially recovered in West Germany to be divided. By late 1987, just prior to the Reagan–Gorbachev Washington Summit, opinion of US foreign policy once again improved: in Britain and West Germany to the level of March 1986 and in Italy to a little below this level. French opinion, which dropped from a net $+39$ in March 1986 to -6 in June 1986 rebounded more quickly, with the net reaching $+14$ in July 1986; this quicker improvement in France may have been because a plurality of the French approved the US bombing raid in Libya.

Results on the other general measure of attitudes toward US foreign policy, confidence, also varied with events to a degree, but not nearly as much or as regularly as on the peace–war question. Confidence in US foreign policy was also at or near its lowest point in Britain, Italy, and West Germany in 1983. Confidence in the USA regained somewhat in 1985 and then fell again in the mid-1986 to mid-1987 period, a time in which the bombing in Libya, the October 1986 Reykjavik Summit, and the late 1986/early 1987 revelations of the Iran–Contra scandal all occurred. However, the magnitude of these changes was much less than those on the peace–war question. Confidence once again rose between early 1987 and mid-1988 to the highest net levels of President Reagan's second term, +4 in Britain, +8 in West Germany and +29 in Italy.

These two measures do not tap exactly the same feelings toward US foreign policy. While they generally vary together within each country, this correlation is by no means perfect; in fact, in some instances, the two questions give very different findings even within the same survey. However, both are valuable: the peace-war question is a more sensitive barometer with changing events, while the confidence question allows us to compare views on US foreign policy in the 1980s with those from the 1960s and 1970s. Overall, the Italians see US foreign policy considerably more negatively on the peace-war question than on the confidence question; this is also true to a less pronounced degree among the British. By contrast, the opposite occurs in West Germany, where results on the confidence question give more negative findings.

In a battery of items asked in Fall 1987 in the four major West European countries in which respondents had to compare US and Soviet foreign policy directly in the same question, the USA received highest marks in comparison to the Soviets on fostering human rights in other countries, willingness to negotiate disputes, and helping poorer nations to develop (see Table 4.11). Except in Britain, where opinion was more mixed, the USA was also generally considered as the more trustworthy in negotiations, though a quarter to a third said both were equally trustworthy. In a survey done when the INF Treaty was almost completed and just two months before it was signed, both the USA and the Soviets received relatively good marks for 'genuinely wanting peace in the world', with the United States doing somewhat better in all four countries. Fewer thought the USA rather than the USSR likely to use military force to attain its goals. However, echoing the finding that many thought US policies tended more to increase the risk of war than to promote peace, sizeable numbers, ranging from 37 to 49 per cent, said that both the USA and the Soviet Union used military force to attain their goals. Among all the items tested, the USA was rated most poorly on two which parallel some of the West European concerns about bilateral relations with the USA: trying to dominate other countries economically or interfering in the affairs of other countries. On trying to dominate other countries economically, seven in ten or more in each of the four countries either said this was true more of the USA than the Soviets or that it was true of both of them, with between 27 and 48 per cent saying it applied more to the

Table 4.11 How the USA and Soviet Union compare on various aspects of foreign policy, 1987 (per cent)

	Britain	France	Italy	West Germany
Fosters human rights in other countries				
Applies more to USA	56	64	64	68
About equally to both	17	13	9	15
Applies more to USSR	6	5	4	2
Uses military force to attain its goals				
Applies more to USA	19	10	16	9
About equally to both	44	37	47	49
Applies more to USSR	32	41	30	40
Willing to negotiate disputes				
Applies more to USA	48	51	43	48
About equally to both	29	24	28	37
Applies more to USSR	10	4	11	5
Trustworthy in negotiations				
Applies more to USA	27	42	36	43
About equally to both	27	25	26	35
Applies more to USSR	10	3	13	9
Neither (volunteered)	27	14	15	9
Tries to dominate other countries economically				
Applies more to USA	43	43	48	27
About equally to both	30	36	33	44
Applies more to USSR	17	9	12	24
Helps poorer nations to develop				
Applies more to USA	53	61	55	66
About equally to both	20	14	10	22
Applies more to USSR	5	3	4	2
Interferes in the affairs of other countries				
Applies more to USA	29	22	27	12
About equally to both	49	52	47	57
Applies more to USSR	17	11	15	27
Genuinely wants peace in the world				
Applies more to USA	21	29	23	28
About equally to both	52	35	34	48
Applies more to USSR	13	4	11	8

Question: Now I am going to read you several statements that might apply to the U.S. or to the USSR in their relations with other countries. For each statement on this card (HAND CARD), please tell me if you think it applies very much more to the US, a bit more to the US, about equally to both, a bit more to the USSR, or very much more to the USSR. Responses do not total 100 per cent because 'don't know' and, except in one case, volunteered 'neither' responses are not included.

Source: September–October 1987 American Image Survey.

USA. On the interference in the affairs of other countries, about half in each country said this was true of both, and an additional 12 to 29 per cent said it applied more to the United States.

On most items, relatively little change occurred if one compares the three times these questions were asked (1982 in all four countries, 1984 in Britain, Italy, and West Germany, and 1987 in all four).[27] Among the four countries, opinion changed the most in Britain, with the US rating dropping somewhat on nearly every item; this drop occurred in most cases between 1984 and 1987. The item on which results changed the most across countries, with the exception of France, was on the use of military force to attain its goals; between 1982 and 1987, the proportion saying this was true primarily of the Soviet Union dropped from 68 to 32 per cent in Britain, from 45 to 30 per cent in Italy, and from 53 to 40 per cent in West Germany.

In the first half of the 1980s, American policymakers at times expressed concern over 'moral equivalence', that is, that the Western Europeans viewed the two superpowers as being about the same. As Chapter 5 will show, this fear was greatly exaggerated. Overall opinion of the Soviet Union and its foreign policy improved only after Gorbachev came to power in 1985 and brought about sweeping change; furthermore, Soviet society still received very negative marks in the late 1980s. However, when looking at foreign policy goals in very broad terms, Western Europeans at times did tar both the USA and the Soviet Union with the same superpower brush. This was true on the items relating to economic domination and interference in the affairs of other countries. In addition, when asked a very general question about the foreign policy goals of the two superpowers in Fall 1987, pluralities in seven of eight countries surveyed and a majority in Italy said that the foreign policy goals of the USA and the USSR are basically the same rather than fundamentally different.[28] Even more dramatically, in Fall 1984 large pluralities in eight of ten West European countries surveyed thought that 'what the Soviet Union is doing in Afghanistan and what the USA is doing in Central America' are about the same thing; in West Germany, a large plurality thought the two things very different.[29]

WESTERN EUROPEANS AND PRESIDENT REAGAN

Ronald Reagan was President for eight years from 1981–89, the first American President since Dwight Eisenhower to serve two full terms. Of special importance to West Europeans the eight years of the Reagan Administration were marked by the key battle over INF deployment in the 1981–85 period; by great change in US–Soviet relations from the 'evil empire' speech and INF deployment in 1983 to the Reagan–Gorbachev Summits in the 1985–88 period, including the INF Treaty signed in Washington in December 1987; and by the Iran–Contra revelations in late 1986/early 1987. Clearly, most Western Europeans had formed some opinion of President Reagan by the 1987–88 period. In Fall 1987, President Reagan had only limited popular support in Western Europe; favourable opinion of President Reagan ranged from 26 per cent to 53 per cent in eight West European countries surveyed. Furthermore, as Table 4.12 shows, favourable opinion clearly prevailed only in France and West Germany; opinion was close to divided between favourable and unfavourable views in Italy. On the other hand, majorities or near majorities in Britain (58 per cent), Denmark (58 per cent), Finland (64 per cent), Norway (50 per cent), and Sweden (53 per cent) held unfavourable views of President Reagan. When asked in a follow-up question to explain their views of Reagan, those with favourable opinions generally cited his friendly, inspiring personality, his trustworthiness, and, in West Germany, his sincerity on arms control. Those with unfavourable opinions of Reagan most often questioned his effectiveness (saying, for example, he was 'too old', 'only an actor', 'makes many mistakes'), his trustworthiness, his policies, and his being tainted by scandal.

Data on President Reagan's popularity for more than this Fall 1987 snapshot are available from only three West European countries, Britain, France, and West Germany. These findings (for the mid-1985 to Spring 1988 period in France, for the late 1985 to mid-1988 period in West Germany, and for practically the entire Reagan

Table 4.12 Overall opinion of President Reagan, Fall 1987 (per cent)

	Britain	Denmark	Finland	France	Italy	Norway	Sweden	West Germany
Very favourable	5	3	1	4	11	6	2	9
Somewhat favourable	31	28	25	43	37	36	31	44
Subtotal	36	31	26	47	48	42	33	53
Somewhat unfavourable	34	44	49	19	33	37	44	29
Very unfavourable	24	14	15	6	11	13	9	8
Subtotal	58	58	64	25	44	50	53	37
Don't know	5	11	9	29	9	8	14	11
Total	99	100	99	101	101	100	100	101

Question: What is your overall opinion of American President Ronald Reagan – do you have a very favourable, somewhat favourable, somewhat unfavourable, or very unfavourable opinion of President Reagan?

Sources: For Britain, France, Italy and West Germany: September 1987 Security Survey. For Denmark, Finland, Norway and Sweden: October 1987 Scandinavian Survey.

Administration (March 1981–July 1988) in Britain) show that opinion differed among the three countries. The British held a predominantly negative view of President Reagan in nearly all surveys, with favourable opinion never clearly prevailing in any of more than 30 results examined. The French had a favourable opinion (at the majority or large plurality level) in all cases; and West German opinion ranged up and down between favourable readings of as high as a net (favourable minus unfavourable) of +25 and unfavourable readings of as low as a net of −18, with opinion divided or close to it in about half the surveys.[30]

Lack of trend data for the entire Reagan Administration from more than one West European country makes it difficult to judge whether President Reagan's popularity eroded or improved or ultimately changed little through his eight years in power. However, the evidence which is available, from Britain, where the same question about whether President Reagan was or was not proving a good President of the USA was asked by Gallup 26 times between March 1981 and July 1988, suggests that there was no consistent trend, but rather variation up and down with events. The most consistently negative findings were in the 1982–84 period, when the net result of those saying he was proving a good President minus those saying he was not ranged from −20 to −32, with an average of −27. For 1985–86, the average net was −8, for three surveys between July 1987 and April 1988, it was −24. President Reagan may have ended his Administration on a more positive note, with opinion on him divided or close to it in June and July 1988. Overall, President Reagan was predominantly viewed negatively by the British in most surveys in the 1980s; the best he did was a rough division between positive and negative views. By contrast, President Reagan's predecessor, Jimmy Carter, was predominantly seen as being a good President seven out of the nine times this question was asked about him between May 1977 and April 1980, in three cases by small pluralities, in three by larger pluralities, and in the first survey by a majority.[31]

While President Reagan did well among West European publics in comparison to Soviet leaders prior to Gorbachev, he suffered by comparison to Gorbachev both in general popularity ratings and in getting credit for the arms control progress in the last two years of his term. For example, Reagan scored well ahead of both Leonid Brezhnev and Yuri Andropov in efforts to achieve an arms control agreement, but has been far behind Gorbachev on the same comparison. In April 1982, the publics in Britain, France, Italy, and West

Germany predominantly viewed Reagan's effort to reduce nuclear weapons as sincere and Leonid Brezhnev's effort as not sincere. In January 1983, more in Britain, France, and West Germany saw Reagan rather than Andropov as credible on the issue of limiting nuclear weapons; only in the Netherlands, where opinion was divided, was Reagan not clearly ahead. By contrast, in three telephone surveys in the May to November 1987 period, Gorbachev rated well ahead of Reagan on who deserved more credit for the progress then occurring in arms control negotiations. In the November survey, large majorities in Britain (61 per cent) and West Germany (61 per cent) and a plurality in France (38 per cent) saw Gorbachev rather than Reagan as doing more for arms control; many fewer in Britain (18 per cent) and West Germany (17 per cent) and somewhat less (25 per cent) in France said Reagan deserved more credit.[32]

On general opinion of the two leaders, Reagan was also far behind Gorbachev in seven of the eight countries surveyed in Fall 1987; the exception was France, where the two were rated about the same. In the other seven countries, the proportion with a favourable opinion of Gorbachev was between 27 and 65 per cent greater than the number with a favourable opinion of Reagan (see Chapter 5 for the detailed Gorbachev results). At the same time, on more specific questions asked in five surveys in the December 1985 to February 1987 period, President Reagan did better, either being rated somewhat ahead of Gorbachev or about the same on five items. These were understanding European problems, wanting world peace, being trustworthy, being flexible in negotiations, and likeliness of using military force to achieve his objectives.[33]

In most West European countries, opinion of President Reagan was either divided or generally unfavourable in the 1987–88 period; among the eight countries from which data are available, opinion of President Reagan was consistently favourable only in France. There is no evidence of a constant trend in West European opinion of President Reagan over his eight years in office; in fact, the evidence that is available suggests variation with changing events. In Britain, his rating reached low points probably associated with INF deployment and the Iran–Contra revelations, but he bounced back in both cases. President Reagan did well when compared to Brezhnev and Andropov, but on general popularity and credit for arms control, he suffered in comparison to Gorbachev. This comparison may not, however, be a totally fair one given the novelty of Gorbachev in 70 years of Soviet history.

CONCLUSIONS

American policymakers and mass media greatly exaggerated the extent of anti-Americanism in Western Europe in the 1980s. They confused dissatisfaction with US foreign policy and opposition to INF deployment with more fundamental attitudes toward the USA. Anti-Americanism is the view of only a limited minority; furthermore, very few Western Europeans consider themselves to be strongly anti-American. While West Europeans have concerns about US–European relations, they generally consider them to be good and do not want to weaken them. Opinion of US foreign policy was at times very negative in many West European countries, with confidence lower in Britain and West Germany in particular and in Italy to a certain extent in the 1980s than in the 1960–75 period. However, the more fundamental attitudes toward the USA as a country, towards most aspects of American society, and towards the American people have remained largely positive and have not changed nearly as much; they certainly have not shifted back and forth between positive and negative as has occurred in some countries in attitudes toward US foreign policy. Among the publics of the four major countries, the greatest changes across the broad range of questions examined in this chapter occurred in France, where overall opinion of the USA and its foreign policy became more positive in the 1980s, and in Britain, where some attitudes about the USA became more negative in the 1980s. Even in Britain, however, overall opinion of the USA did not decline in the decade, and many of the fundamental attitudes toward the United States remained predominantly favourable. After eight years of Ronald Reagan as President, overall opinion of the United States in Western Europe as a whole, while probably no more positive, does not appear to be any more negative as we begin the 1990s than it was when we entered the 1980s.

5 Soviet Image and Public Diplomacy

The transformation of public attitudes toward the Soviet Union after Gorbachev became the Soviet leader in March 1985 represents the most dramatic change in West European public opinion in the 1980s. This chapter documents the general perceptions of the Soviet Union and its leaders, as well as West European attitudes on specific Soviet-related issues such as human rights, Afghanistan and the Soviet political system. Although the Soviet Union enjoyed a positive overall image in latter half of the 1980s throughout Western Europe, Europeans did not approve of many specific Soviet actions and policies nor of Soviet human rights policies. However, many of these attitudes can be expected to improve as democratic reforms take hold inside the Soviet Union in the 1990s, and as further changes in Soviet foreign policy occur. The last section of the chapter discusses the various Soviet public diplomacy efforts during the 1980s in Western Europe designed to improve the image of the Soviet Union as well as drive a wedge between Western Europe and the United States.

The USSR has, to a large extent, framed the relationship between the United States and Western Europe during the postwar period. Western perceptions of the Soviet Union form the cornerstone of numerous Allied security, political and economic policies. As attitudes toward the Soviet Union have improved across West European publics, so too one can anticipate a re-examination of West European attitudes toward the special Allied relationship that has existed since World War II. Clearly the rise of Mikhail Gorbachev was central to the improvement of the overall Soviet image among many West Europeans. Since Gorbachev became the leader of the Soviet Union in 1985, a substantially greater number of West Europeans say they have a favourable image of the Soviet Union, have confidence in its foreign policy to solve world problems, and perceive Soviet policies as promoting peace rather than increasing the risk of war. However, this improved overall image of the Soviet Union among Western Europeans should not be interpreted as a blanket endorsement of the condition of Soviet society, including the status of human rights, or specific Soviet foreign policies.

In tracking the Soviet image among Western Europeans during the 1980s, two distinct time frames emerge: before and after Gorbachev. The before Gorbachev period was characterised by a negative perception of the Soviet Union as it went through a series of leaders, none of whom generated much public support in Western Europe. By stark contrast, West European opinion of the Soviet Union reached new heights once Gorbachev became established as the new Soviet leader.

The traditionally negative perception of the Soviet Union was a significant factor in the glue that held the Western political, economic and military Alliance together throughout the postwar period. Once this glue began to dissolve, Western leaders faced an increasingly difficult task of stimulating Allied support for continued defence expenditures. Furthermore, the perceived transformation of the Russian bear sparked an intense debate within the Alliance over the appropriate Western response. This debate focused on such issues as whether the USA and Western Europe should encourage Soviet reforms by helping to shore up the devastated Soviet economy through liberalising trade policies or by entering into arms control agreements to reduce the Soviet defence burden. British Prime Minister Margaret Thatcher noted 'The Russian bear was easier to deal with when it looked more like a bear'.[1]

As Gorbachev has brought about a change in the Soviet image throughout Western Europe, so too has he modernized Soviet public diplomacy efforts targeted to Western Europe. The new Soviet leader introduced a more sophisticated charm offensive to replace the crude peace offensive strategy of the Brezhnev era. Gorbachev's more open international diplomacy emphasized 'his dedication to peace and international stability' as well as his domestic policies of glasnost and perestroika to improve the Soviet image abroad (Szabo, 1989, p. 153).

THE OVERALL IMAGE OF THE SOVIET UNION

Throughout the 1980s, three survey questions were asked primarily in the four major West European countries to measure overall attitudes toward the Soviet Union and its foreign policies. These questions inquire about overall opinion of the Soviet Union, confidence in Soviet foreign policy, and whether Soviet policies promote peace or increase the risk of war. Other variations of these measures were asked sporadically throughout the decade and are discussed where relevant.

Prior to Mikhail Gorbachev, Soviet leaders did not convey an image which endeared them to Western publics. Drearily clad ageing men atop the Kremlin, stiffly reviewing May Day military parades in Moscow, was probably one of the most familiar images Western audiences had of Soviet leaders. This gloomy perception of Soviet leadership, coupled with extremely unpopular actions such as the invasion of Czechoslovakia in 1968 and then Afghanistan in 1979, and the support for martial law in Poland in the early 1980s, provided little reason for West European publics to develop a favourable image of the Soviet Union or its leaders. When asked in 1981 and 1982, no more than two in ten in Britain, France and West Germany and three in ten in Italy said they had a favourable overall opinion of the Soviet Union (Figure 5.1). This unfavourable view of the Soviet Union generally mirrored that found among West European publics in the late 1950s, the 1960s and the 1970s.[2]

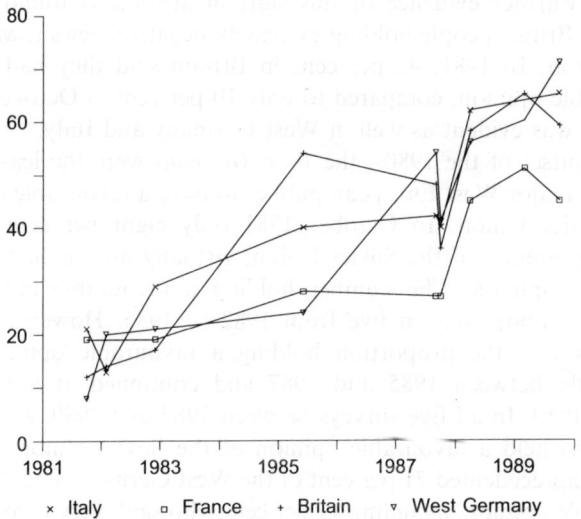

Question: What is your overall opinion of the Soviet Union – do you have a very favourable, somewhat favourable, somewhat unfavourable, or very unfavourable opinion of the Soviet Union? Figures represent total of 'very favourable' and 'somewhat favourable'.

Sources: USIA Surveys listed in Table A.3 in Appendix 3.

Figure 5.1 Favourable image of the Soviet Union, 1981–89 (per cent having a favourable opinion)

In the second half of the 1980s, the improved Soviet image was especially evident in Britain, Italy and West Germany, while the least dramatic increase was found among the French. The *British* were the first to register their change of opinion of the Soviet Union in the wake of Gorbachev. In June 1985, just a few months after Gorbachev came to power, a majority of British (54 per cent) said they had a favourable opinion, a dramatic increase from the 12 per cent who held this view in 1981, and more than that found in any of the other three major countries. A seven country survey in June 1985 found that, using another measure, only in Britain did more (54 to 35 per cent) say they had a good opinion rather than bad opinion of the Soviet Union. Half or more in the other six countries (Denmark (58 per cent), France (52 per cent), Italy (51 per cent), the Netherlands (61 per cent), Norway (61 per cent), and West Germany (55 per cent)) held a bad opinion of the Soviet Union.[3] By March 1989, two-thirds (65 per cent) of the British said they had a favourable opinion of the Soviet Union. British opinion of the Soviet Union remained favourable by October 1989 (59 per cent). Further evidence of this shift in attitude is found in the number of British people holding extremely negative views toward the Soviet Union. In 1981, 42 per cent in Britain said they had a *very* unfavourable opinion, compared to only 10 per cent in October 1989. This trend was evident as well in West Germany and Italy.

At the outset of the 1980s, the *West Germans* were the least likely among the major West European publics to have a favourable opinion of the Soviet Union. In October 1981 only eight per cent had a favourable opinion of the Soviet Union, virtually no one had a 'very favourable' opinion. The number holding a favourable impression increased to about one in five from 1982 to 1985. However, in the Gorbachev era, the proportion holding a favourable opinion rose dramatically between 1985 and 1987 and continued at a majority level into 1989. In all five surveys between 1987 and 1989, a majority of Germans held a favourable opinion of the Soviet Union. In Fall 1989, an unprecedented 71 per cent of the West Germans said they had a favourable opinion, including 17 per cent who said 'very favourable', of the Soviet Union. The favourable German attitude toward the Soviet Union can be expected to continue into the 1990s, due in part to Soviet acquiescence to the October 1990 German reunification.

The Soviet image also improved greatly among the *Italians*, reaching majority status by 1988 from a low of 13 per cent in 1982. In October 1981, 21 per cent in Italy said they had a favourable opinion of the

Soviet Union. This figure improved to 40 per cent in June 1985 and eventually tripled to 65 per cent by October 1989.

The *French* have taken the longest to develop a favourable image of the Soviet Union during the Gorbachev era. Gorbachev's popularity has not 'sparked the same enthusiasm' in France as it has elsewhere in Western Europe (Imbert, 1989, p. 54). Even by October 1989 only a plurality (45 per cent) of the French said they held a favourable opinion of the Soviet Union. While this is one of the highest levels of favourable Soviet opinion registered by the French throughout the entire 1980s, it is the lowest figure among the four major West European publics (Table 5.1). In an October 1989 survey only the Portuguese, among 11 publics surveyed, held as low a level of favourable opinion toward the Soviet Union as the French. Some of this reluctance to endorse the new Soviet image may stem from French President Mitterrand's prudent approach to East–West relations and arms control (Imbert, 1989, pp. 52–54; Moisi, 1988, pp. 152–157).

As Table 5.1 demonstrates, in Fall 1989 majorities in 9 of 11 West European countries surveyed (ranging from 55 per cent in Ireland and Spain to 71 per cent in West Germany) had a favourable image of the Soviet Union. In France, opinion was evenly divided (45–43 per cent), and the plurality view in Portugal was favourable (44 per cent) with a sizable proportion (30 per cent) not having an opinion. While these figures are historical highs for the Soviet Union, only in Greece and Spain do they exceed the proportion with a favourable opinion of the United States, and in these two cases the margin is slight (see Chapter 2 on the American image). A positive image of the Soviet Union is found among West European publics across the ideological spectrum. For example, a majority of those who identify themselves on the right of the political spectrum (56 per cent) as well as those on the left (70 per cent) hold a favourable image.[4]

An improvement in West European attitudes toward the Soviet Union was also recorded in a question which asks if the respondent is pro- or anti-Soviet. This question was asked twice during the Gorbachev era to date, in September 1987 and July 1988.[5] The number identifying themselves as anti-Soviet decreased in the 1987–8 surveys compared to the pre-Gorbachev era. However, as Table 5.2 shows, this decrease in anti-Soviet feelings did not necessarily result in a corresponding increase in the number having a 'pro-Soviet' attitude in all four countries. For example in Britain this manifested itself in a doubling of the number (18 to 36 per cent) of respondents who

Table 5.1 Soviet image in Western Europe, October 1989 (per cent)

	Belgium	Denmark	West Germany	Greece	Spain	France	Ireland	Italy	The Netherlands	Portugal	Britain
Favourable											
Very	9	10	17	12	16	4	12	17	10	10	7
Somewhat	47	57	54	47	39	41	43	48	60	34	52
Subtotal	56	67	71	59	55	45	55	65	70	44	59
Unfavorable											
Somewhat	28	24	16	20	16	30	16	16	21	19	23
Very	9	6	3	7	10	13	10	6	4	7	10
Subtotal	37	30	19	27	26	43	26	22	25	26	33
Don't know	7	4	9	14	18	11	18	13	6	30	8
Total	100	101	99	100	99	99	99	100	101	100	100

Question: What is your overall opinion of the Soviet Union? Is your opinion of the Soviet Union very favourable, somewhat favourable, somewhat unfavourable, or very unfavourable?

Source: October 1989 Eurobarometer.

volunteered that they were 'neither pro- nor anti-Soviet' rather than a corresponding increase in the number giving a 'pro-Soviet' response. The number of British holding anti-Soviet feelings in the late 1980s is much less than that in the early 1980s. Surveys in the early 1980s, using somewhat different response categories, found that majorities of 61 per cent (1983) and 62 per cent (1984) said they were anti-Soviet.[6] The relatively low French regard for the Soviet Union, demonstrated earlier, was found on this measure as well. When asked in 1987 and 1988 to describe their feelings as pro- or anti-Soviet, the French, registering 7 and 14 per cent respectively, were the least 'pro-Soviet' compared to the other three major West European publics. This question was not asked in France in 1983.

Attitudes among the Italians became much less negative and more neutral in outlook in the late 1980s as compared to the pre-Gorbachev era. Half or more in 1983 (52 per cent) and 1984 (58 per cent) said they held 'anti-Soviet' feelings. From 1987 to 1988 the number who said they were anti-Soviet dropped from 50 per cent to about 30 per cent. The West Germans also became less anti-Soviet during the 1980s. Survey questions which did not use the option of 'neither pro- nor anti-Soviet' found that majorities in 1983 (68 per cent) and 1984 (67 per cent) described their feelings as 'anti-Soviet'. In 1987 (46 per cent) and 1988 (35 per cent), a diminishing plurality of West Germans, continued to hold this feeling, although this shift in opinion did not necessarily translate into a sizeable pro-Soviet increase.

This question was asked in Spain only in 1987 and found a plurality of Spanish with anti-Soviet feelings. This question was also asked only once (September 1988) in Belgium and the Netherlands. In Belgium, a large plurality (48 per cent) said they were neither pro- nor anti-Soviet. Data from the Netherlands is not comparable because the category of 'neither pro- nor anti-Soviet' was not used. Nevertheless, a sizeable plurality of the Dutch described their feelings as 'pro-Soviet'.

Using yet another measurement to gauge West European attitudes toward the Soviet Union, the April 1987 Eurobarometer asked publics in 11 of the 12 European Community countries whether they had a very good, fairly good, fairly bad or very bad opinion of the Soviet Union. Respondents who volunteered a 'neither good nor bad' were recorded. When the question was asked in this manner, a rather substantial number, ranging from 16 per cent in Great Britain to 52 per cent in West Germany, volunteered that their opinion of the Soviet Union was neither good nor bad. In Germany, Ireland, Italy, Britain, Greece, and Portugal the prevailing view among those expressing an

Table 5.2 Pro- and anti-Soviet feelings among Western Europeans, 1983–88 (per cent)

	Belgium	Britain				France			Italy			
	Jul. 1988	Dec. 1983	Feb. 1984	Oct. 1987	Jul. 1988	Oct. 1987	Jul. 1988	Jul. 1983	Dec. 1983	Feb. 1984	Oct. 1987	Jul. 1988
Pro-Soviet												
Strongly	2	3	1	2	3	—	1	2	1	1	2	3
Somewhat	17	13	18	30	28	7	13	12	9	7	14	26
Subtotal	9	16	19	32	31	7	14	12	10	8	16	29
Neither (volunteered)	48	N/A	N/A	18	36	38	35	31	32	29	31	36
Anti-Soviet												
Somewhat	22	38	39	34	17	33	29	27	30	31	31	21
Strongly	10	23	23	12	7	18	31	24	22	27	17	10
Subtotal	32	61	62	46	24	51	42	51	52	58	50	31
Don't know	2	23	18	4	9	4	10	4	6	5	5	5
Total	101	100	99	100	100	100	101	100	100	100	100	100

	The Netherlands Jul. 1988	Spain Oct. 1987	West Germany Jul. 1983	Dec. 1983	Feb. 1984	Oct. 1987	Jul. 1988
Pro-Soviet							
Strongly	2	2	2	2	2	1	4
Somewhat	45	15	27	8	10	19	21
Subtotal	47	17	29	10	12	20	25
Neither (volunteered)	N/A	29	N/A	N/A	N/A	31	28
Anti-Soviet							
Somewhat	28	23	44	42	41	38	26
Strongly	5	15	19	26	26	8	9
Subtotal	33	38	63	68	67	46	35
Don't know	20	16	8	22	20	3	12
Total	100	100	100	100	99	100	100

Question: Generally speaking, would you describe your feelings about the Soviet Union as strongly pro-Soviet, somewhat pro-Soviet, somewhat anti-Soviet, or strongly anti-Soviet? (Accept 'neither pro- nor anti-Soviet' as volunteered response only).

Sources: July–August 1983 INF Intensive Survey, December 1983 INF Survey, February 1984 Middle East Issues Survey, September–October 1987 American Image Survey and July 1988 Security Survey.

opinion was a good perception of the Soviet Union. Only in France did more say they had bad rather than good feelings about the Soviet Union. In the remaining survey countries of Belgium, Denmark, the Netherlands, and Spain, proportions which said they had good feelings were about equal to those who held bad feelings toward the Soviet Union.[7]

Indicating the changed perceptions toward the Soviet Union, in 1987 large numbers in Britain (47 per cent), Italy (48 per cent) and West Germany (53 per cent) said their opinion about the Soviet Union had changed *for the better* over the past year. Many fewer in France (28 per cent) and Spain (17 per cent) said their opinion had improved (Table 5.3).

Table 5.3 Improvement in opinion toward the Soviet Union, October 1987 (per cent)

	Britain	France	Italy	Spain	Germany
Better	47	28	48	17	53
Worse	5	3	5	4	5
No change	47	64	44	63	37
Don't know	3	5	3	16	5
Total	100	100	100	100	100

Question: Has your opinion about the Soviet Union changed for the better or worse over the past year or so, or is it about the same?
Source: September–October 1987 American Image Survey.

A survey among Scandinavian publics in Fall 1987 found that a majority in Finland (75 per cent), about half in Norway (53 per cent) and a large plurality in Denmark (47 per cent) said they had a favourable view of the Soviet Union. By contrast, only 28 per cent of the Swedes had a favourable opinion. When asked to explain their overwhelmingly favourable image of the Soviet Union, the Finns most frequently mentioned their unique relationship with the USSR which they said includes good trade and employment opportunities. Those who held favourable opinions of the Soviets in Denmark, Norway and Sweden most frequently said that Gorbachev and the more open Soviet society or glasnost caused them to have such an opinion.[8]

Those who held unfavourable opinions of the Soviet Union said these were based on the lack of freedom in the Soviet Union and their own dislike of the Soviet political system. Large majorities in Denmark (72 per cent), Norway (77 per cent) and Sweden (73 per cent) said their opinion of the Soviet Union had changed because of Soviet leader Gorbachev. Only half (51 per cent) in Finland said their opinion had changed.

SOVIET FOREIGN POLICIES

Two general questions were asked regularly throughout the 1980s in the major West European countries to gauge public reaction to Soviet foreign policy. Respondents were asked how much confidence they had in the ability of the Soviet Union to deal responsibly with world problems and whether they think Soviet policies and actions during the past year did more to promote peace or to increase the risk of war. Responses to these questions, much like those found in the overall image questions, changed after Gorbachev took power.

Although West European confidence in Soviet foreign policy also improved substantially during the Gorbachev era, it did not improve as quickly or quite as much as the overall Soviet image (Figure 5.2). It was not until July 1988 that a majority in any of the four major West European countries said they had at least a fair amount of confidence in the Soviet Union's ability to deal responsibly with world problems. This July 1988 majority was found in Italy (60 per cent) and Britain (58 per cent).[9]

Among the four largest West European publics, the French remained the least enchanted with Soviet foreign policy during the 1980s. Although the level of French public confidence has increased during the Gorbachev era, either majorities or pluralities since the question was first asked in 1982 said they did *not* have confidence in Soviet foreign policy. On this issue, the most dramatic contrast to the French is found among the West Germans, where confidence levels increased from a mere 5 per cent in 1983 to 68 per cent in October 1989. In surveys conducted from 1982 until early 1989, less than half in West Germany said they had confidence in Soviet foreign policy. In February 1989, this figure grew to 43 per cent and reached a substantial majority of 68 per cent by October 1989. A similar, increase was found in Britain and Italy. British confidence levels, which hovered around one in five to one in three during the pre-

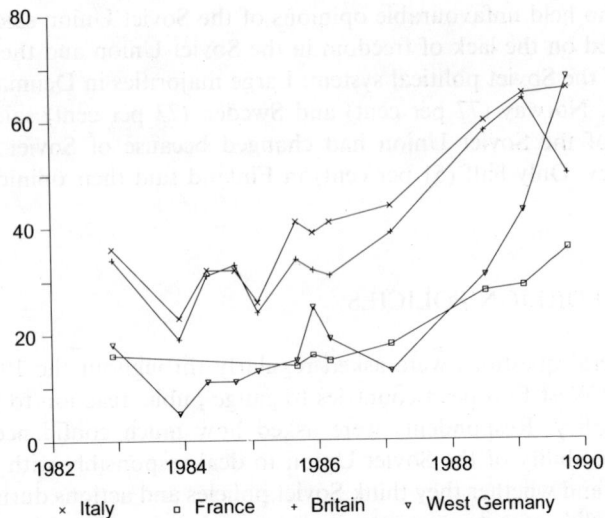

Question: How much confidence do you have in the ability of the Soviet Union to deal responsibly with world problems – a great deal, fair amount, not very much or none at all? Figures represent total of those saying 'great deal' and 'fair amount' of confidence.

Sources: USIA surveys listed in Table A.4 in Appendix 3.

Figure 5.2 Confidence in the Soviet Union foreign policy (per cent having confidence in the Soviet Union)

Gorbachev era, increased to majority and near majority status in the latter 1980s. The number of Italians who had confidence almost tripled from the low point in 1983 (23 per cent) to October 1989 (66 per cent).

An October 1989 ten country Eurobarometer survey found that Western Europeans' confidence in Soviet foreign policy did not match their overall favourable image of the Soviet Union. As Table 5.4 indicates, in only three countries (Italy (66 per cent), the Netherlands (61 per cent), and West Germany (68 per cent)) did majorities have confidence in the Soviet ability to deal responsibly with world problems compared to the nine countries in which majorities held a favourable image of the Soviet Union. However, pluralities in five other countries had confidence in Soviet foreign policy. Only in France did a negative view of Soviet ability prevail. The 1989 survey found the French to have the lowest level of confidence (36 per cent) among the EC publics in Soviet ability to handle world problems.

Table 5.4 European confidence in Soviet foreign policy, 1989 (per cent)

	Belgium	Denmark	Germany	Greece	Spain	France	Ireland	Italy	Netherlands	Portugal	Britain
Confidence											
Great deal	7	7	14	13	12	5	12	15	8	13	6
Fair amount	44	40	54	30	37	31	40	51	53	31	44
Subtotal	51	47	68	43	49	36	52	66	61	44	50
No confidence											
Not much	32	40	22	27	20	37	17	21	30	18	33
None	11	11	4	15	12	17	14	6	3	10	11
Subtotal	43	51	26	42	32	54	31	27	33	28	44
Don't know	5	3	5	15	20	9	17	8	7	29	6
Total	99	101	99	100	101	99	100	101	101	101	100

Question: How much confidence do you have in the ability of the Soviet Union to deal responsibly with world problems? Do you have a great deal of confidence, a fair amount, not very much or none at all?

Source: October 1989 Eurobarometer.

The third overall image question asked throughout the 1980s was whether Soviet policies and actions during the past year have done more to promote peace or to increase the risk of war. The number who said Soviet policies do more to promote peace remained at a consistently low level during the first half of the 1980s. However, similar to other indicators of general Soviet image, this number has increased dramatically in each of the four major West European countries since Gorbachev took office (Table 5.5).

In April 1982, only one in ten in each of the four major West European countries said they thought Soviet policies did more to promote peace than increase the risk of war. Despite the Brezhnev 'peace offensive' in Western Europe designed to exploit the anti-INF missile fever by portraying the US deployment of missiles as a quest for military superiority and a major threat to peace (without mentioning Soviet installation of SS–20 missiles), surveys throughout the first half of the 1980s demonstrated that few Western Europeans believed Soviet policies and actions matched their public diplomacy themes emphasising peace (Wettig, 1986, pp. 273–281). Rather, Soviet actions such as the invasion of Afghanistan and the installation of the SS–20s contributed to the prevailing West European opinion during the pre-Gorbachev early 1980s that Soviet policies and actions increased the risk of war.

West European attitudes toward Soviet foreign policies and actions began to change in late 1985 with the combination of Gorbachev coming to power in March 1985 and the subsequent superpower summit in Geneva in November 1985. By the end of 1985, half in Britain (50 per cent) and approximately one-third in France (32 per cent), Italy (39 per cent), and West Germany (35 per cent) said Soviet actions promoted peace. These figures represented sizeable increases over those found just three months earlier in September 1985.[10] At an erratic pace this proportion, which reached record levels by March 1989, increased throughout the latter half of the decade, even in France. In March 1989, very large majorities in Britain (85 per cent), France (66 per cent) and West Germany (78 per cent) said Soviet policies did more to promote peace than increase the risk of war. The most recent survey data for Italy (November 1987) indicated that 56 per cent held this view.

Western Europeans were anxious for improved relations with the Soviet Union which would signal a thaw in the Cold War as well as greater economic co-operation. Given this environment, it is not

Table 5.5 Soviet policies promote peace, 1982–89 (per cent)

	Apr. 1982	Apr. 1983	Dec. 1983	May 1984	Feb. 1985	May 1985	Sep. 1985	Dec. 1985	Jul. 1986	Nov. 1987	Mar. 1989
Britain	9	11	10	10	27	32	25	50	43	65	85
France	11	N/A	N/A	11	N/A	N/A	17	32	N/A	35	66
Italy	11	16	12	13	25	26	26	39	46	56	N/A
West Germany	9	17	9	11	18	19	20	35	31	51	78

N/A indicates question was not asked in that country.

Question: On balance, do you think Soviet policies and actions during the past year have done more to promote peace or more to increase the risk of war?

Sources: USIA surveys listed in Table A.5 in Appendix 3.

surprising that the Western Europeans were eager to embrace a new image of the Soviet Union shaped by Gorbachev.

THE GORBACHEV FACTOR

Since Gorbachev's rise to power, the Soviet leader and his policies have been the focus of almost nonstop attention by Western journalists, governments, marketing firms, business interests and others fascinated by the actual changes he has initiated and the potential for change he represents. The Gorbachev factor has achieved such a status as even to play a major role in world stock exchange markets. For example, in December 1988, stock prices soared in New York, London and Frankfurt in response to Gorbachev's proposal to reduce the Soviet military presence in Europe.[11] While it may be difficult to measure precisely Gorbachev's impact on the grand issues of Soviet society and the Western Alliance, it clearly can be demonstrated that he has changed the way in which West European publics generally view the Soviet Union and its leader. In September 1987, majorities in three major West European countries, Britain (63 per cent), Italy (59 per cent), and West Germany (63 per cent), said their opinion of the Soviet Union had changed because of Gorbachev. The French were evenly divided (41 to 41 per cent) on this question.[12] A separate October 1987 survey in the Scandinavian countries demonstrated that large majorities in Denmark (72 per cent), Norway (77 per cent) and Sweden (73 per cent) and 51 per cent in Finland said Gorbachev had changed their opinion of the Soviet Union. As the previous presentation of data on the overall attitudes toward the Soviet Union and its policies indicate, the Gorbachev era barely resembles that of his predecessors.

In general, Gorbachev has enjoyed a remarkably high level of popularity among Western Europeans. In fact, Gorbachev's overall image is the highest of any Soviet leader 'in the postwar history of polling in the West' (Szabo, 1989, p. 152). Furthermore, European publics generally approve of his policies for change inside the Soviet Union and believe he has permanently changed the Soviet political and social landscape. As Table 5.6 demonstrates, large majorities throughout Western Europe hold a favourable opinion of Gorbachev. This includes seven countries in which about one-third say they have a very favourable opinion. Even among the French, who have been the most reluctant to change their attitudes toward the Soviet Union, seven in ten hold a favourable attitude toward Gorbachev. Except in France,

Table 5.6 Gorbachev image in Western Europe, October 1989 (per cent)

	Belgium	Denmark	Germany	Greece	Spain	France	Ireland	Italy	Netherlands	Portugal	Britain
Favourable											
Very	24	33	39	31	29	13	39	32	32	22	38
Somewhat	58	55	48	45	37	57	39	50	52	38	47
Subtotal	82	88	87	76	66	70	78	82	84	60	85
Unfavourable											
Somewhat	8	6	6	6	8	13	4	7	4	6	6
Very	3	2	2	3	5	6	4	3	1	4	3
Subtotal	11	8	8	9	13	19	8	10	5	10	9
Don't know	7	4	5	16	21	12	14	8	5	31	6
Total	100	100	100	101	100	101	100	100	99	101	100

Question: What is your overall opinion of the Soviet leader Mikhail Gorbachev? Do you have a very favourable, somewhat favourable, somewhat unfavourable, or very unfavourable opinion of Soviet leader Gorbachev?

Source: Eurobarometer, October 1989.

the level of favourable West European attitudes toward Gorbachev is much higher than toward Ronald Reagan (see Chapter 4 for discussion of Reagan's image).

A survey in September 1987 found similarly high numbers holding a favourable opinion of Gorbachev in Britain, Italy and West Germany. In 1987, only half in France (51 per cent) had an overall favourable opinion. When asked for some of the reasons for their opinion, most respondents cited Gorbachev's being more open and democratic than his predecessors and his perceived desire to bring about reforms in the Soviet Union. Those who had an unfavourable opinion said he was untrustworthy and too similar to his predecessors.[13]

When one compares the more stylish Gorbachev to his predecessors, it is not surprising that he enjoys higher approval ratings. Western Europeans believe Gorbachev represents a quantum leap from his predecessors as a new, modern-era leader intent on making fundamental changes in the Soviet Union that will, in all probability, remain. For example a December 1985 telephone survey found that majorities in Britain (60 per cent), Italy (59 per cent), the Netherlands (69 per cent), and West Germany (66 per cent) and 52 per cent in France believed that Mr Gorbachev would do more than previous Soviet leaders to reduce tensions in the world.[14] These figures increased by November 1986 in Britain (69 per cent), France (61 per cent) and West Germany (74 per cent).[15]

Furthermore when asked in June 1988 majorities in Britain (58 per cent) and especially in West Germany (78 per cent), and a plurality in France (47 per cent), said the current Soviet reforms were not inevitable but rather occurred only because of Gorbachev's efforts.[16] Sizeable majorities in four Scandinavian countries – Denmark (67 per cent), Finland (82 per cent), Norway (70 per cent) and Sweden (64 per cent) – thought the changes Gorbachev made were so fundamental that they would be permanent.[17] The prevailing view in Britain (61 per cent), France (52 per cent) and West Germany (62 per cent) in March 1989 was that the changes Gorbachev made would be permanent.[18] Moreover, majorities in these three countries agreed that it is likely that Gorbachev would still be the leader of the Soviet Union in five years.

West European approval of Gorbachev may continue into the 1990s as the Soviet repression of Eastern Europe becomes a more distant memory and these countries continue their march toward democracy and a closer economic and political relationship with the European Community. Western Europeans may also come to expect continued dramatic results in Soviet foreign policies under Gorbachev. Asked in September 1987 about Gorbachev's foreign policy making ability, majorities in Britain (81 per cent), France (66 per cent) and West Germany (79 per cent) thought Gorbachev would be effective in dealing with world problems over the next several years.[19] While this dramatic change in West European attitudes toward the Soviet leader has spilled over into more generally positive opinions of the Soviet Union, it does not mean that all of Gorbachev's actions have enjoyed, or for that matter will enjoy, majority support among West European publics.

HUMAN RIGHTS IN THE SOVIET UNION

By May 1989, Gorbachev still had a long way to go to convince Western Europeans that human rights were being well protected in the Soviet Union. While this image is most likely to improve in the 1990s as immigration policies are relaxed and civic freedoms are promoted, in 1989 the overall West European impression that human rights are poorly protected in the Soviet Union had not changed since 1977, despite Gorbachev's effort to promote an improved Soviet image. In 1977, only a handful in each of the four major West European countries, ranging from 6 per cent in Britain to 13 per cent in Italy, said that human rights were protected in the Soviet Union. As demonstrated by Table 5.7, this grim assessment of the status of human rights in the USSR improved little, if any, during the 1980s. Noticeable improvement can only be found in Italy, where positive assessment of human rights in the Soviet Union increased from 13 per cent of the public in 1977 to 30 per cent in 1989.

Data from 1987, when the largest number of countries was surveyed, indicate that the negative perception of human rights in the Soviet Union was widespread across Europe. These 1987 USIA surveys, displayed in Table 5.8, found that large majorities in Britain (64 per cent), Denmark (74 per cent), France (75 per cent), Italy (64 per cent), Norway (73 per cent), Sweden (84 per cent), and West Germany (86 per cent) and a plurality in Finland (47 per cent) thought human rights were poorly protected in the Soviet Union.[20] This represented a slight increase in the number who held such views since surveys in September 1985 in Britain (59 per cent) and France (66 per cent). The number in Italy remained the same since 1985.

Table 5.7 Protection of human rights in the Soviet Union, 1977–89 (Per cent saying human rights are well protected)[a]

	Jul. 1977	Sep. 1985	Feb. 1987	Oct. 1987	May 1989
Britain	6	9	14	19	11
France	10	9	10	11	13
Italy	13	14	23	23	30
West Germany	7	4	7	7	15

[a] Figures displayed are total of very well and rather well.

Question: How well do you think human rights are protected in the Soviet Union – very well, rather well, rather badly, or very badly? In October 1987 the question included the phrase 'at the present time'.

Sources: July 1977 Human Rights Survey, September 1985 Security Survey, February 1987 Security Survey, September–October 1987 American Image Survey and May 1989 Paris Economic Summit Survey.

West European assessment of human rights in the Soviet Union did not improve by July 1988 when majorities of seven in ten or more in Belgium, Britain, France, Italy, the Netherlands, and West Germany said individual freedoms were poorly protected in the Soviet Union. Furthermore, among those that said individual freedoms were poorly protected, very few agreed with the question statement that the 'economic benefits the Soviets say their people get – like a guaranteed job or a high standard of living – compensate for poor individual liberties'.[21] A May 1989 survey continued to support the finding that human rights are not thought to be well protected in the USSR: large majorities in Britain (74 per cent), France (74 per cent), Italy (69 per cent), and West Germany (76 per cent) thought that individual freedoms were being badly protected in the Soviet Union.[22]

Although, Western Europeans have not perceived much progress in improved Soviet human rights, a sizeable number in Britain (54 per cent), France (31 per cent), and West Germany (45 per cent) gave Gorbachev some credit for promoting human rights in his country.[23] In July 1987, majorities in Britain (74 per cent), France (67 per cent), and West Germany (61 per cent) thought Mr Gorbachev's policies were making the Soviet Union become a less repressive society.[24]

While Gorbachev enjoys a high level of popularity throughout Western Europe, it is to some extent based on comparative perceptions between Gorbachev and his predecessors. A series of questions

Table 5.8 Soviet protection of human rights, September 1987 (per cent)

	Denmark	Finland	Norway	Sweden	Britain	France	Italy	Spain	West Germany
Very well	1	1	2	0	2	2	2	4	1
Rather well	7	26	13	6	17	9	21	18	6
Subtotal	8	27	15	6	19	11	23	22	7
Rather badly	41	39	39	44	46	37	39	26	56
Very badly	33	8	34	40	18	38	25	17	30
Subtotal	74	47	73	84	64	75	64	43	86
Don't know	18	26	12	10	17	13	12	36	7
Total	100	100	100	100	100	100	100	101	100

Question: How well do you think human rights are being protected in the Soviet Union – very well, rather well, rather badly, or very badly? The question in Spain included the phrase 'at the present time'.

Sources: October 1987 Scandinavian Survey for Denmark, Finland, Norway and Sweden; and September–October 1987 American Image Survey for Britain, France, Italy, Spain and West Germany.

throughout the latter 1980s asked respondents to identify which characteristics best described President Reagan or Mr Gorbachev. Reagan consistently, and by a wide margin, outpaced Gorbachev on the question of who 'promotes human rights'. On other factors such as 'trustworthiness' and 'understands world problems', the results are much more mixed across the publics (see Chapter 6). On the issue of arms control, the prevailing opinion in the four major West European countries gives more credit to Gorbachev than Reagan. This credit may be a partial result of Gorbachev's halo effect since Reagan was in fact the first to propose the elimination of intermediate-range nuclear missiles.

AFGHANISTAN

Despite an improved overall Soviet image in Western Europe, the Soviet invasion of Afghanistan received very unfavourable reactions from the European publics. The Soviet invasion of Afghanistan in December 1979 was widely criticised by the international press as well as by most governments. Additionally, this act of aggression put a strain on US–Soviet relations (Garthoff, 1985). Not unlike the rest of the Western world, Western Europeans overwhelmingly disapproved of the 1979 Soviet invasion. A 1980 survey found that most of the public in three major West European countries did not think the Soviets acted with justification. Majorities in Britain (73 per cent), France (59 per cent), and West Germany (75 per cent) agreed that the Soviets entered Afghanistan to take over control of the Afghan government rather than to help the legitimate government handle rebellious groups from outside.[25]

An October 1987 survey found virtually no approval for Soviet actions in Afghanistan among the British (4 per cent), French (4 per cent), Italians (4 per cent), Spanish (5 per cent) or West Germans (5 per cent). Majorities in Britain (83 per cent), France (75 per cent), Italy (83 per cent), Spain (58 per cent) and Germany (84 per cent) said they disapproved, including 60 per cent or more in each country except Spain who said they *strongly* disapproved.[26] Despite the almost unanimous opposition to Soviet troops in Afghanistan, Western Europeans, for the most part, did not view the situation as posing much of a threat to their interests and did not expect their own governments to take very serious action.[27] Surveys in 1980 and 1984 found little support for supplying military equipment to the Afghan resistance. In 1980, 42 per cent in France, 25 per cent in West Germany, and 17 per cent in Britain said no special action should be taken regarding Soviet troops in Afghanistan.[28] A ten country Eurobarometer survey in 1984 found that a sizable number (ranging from 19 per cent in the Netherlands and West Germany to 39 per cent in Belgium and Greece) preferred their country to do nothing to deal with the Soviet war in Afghanistan.[29] As further evidence of this lack of concern over the issue, a survey in February 1987 found only a handful in Britain (8 per cent), France (10 per cent), and Italy (9 per cent) said that Soviet troops in Afghanistan posed the greatest threat to Western interests when asked to choose from a list of six international problems. The conflict in Lebanon was identified most frequently as the greatest threat. The other international problems listed were the conflicts in Nicaragua, Angola, Kampuchea, and South Africa. Sizeable numbers, ranging from 16 per cent in Britain to 34 per cent in West Germany, did not offer an opinion.[30]

From the time he took office in 1985, Gorbachev hinted at his uneasiness with the Soviet policy toward Afghanistan as indicated by his reported desire to withdraw Soviet troops. In part Gorbachev was responding to international political and economic pressure and, possibly of greater importance to him, to the disenchantment with the war among the Soviet people themselves. During the run-up to the Soviet troop withdrawal starting in 1988, a series of Geneva negotiating sessions and policy statements were widely reported in the international press, raising people's expectations for a settlement of the war. During this time Western Europeans were somewhat dubious of Gorbachev's announced intentions to withdraw Soviet troops from Afghanistan. In July 1987 the prevailing opinion among the French (51 per cent) and West Germans (45 per cent) was that Gorbachev's statements about withdrawing troops were 'merely propaganda'. The British were roughly divided (37 to 31 per cent), with slightly more saying Gorbachev was serious.[31] By June 1988, the prevailing opinion in Britain and West Germany had changed from that found in 1987 to the view that Gorbachev was serious about withdrawing troops from Afghanistan. Finally, by the time Soviet troops actually started to withdraw in 1988, European publics began to believe Gorbachev's policies represented a change. The prevailing opinion in three of the major West European countries, Britain (55 per cent), France (46 per cent), and West Germany (58 per cent), was that the Soviet military withdrawal from Afghanistan indicated a basic change in Soviet foreign policy.[32] Judging from Gorbachev's high approval ratings even before the withdrawal, it appears that West Europeans did not consider the continued Soviet war in Afghanistan as the primary factor in determining their image of Gorbachev.

WEST EUROPEAN–SOVIET RELATIONS

Western Europeans' postwar negative perception of the USSR, fuelled by the heavy-handed Soviet control over the eastern half of the continent, their persistent Third World adventurism, and the dismal state of Soviet society and economy, contributed to a strained relationship with the USSR over the last 40 years. Furthermore, Europe's geographic proximity to the Soviet Union is a constant reminder to Western Europeans that their part of the world would almost certainly be the battlefield for the next war, regardless of who fired the first volley. Moreover, a number of West European countries conduct considerable trade with the Soviets (see Chapter 9 on US–West European economic relations). This factor has led to occasional confrontations within the Alliance over how to protect high technology products from going to the Soviets. Given this landscape, it may be understandable that the West Europeans are anxious to improve relations with Gorbachev's Soviet Union.

Public assessment of West European–Soviet relations improved in the latter half of the 1980s. As Table 5.9 demonstrates, in 1985 only a small majority in Italy, about half in Britain and in France, and only a quarter in West Germany said their country's relations with the Soviets were good. Furthermore, in June 1985, the prevailing view in six of seven surveyed NATO countries was that it would be better for them in the long run if their country's ties to the Soviet Union continued as they were rather being improved.[33] However, by September of 1987 majorities in each of the four major countries described their government's current relations with the Soviet Union as good.

To some extent, West European public expectations that the Soviet Union was becoming a more responsible actor in the global community, and one with which relations should be encouraged, were damaged by its handling of the nuclear accident at Chernobyl in April 1986. This accident released a substantial amount of radiation into the atmosphere, which directly affected the environment and health conditions in neighbouring countries, particularly the Scandinavian countries. The Soviet Union was widely criticised for withholding

Table 5.9 West European relations with the Soviet Union, 1985-87

	Britain		France		Italy		West Germany	
	Jun. 1985	Sep. 1987	Jun. 1985	Sep. 1987	Jun. 1985	Sep. 1987	Jun. 1985	Sep. 1987
Very Good	1	6	2	1	3	7	0	2
Fairly Good	52	69	44	58	55	66	28	65
Subtotal	53	75	46	59	58	73	28	67
Fairly Bad	26	17	23	17	22	16	34	19
Very Bad	6	3	6	3	5	2	11	2
Subtotal	32	20	29	20	27	18	45	21
Don't know/haven't heard enough to say	15	5	24	21	15	9	27	12
Total	100	100	99	100	100	100	100	100

Question: How would you describe the current relations between the Soviet Union and [survey country]? Would you say that relations are very good, fairly good, fairly bad or very bad? In June 1985 'or haven't you heard enough to say?'

Sources: June–July 1985 Baseline Survey, September 1987 Security Survey.

essential information about the accident which would have aided relief efforts. Two-thirds or more in Denmark, Finland, Norway and Sweden agreed that the Soviet Union had not done all it could have in disseminating vital information to government officials throughout Europe.[34] The initial effort by the USSR to shroud the Chernobyl disaster in secrecy damaged Soviet credibility as well as Gorbachev's stated commitment to 'openness' in the press. Many in the western press compared the handling of Chernobyl with the Soviets' reluctant admission of shooting down a Korean passenger airliner in 1983. However, the dramatic events inside the Soviet Union and Eastern Europe in 1989 and the early 1990s provided reason for many Western Europeans to want their country to develop closer ties to the USSR. For example, in Fall 1990 three-quarters of the EC citizens believed the EC should provide aid to the Soviet Union to promote its political and economic reforms.[35]

SOVIET PUBLIC DIPLOMACY EFFORTS IN WESTERN EUROPE

Throughout the postwar period the Soviet Union has mounted great efforts, ranging from clumsy forgeries and disinformation campaigns to sophisticated public relations blitzes, designed to influence West European public opinion and drive a wedge between the United States and Western Europe.[36] Among other enterprises, the Soviets have actively supported and encouraged local West European communist parties, anti-nuclear demonstrations, and propaganda organs in an attempt to de-nuclearize Western Europe and wear down the Atlantic Alliance.[37] The West has long been impressed with the clumsy, yet to some extent successful, Soviet propaganda effort. Arms control expert Paul H. Nitze, in reference to the Soviets' peace theme, has said he was 'amazed at what the Soviets can do with absolutely rotten material' (Nitze, 1990).

Soviet public diplomacy efforts during the Reagan years were first characterized by Brezhnev's 'peace offensive' in the early 1980s and Gorbachev's 'charm offensive' during the latter part of the decade. Both emphasized the traditional Soviet theme stating its commitment to peace and pledge of no first use of nuclear weapons.[38] Critics of the Soviet 'peace' theme contend that it has been traditionally 'in terms of world domination by communism' (Nitze, 1990).

Brezhnev's 'Peace Offensive'

For many Soviet observers, Brezhnev's peace offensive during the late 1970s and early 1980s was a rehash of an old Soviet theme.

'Peace offensives' have been periodically launched from Moscow not only during the 24 long years of Mr Andrei Gromyko's service as foreign minister but even earlier, when his predecessor and tutor Vyacheslav Molotov, was directing Soviet diplomacy. These campaigns have all borne a strong family likeness to each other. Presumably, a standard assembly kit for them, dating back to the vintage Molotov years, is kept in a foreign ministry drawer and dusted off at intervals.

The standard kit includes a demand that the West should refrain from (a) doing certain things that the Russians dislike, and (b) complaining about certain Soviet actions that it dislikes. The things cited under (a) have two common characteristics. They are Western responses to Soviet actions that come under the (b) heading; and they are controversial in the West.[39]

The peace offensive centred on charges that the 1979 NATO decision to deploy intermediate-range nuclear missiles in Western Europe would upset superpower nuclear parity and increase the risk of war. The Soviets were determined to derail the missile deployment by doing what they could to encourage already existing, widespread anti-INF feelings in Western Europe. To implement this strategy, the Soviets actively encouraged the large anti-INF demonstrations which took place throughout the Western European capitals in the early 1980s. This issue is discussed in detail in Chapter 3. Although the anti-INF movement in Western Europe needed little external assistance, the Soviet attempt to create public support against the INF deployment was perhaps the most aggressive Soviet public diplomacy campaign in Western Europe since the creation of NATO in 1949. The Soviets sought to persuade public opinion in Western Europe that the NATO response to the Soviet SS–20 missiles was actually a provocation to the defence-minded USSR. In order to influence public opinion the Soviets used a variety of measures, including: the 'staging of rare opportunities for "news" from Moscow, where useful access by Western press was sharply limited'; the use of well-organised front groups; and political influence operations (Sorrels, 1983, p. 2).

The large demonstrations in 1982–83, particularly in the INF basing countries, caused great concern in Washington and other NATO capitals (Wirthlin, 1990). However, some observers believed the Soviets, counting on public demonstrations to undermine INF deployment, overplayed their INF hand.

> The Soviet leaders . . . undertook a major campaign to influence Western public opinion against deployment. They placed the INF issue in the political forefront and made it a much more important political-military factor than it inherently was. In doing so, they only increased the significance of their failure. By making support for INF deployment a touchstone of political intentions and detente, they damaged East–West political relations (particularly with West Germany, the key country) . . . Overall, deployment became a defeat for the Soviet Union of larger political dimensions than it would otherwise have been (Garthoff, 1985, p. 1032).

The activist Soviet strategy to encourage public demonstrations was coupled with a stream of arms control proposals from Moscow, such as their much-heralded call for a nuclear freeze. One of the major prongs of the Soviet public diplomacy campaign was to emphasise their commitment to peace by citing their numerous proposals for arms reductions.[40] These proposals, directed at a West European audience anxious for a reduction in the superpower arms race, generally found public support. A May 1984 survey in seven NATO countries found that, despite their dislike and mistrust of the Soviet Union at that time, most Western Europeans favoured the major peace initiatives proposed by the Soviet Union. These proposals included a ban on the production, possession, and use of chemical weapons; a non-aggression pact renouncing the use of military force except in self-defence; creation of a nuclear free zone in East and West Europe; and an agreement that neither side will be the first to use nuclear weapons (Adler, 1984b). However, while many Western Europeans approved of the Soviet 'peace initiatives', they were sceptical of Soviet sincerity. An April 1981 survey indicated that in Britain (44 to 18 per cent), France (53 to 22 per cent), and the Netherlands (46 to 38 per cent) a larger number considered Soviet proposals an attempt to divide and weaken the Western Alliance rather than a genuine concern for peace.[41] A sizeable proportion of Western Europeans believed the Soviet Union was using disinformation campaigns to further its goals. A 1984 survey asked respondents to indicate whether the statement 'spreads lies to attain its goals' applies more to the USA, the USSR, or to both equally. More than one-third in Britain (38 per cent), Italy (36 per cent) and West Germany (44 per cent) said it applied more to the Soviet Union. Fewer than one in ten said such a statement applies more to the USA. However, a sizeable number in each of these three countries, between 37 and 42 per cent, said the statement applied to both equally.[42]

Gorbachev and the Power of the Press

On assuming power in 1985, Gorbachev recognized that the Soviet campaign to stop INF deployment had backfired. Despite some large demonstrations and a Soviet walk-out from the Geneva arms control negotiations, the NATO alliance deployed the missiles and held their ground in what was to be the last major contest of the Cold War. Furthermore, Soviet efforts to turn West Germany, the cornerstone of the NATO Alliance, into a neutral state failed miserably. Given this inherited environment, Gorbachev struck out to revamp the Soviet public diplomacy machine. Recognising the power of the media for modern public diplomacy strategies, Gorbachev quickly exploited the media by staging numerous press conferences, including a two hour press briefing after the 1985 Geneva Summit, and state visits throughout Western Europe (Walker, 1986, p. 256). During the 27th Party Congress in 1986, Gorbachev, in an effort to modernise and emphasise the Soviet public relations apparatus, made major personnel changes in the propaganda and information offices by installing individuals with intimate knowledge of the West (Grant, 1986).

Gorbachev's tenure as Soviet leader brought with it several new weapons to the Soviet public diplomacy arsenal. Complementing Gorbachev's powerful and charming personality, Soviet diplomacy emphasised the need for 'new thinking' in Soviet foreign policy, the importance of arms control negotiations and the concept of a common European home characterised by broad economic co-operation and broad disarmament. In a rare appearance for a Soviet leader before the Council of Europe in Strasbourg, Gorbachev called for a united Europe to include the Soviet Union.

> Europeans can meet the challenges of the next century only by pooling their efforts. We are convinced that they need one Europe – peaceful and democratic – a Europe that preserves all of its diversity

and abides by common humane ideals, a prospering Europe that extends a hand to the rest of the world. A Europe that confidently marches into the future. We see our own future in this Europe.[43]

Gorbachev's initial theme of a common European home had not resonated throughout Western Europe by late 1987. For example, sizeable numbers, ranging from 15 per cent in France to 31 per cent in Belgium, in six countries did not even agree that their own country and the other nations of Western Europe constitute a community of nations which have much in common. Furthermore, of those that did agree with the existence of such a European community, majorities in Belgium (83 per cent), Britain (64 per cent), France (68 per cent), Italy (64 per cent), the Netherlands (56 per cent), and West Germany (79 per cent) did not think the Soviet Union was part of this community.[44] In addition, almost nobody in three of the major West European countries thought their society's values resembled those of the Soviet Union. In a September 1987 telephone survey, vast majorities in Britain (87 per cent), France (80 per cent), and West Germany (92 per cent) said the values of their own society are closer to the values of the US rather than the Soviet Union.[45] Furthermore, in 1985 large majorities, exceeding three out of four in Britain, France, Italy, the Netherlands,and West Germany, thought that what the people of their own country value in life was different from what Russians value.[46]

A European Community-wide survey in 1986 found that only a third or fewer in each of the 12 EC countries said they thought the Russian people were trustworthy. However, the level of mistrust of the Russians has declined since the 1970s 'probably reflecting the improvement in their world image, albeit relative, after Mr Gorbachev came to power in March 1985'.[47]

The Soviet public diplomacy strategy to churn out arms control initiatives during the middle to late 1980s failed in many cases to reach a broad audience throughout Western Europe. For example, in 1986 majorities in Britain (67 per cent), France (68 per cent) and Italy (57 per cent) and half in West Germany (51 per cent) said they had not heard or read about the widely publicised Soviet proposal to eliminate nuclear weapons by the year 2000. Furthermore, among those that were familiar with the proposal, opinion was about evenly divided as to whether the proposal had been made for propaganda purposes or was sincere.[48] Likewise in July 1986 large majorities in Britain, France, Italy and West Germany said they were unfamiliar with the then recent Soviet proposal for both the USA and USSR to stop all testing of nuclear weapons. The prevailing opinion among those that had heard or read at least something about the Soviet initiative was that it represented mere propaganda rather than a sincere proposal.[49] In June 1985 publics in five West European countries were asked for which country the statement 'spreads lies in other countries to attain its goals' was most applicable, providing the respondent with the opportunity to mention any country, not just the USA or the USSR. The Soviet Union was the most frequently named country by a very wide margin in Britain (34 per cent), France (27 per cent), Italy (30 per cent), the Netherlands (43 per cent), and West Germany (42 per cent).[50]

Gorbachev's new public diplomacy strategies included expanded cultural and information activities throughout West Europe. These activities included Soviet public appearances, press conferences, interviews with local media, exchange programmes, distribution of films emphasising glasnost, and Soviet cultural exhibits (Olds, 1988). These efforts contributed to an improved West European perception of Gorbachev, both at the elite and public level. They also helped create a new interest in Soviet developments under Gorbachev among the Western Europeans. For example, the improved Soviet image opened the door for numerous exchange programmes and sister-cities relations in West Germany and other countries.[51]

The US Department of Defence in its 1988 edition of the annual *Soviet Military Power* entitled *An Assessment of the Threat* dismissed the early Gorbachev diplomacy as merely new efforts to weaken the Atlantic Alliance:

> Under Gorbachev, the Soviet Union's longstanding policy of seeking to drive a wedge between the United States and NATO by, among other things, generating concern within Western Europe over US defense programs has been given new impetus. The basic Soviet goal remains the transformation of the political status quo in Europe to favour the USSR.[52]

By 1990, however, the Department of Defense acknowledged the evolution of Gorbachev's 'new thinking' as a positive contribution to the international community.[53] In the wake of the end of the Cold War, one can expect Soviet public diplomacy efforts to reflect its desire to become more thoroughly integrated in Western political and economic environment rather than an attempt to drive a wedge through the Western Alliance.

CONCLUSION

While not all of Gorbachev's policies and actions enjoy West European public support, the novelty of a modern Soviet leader and his skillful use of the media have given Gorbachev unprecedented positive recognition in the West. In fact, Gorbachev was named *Time* magazine's 'Man of the Decade' for the 1980s, and won the Nobel peace prize in 1990, in large part for his role in reforming the Soviet Union and raising the Iron Curtain.[54] It is clear that Gorbachev is the driving engine behind the improved Soviet image across Western Europe. The overall image of the Soviet Union was the first to improve in Western Europe, reaching unprecedented highs in the late 1980s. Along with this attitude, confidence in Soviet foreign policy also improved, although to a lesser degree. However, as successful as Mr Gorbachev has been in polishing the general image of the Soviet Union, Western Europeans still harbour negative feelings toward the Soviet political and economic system.

The shift in attitudes toward the Soviet Union represents the most dramatic change in Western European public opinion in the 1980s and, in all likelihood, in the postwar period. The rise of Gorbachev and the corresponding improvement in the Soviet image in Western Europe, along with the flood of changes in Eastern Europe, have dramatically changed the calculus of US–West European relations and the Alliance's relationship with the USSR. Fundamental security and political alliances, previously built on a foundation of the Cold-War Soviet threat, are now being re-examined.

6 US–Soviet Relations

This chapter examines West European attitudes on US–Soviet relations, with specific focus on the four superpower summits held during the Reagan years. It also provides an historical overview of West European perspectives on postwar US–Soviet summits. Throughout the postwar period West European economic, political and security interests have been inextricably tied to the state of US–Soviet relations. During the Reagan years, superpower relations affected important European security interests as well as East–West trade relations. This was especially true during the 1980s because the Reagan foreign policy

> was, above all, a policy centered on the Soviet Union, whether as an enemy threatening destruction and chaos that could be dealt with only through military force, or as a partner in a broad relaxation of tensions and a search for arms reductions and regional disengagement. (Deibel, 1989 p. 36)

The 1980s were a period of extreme highs and lows in US–Soviet relations; the early 1980s were characterised by confrontation and the longest gap in US–Soviet summits (Table 6.1). From 1985 to the end of the Reagan years, superpower relations vastly improved, evidenced by four summits in three years and the eventual signing of the INF Treaty.

West European security interests often have been the central focus of superpower summits. During the four Reagan–Gorbachev summits held in the 1980s arms control issues, which directly affected Western European security, dominated the agenda. Following World War II, meetings of American and Soviet leaders frequently have been held at centre stage with extensive press coverage. Both superpowers have taken advantage of the broad media attention with the aim of bolstering their image among the domestic, as well as the international, public. US–Soviet summits during the Reagan years epitomised the importance of public relations and media coverage.

In examining West European attitudes toward the numerous postwar summits, several characteristics emerge. First, although most Western Europeans think it is important for the superpowers to meet in the hope of promoting a more peaceful and stable environment in

Table 6.1 US–Soviet summits, 1955–90

1.	July 1955	Eisenhower/Khrushchev, Four Power Conference in Geneva.
2.	September 1959	Eisenhower/Khrushchev, Camp David.
3.	May 1960	Eisenhower/Khrushchev, Paris Heads of Government Conference.
4.	June 1961	Kennedy/Khrushchev, Vienna.
5.	June 1967	Johnson/Kosygin, Glassboro, NJ.
6.	May 1973	Nixon/Brezhnev, Moscow.
7.	June 1973	Nixon/Brezhnev, Washington and San Clemente.
8.	July 1974	Nixon/Brezhnev, Moscow.
9.	November 1974	Ford/Brezhnev, Vladivostok.
10.	June 1979	Carter/Brezhnev, Vienna.
11.	November 1985	Reagan/Gorbachev, Geneva.
12.	October 1986	Reagan/Gorbachev, Reykjavik.
13.	December 1987	Reagan/Gorbachev, Washington.
14.	May–June 1988	Reagan/Gorbachev, Moscow.
15.	December 1989	Bush/Gorbachev, Malta.
16.	May–June 1990	Bush/Gorbachev, Washington.
17.	September 1990	Bush/Gorbachev, Helsinki.

the nuclear world, particularly when they address critical security issues, many are uncomfortable in allowing their security interests to be decided in proxy by the two superpowers. Despite the attempts of various American administrations to inform and consult the Western Alliance, many West Europeans believe that their interests are not well protected by the United States during superpower meetings, even when they approve of the summit outcome. Secondly, while West Europeans encourage improved superpower relations, they are more likely to perceive US–Soviet summits as primarily reducing general East–West tensions than as actually resolving specific international problems.

West Europeans view the ebb and flow of US–Soviet relations through the perceived success and failure of superpower summitry. As demonstrated in Table 6.2, West European perceptions of the state of superpower relations were strongly influenced by the outcome of the four summits during the Reagan years. For example, West Europeans generally considered US–Soviet relations as more positive after the

Table 6.2 US–Soviet relations, 1985–88 (Per cent saying relations are very good/fairly good)[a]

	Nov. 1985	Dec. 1985	Oct. 1986	Nov. 1986	Jan. 1987	Nov. 1987	Dec. 1987	Mar. 1988	Jun. 1988
Britain	48	60	47	34	35	77	89	88	89
France	48	60	49	33	42	62	78	71	78
Italy	56	68	—	—	—	—	94	—	—
Netherlands	35	48	—	—	—	—	88	—	—
West Germany	35	55	46	39	23	72	84	79	88

[a] For complete data see Table A.6 in Appendix 3.

Question: How would you describe the current relations between the United States and the Soviet Union? Would you say that relations between these two countries are very good, fairly good, fairly bad, or very bad?

Sources: November 1985 Pre-Geneva Summit Telephone Survey; December 1985 Geneva Summit Telephone Survey; October 1986 Post-Reykjavik Summit Telephone Survey I; November 1986 Post-Reykjavik Summit Telephone Survey II; January 1987 Security Telephone Survey; November 1987 Pre-Washington Summit Telephone Survey; December 1987 Post-Washington Telephone Survey; March 1986 Pre-Moscow Summit telephone Survey; June 1988 Post-Moscow Summit Telephone Survey.

first Reagan–Gorbachev meeting in Geneva in late 1985 despite the lack of any clear arms control agreement. However, this positive assessment dropped precipitously after the hurriedly conceived Reykjavik summit held in October 1986 which was in general considered a setback during what otherwise was viewed as an era of improving US–Soviet relations.[1]

Just prior to the Geneva summit, a telephone survey found a majority in Italy, about half in Britain and France, and only a third in the Netherlands and West Germany judged US–Soviet relations to be at least fairly good. After the Geneva summit, the assessment of US–Soviet relations became more optimistic in all five countries. However, this positive assessment dimmed quickly after the unsuccessful Reykjavik summit in October 1986 and dropped even further in the following months. By January 1987, only between two in ten in Germany and four in ten in France called US–Soviet relations 'good'. After the post-Reykjavik low, perceptions improved dramatically as the prospects for an INF arms control agreement increased. Immediately after the December 1987 Washington summit at which Reagan and Gorbachev signed the INF Treaty, overwhelming majorities in Western Europe, ranging from 78 per cent in France to 94 per cent in Italy, said US–Soviet relations were good. Similarly large majorities described superpower relations as good in a telephone survey following the Spring 1988 Moscow summit. Despite the generally favourable view of superpower relations in the late 1980s, sizeable majorities of approximately 70 per cent in each of these three countries said relations between the two countries could be improved.[2]

OVERVIEW OF THE PRE-REAGAN SUMMITS

Available post-World War II survey data from selected summits indicate that Western Europeans have generally encouraged US–Soviet summitry as an instrument to relax general East–West tensions, but hold rather modest expectations of summits as a means of solving major world problems. During the Eisenhower Administration, European capitals called on the President to meet with Soviet Premier Khrushchev to resolve numerous East–West problems, especially the Berlin question. This resulted in the first postwar summit, the Four Power Conference (Britain, France, USA, USSR) held in Geneva in July 1955. At this conference President Eisenhower made his 'Open Skies' proposal which 'won favourable world attention even though it was rejected almost out of hand by the Soviets' (Weihmiller and Doder, 1986, p. 26). Western Europeans, although supportive of the Conference, were not overwhelmed by the meeting's chances of achieving concrete results. A June 1955 survey indicated that only minorities in Austria (30 per cent), Britain (40 per cent), France (13 per cent), Italy (15 per cent) and West Germany (22 per cent) thought the chances for a successful summit outcome were good.[3] Despite the pessimistic outlook for specific summit results, Western Europeans held a widespread belief that the Four Power Conference 'contributed to the relaxation of international tensions'.[4]

Large majorities throughout Western Europe approved of the second Eisenhower–Khrushchev meeting held at Camp David in September 1959, although expectations that such a visit would ease cold war tensions were quite tempered.[5] Even this limited West European optimism regarding superpower relations was quickly dashed after the failure of the May 1960 Paris Summit Conference to improve superpower relations, due, in part, to the shooting down of an American U2 surveillance plane over Soviet territory. Although the Soviets were primarily blamed for the collapse of the summit (when Khrushchev walked out), the image of both superpowers declined in Britain, France and to a lesser extent in West Germany.[6]

As was the case after the Eisenhower–Khrushchev Camp David summit, the June 1961 Kennedy–Khrushchev Summit in Vienna was not considered by Western Europeans as having accomplished much in resolving East–West disputes. A June–July 1961 survey found that one-fifth or less in Britain (17 per cent), France (8 per cent), Italy (16 per cent), and West Germany (19 per cent) felt the meeting accomplished much in 'settling disputes between the Western powers and the Soviet Union'.[7] In 1972, on the eve of President Nixon's trip to Moscow to finalise the SALT I Treaty, publics surveyed in Britain, France, Italy and West Germany overwhelmingly thought it was a good idea for the two leaders to meet, but many fewer thought the visit would achieve much success in reducing world tensions.[8]

THE REAGAN–GORBACHEV SUMMITS

A relationship of detente between the two superpowers evolved during the 1970s, characterised by a series of arms control agreements including SALT I in June 1972 and SALT II in June 1979. This improving relationship was severely damaged, however, by the December 1979 Soviet invasion of Afghanistan and the Soviet-endorsed imposition of martial law in Poland in December 1981.[9] The 1979 Soviet invasion of Afghanistan led the USA to impose a grain embargo on the USSR and the US Senate to abandon SALT II ratification. The results of the 1980 US presidential election appeared to further strain US–Soviet relations. Americans, reacting to a perceived decline in their relative superpower standing exacerbated by the Iran hostage crisis, elected Ronald Reagan, a conservative Republican whose speeches were frequently laced with staunch anti-Soviet rhetoric (Talbott, 1989, p. 4). President Reagan's 1983 confrontational characterization of the Soviet Union as an evil empire attracted widespread attention and was frequently used by the Western press to portray President Reagan's perception of the Soviet Union. Arms control analyst Strobe Talbott (1989, p. 4) wrote:

When, in a speech in Florida on March 8, 1983, Reagan spoke of the Soviet Union as 'the focus of evil in the modern world' . . . he was also expressing a deeply and widely held conviction that the Russian Bear armed with the Bomb posed a special threat not so much because of the nature of the Bomb as because of the nature of the Bear.

Soviet relations with the West continued to deteriorate when, in September 1983, the Soviet Union shot down a Korean passenger airliner over the Sea of Japan, sparking world condemnation. This stormy period of US–Soviet relations spilled over into the arms control arena as well, including the Soviet deployment of SS–20 missiles and NATO's 1979 decision to deploy their own intermediate-range land-based missiles. The beginning of cruise and Pershing II missile deployment in Western Europe in late 1983 prompted the Soviet delegation to walk out of the on-going Geneva arms talks conference. The Soviets were particularly upset over the state of nuclear arms control issues when, in March 1983, President Reagan unveiled his plan for a defensive shield against ballistic nuclear weapons, the Strategic Defense Initiative. All of these factors, coupled with a deteriorating Soviet leadership, produced strained superpower relations which resonated quite strongly throughout the West European public.

The apprehension among West Europeans over tense superpower relations was eased somewhat as the new Soviet leader Mikhail Gorbachev took power in 1985. As Chapter 5 illustrates, Gorbachev was seen as a Soviet leader intent on reaching an arms control agreement and reducing the superpower tensions which made the West Europeans quite nervous.[10] President Reagan, through his Vice Presidential emissary to the March 1985 funeral of Soviet leader Chernenko, broached the topic of a superpower summit with the new Soviet Secretary-General Gorbachev (Weihmiller and Doder, 1986, p. 199). As a result, the November 1985 meeting between Reagan and Gorbachev in Geneva was the first such meeting of American and Soviet leaders since Jimmy Carter and Leonid Brezhnev signed the SALT II Treaty in Vienna in June 1979. The Geneva summit produced no major arms control agreements as progress on such issues became especially difficult given the US enthusiasm for, and the harsh Soviet opposition to, the American Strategic Defense Initiative. Going into the Geneva summit, the USA had three rather modest objectives:

establish a personal relationship with Gorbachev; obtain a commitment from the Soviet leader that their talks on arms reductions would continue; and agree on a place and approximate time of the next summit. (Regan, 1988, p. 339)

From this American perspective, the Geneva summit was a success.

West European Reaction to the Geneva Summit

The Geneva summit was a media extravaganza. The carefully choreographed movements of the two superpower leaders played wonderfully to the more than 3,000 journalists in Geneva. Each side attempted to manipulate their image at the summit to gain an edge in world public opinion. The Geneva summit was the first major test for the newly developed Soviet public relations strategy for Western audiences. However, on several occasions the carefully orchestrated Soviet press conferences were disrupted by persistent questioning about human rights abuses in the USSR.

The major West European television stations in Britain, France, Italy and West Germany gave lead story coverage to the summit events and personalities on their nightly newscasts throughout the summit. The major West European television nightly news coverage sounded several themes:

> despite limited accomplishments, the meeting established a much needed dialogue; SDI was the main factor blocking an arms control agreement and; the two leaders came to Geneva with different agendas, President Reagan emphasized his desire for a fresh start and his commitment to SDI research, while Gorbachev focused on his attempt to block SDI and gain world respect for the Soviet Union. (Smith, 1985, p. 1)

Immediately prior to the Geneva summit, West European television news broadcasts reported little optimism for the summit's outcome. Typically, BBC 1 editorialised that 'this summit needs saving even before it starts'. However, this negative coverage was transformed during the summit as networks showed images of the smiling leaders as friendly and relaxed. West Germany's ZDF 2 reported 'the talks have been valuable for both sides. However, on a lot of topics there are great differences' (Smith, 1985, p. 2).

The Geneva summit served to boost Western Europeans' image of the superpower relations. The percentage of those who said US–Soviet relations were good increased between 12 and 20 percentage points in Britain, France, Italy, the Netherlands and West Germany compared to immediately before the summit (Table 6.2). Additionally, almost half or more believed that superpower relations would improve as a result of the summit. Furthermore, very large majorities of seven in ten or more in all five countries said that if the President of the United States and the leader of the Soviet Union met more often it would increase, rather than reduce, the chances for world peace.[11] President Reagan himself found the summit advantageous as an opportunity to meet the new Soviet leader and size him up. Coming home from the Geneva summit, Reagan told a key aide that 'Gorbachev was truly a different type of Soviet leader; that he really believed in democracy' (Wirthlin, 1990). While many of the President's inner circle remained sceptical of his assessment of Gorbachev, events in the Soviet Union and Eastern Europe appeared to have justified his judgment.

Despite the euphoria over improved relations, few Western Europeans credited the Geneva summit with accomplishing much towards resolving arms control issues, human rights in the Soviet Union, or regional conflicts outside of Europe (Such as Nicaragua or Afghanistan). Post-summit public evaluation of the meeting's accomplishments, shown in Table 6.3, met the rather modest expectations expressed by many West European publics. Prior to the meeting, a telephone survey indicated that only about a third or less in Britain (34 per cent), France (37 per cent), the Netherlands (13 per cent), and West Germany (15 per cent) thought the meeting would contribute much to resolving various US–Soviet issues. The Italians were the exception in that somewhat more actually saw progress after the meeting than expected it before. Prior to Geneva only about one-third (36 per cent) in Italy thought the summit would produce significant results, but afterwards half (51 per cent) said the summit helped resolve US–Soviet issues.[12] Among those who said the summit did not accomplish very much in resolving issues between the USA and the Soviet Union, a vast majority in each country, ranging from 67 per cent in France to 75 per cent in West Germany, did not fault either President Reagan or Mr Gorbachev, but rather, said both leaders were to blame for the lack of progress.[13]

US–Soviet Prospects After Geneva

The bleak evaluation of specific Geneva accomplishments affected future West European public expectations for progress toward an arms control agreement, even though Western Europeans thought US–

Table 6.3 Geneva summit accomplishments, December 1985 (Per cent saying great deal/fair amount was accomplished)

	Britain	France	Italy	Netherlands	Germany
Summit Issues					
US–Soviet issues	38	39	51	21	26
Arms control	22	25	27	11	11
Soviet human rights	12	20	21	8	5
Regional conflicts	9	11	10	6	5

Question: In general, how much do you think this meeting accomplished in resolving various issues between the United States and the Soviet Union – a great deal, a fair amount, not very much, or nothing at all?

Question: In particular, how much do you think this meeting accomplished in [resolving arms control issues, resolving the issue of human rights in the Soviet Union, the resolution of conflicts outside of Europe such as Afghanistan and Nicaragua] – a great deal, a fair amount, not very much, or nothing at all?

Source: December 1985 Geneva Summit Telephone Survey.

Soviet relations would improve as a result of Geneva.[14] For example, only about one-third in Britain, France, the Netherlands and West Germany, and slightly less than half in Italy thought it likely that the USA and Soviet Union would reach an arms control agreement within the next two years. Arms control advocates generally considered President Reagan's determination to proceed with research into an anti-missile defence system, the Strategic Defense Initiative, as a major stumbling block to arms control progress at the Geneva summit. As Table 6.4 shows, the prevailing opinion in four of the five countries surveyed immediately after the Geneva Summit was that the USA should give up research on an anti-nuclear missile defence system if that were necessary in order to reach a nuclear arms control agreement with the Soviet Union. Only in France did more hold the view that SDI research was 'too important' to give up for the sake of an arms control agreement (see Chapter 2 for further discussion of SDI).

West European assessment of superpower leaders at Geneva
Although President Reagan and Mr Gorbachev were occasional visitors to European capitals and recipients of almost constant inter-

Table 6.4 SDI and arms control, November–December 1985 (per cent)

	Britain	France	Italy	Netherlands	West Germany
Should give it up	49	40	55	57	64
Too important to give up	42	53	33	33	24
Don't know	9	7	12	10	12
Total	100	100	100	100	100

Question: Do you think the USA should give up research on an anti-missile defence system if that were necessary in order to reach a nuclear arms control agreement with the Soviet Union or is this research too important to give up?

Source: December 1985 Geneva Summit Telephone Survey.

national media coverage, the Geneva Summit provided Western Europeans with their first look at both leaders side by side. Table 6.5 shows that among those who said that a given characteristic is more attributable to one leader over the other, a larger number in all five countries identified President Reagan rather than Mr Gorbachev as one who understands West European problems, wants world peace, and is trustworthy. On the issue of military force, only in France did a larger number judge Gorbachev as more likely than Reagan to use military force to achieve his objectives. Attitudes in the other four countries on this issue were closely divided between the two leaders. However, on each of these four questions, large numbers in all five countries said the attribute applied to both or neither of the leaders. The prevailing view in each country, Britain (61 per cent), France (47 per cent), Italy (59 per cent), the Netherlands (70 per cent) and West Germany (74 per cent), was that both Reagan and Gorbachev want world peace. The Geneva summit represented a breakthrough for US–Soviet relations during the Reagan years and served to improve West European attitudes about the superpower relations. While West European publics did not consider the Geneva summit to have accomplished much in resolving particular issues between the USA and the Soviet Union, they widely believed that if Reagan and Gorbachev met more often, chances for world peace would increase.

Table 6.5 Western Europeans judge Geneva summit leaders, December 1985 (per cent)

	Britain	France	Italy	Netherlands	West Germany
Understands European problems:					
Reagan	34	41	34	30	41
Gorbachev	17	6	8	14	12
Both	16	19	22	26	27
Neither	27	27	20	23	13
Don't know	6	8	16	6	6
Total	100	101	100	99	99
Wants world peace:					
Reagan	21	29	15	12	11
Gorbachev	6	4	4	4	6
Both	61	47	59	70	74
Neither	9	14	13	9	5
Don't know	3	5	9	5	4
Total	100	99	100	100	100
Is trustworthy:					
Reagan	20	35	24	14	22
Gorbachev	5	5	10	7	14
Both	20	21	37	21	30
Neither	43	27	14	44	19
Don't know	11	11	14	13	15
Total	99	99	99	100	100
Is likely to use military force to achieve his objectives:					
Reagan	17	9	13	16	13
Gorbachev	22	26	15	17	18
Both	37	34	40	50	34
Neither	18	20	17	11	27
Don't know	6	11	15	6	8
Total	100	100	100	100	100

Question: Now I am going to read several statements. For each one, please tell me if you think it best describes President Reagan or Soviet leader Gorbachev, or does it describe both of them or neither of them – is understanding of European problems, wants world peace, is trustworthy, is likely to use military force to achieve his objectives?

Source: December 1985 Geneva Summit Telephone Survey.

The Reykjavik Summit, October 1986

Following the Geneva summit throughout 1986 a series of summit invitations and rejections volleyed back and forth between the superpowers as each was posturing for the best advantage in the arms control sweepstakes. Western Europeans were anxious for the superpower summit momentum started in Geneva to continue. In March 1986 publics in Britain (82 per cent), France (79 per cent), Italy (88 per cent) and West Germany (70 per cent) overwhelmingly thought that it would be useful for Reagan and Gorbachev to meet during that year, even if it was unlikely that an arms control agreement would be signed.[15]

Finally, in September 1986, just days before the summit, the superpowers announced they would meet next month in Reykjavik, Iceland. President Reagan perceived the hurriedly prepared meeting as an Icelandic 'base camp before the summit' with hopes of laying the foundation for a future arms control agreement.[16] Mr Gorbachev, under pressure at home to derail SDI, held larger expectations for the summit. Gorbachev presented a dramatic proposal at Reykjavik to make deep cuts in each country's huge strategic nuclear stockpiles in exchange for significant constraints on SDI (Mandelbaum & Talbott, 1987). This came as a total surprise to the USA because the Soviets had indicated all along that INF would be the major issue for Reykjavik. During the course of the summit, both Reagan and Gorbachev 'engaged in a bout of feverish one-upmanship, with each trying to outdo the other in demonstrating his devotion to the dream of a nuclear free world' (Mandelbaum & Talbott, 1987, p. 227). President Reagan offered a plan to eliminate all ballistic missiles in ten years; Gorbachev countered with a proposal to eliminate all nuclear weapons. As in Geneva, Gorbachev's proposals hinged on limiting SDI research to the laboratory. But President Reagan, under extreme domestic pressure by the right wing of his Republican party not to compromise on the question of SDI, did not accept the Soviet offer.[17] Consequently, the two world leaders, locked in a stalemate over SDI, abruptly ended the Reykjavik summit.[18]

Both sides, concerned over the negative media interpretation of Reykjavik on world opinion, turned their communication machines into action.[19] Usually inaccessible Reagan Administration officials actively sought out the press to spread an upbeat message that, despite the lack of an actual agreement, historic breakthroughs had been made at Reykjavik.[20] As well, high level Soviet officials were dispatched to European capitals to talk of possible arms control agreements in the wake of Reykjavik. Despite superpower efforts at spin control, few quarters considered the Reykjavik summit a success. The Western media provided the public with little reason to be optimistic in the wake of the meeting. The parting television image of the Reykjavik summit, unlike Geneva where the two leaders were portrayed as amiable partners, was that of the two sombre leaders exchanging stiff goodbyes (Regan, 1988).

Almost all sectors of European public and elite opinion took offence at the outcome of the Reykjavik summit.

> The forces of the [West European] right were everywhere horrified by the presidents's declared objective of 'eliminating all ballistic missiles from the face of the earth' by 1996 and his aspiration to create a 'world without nuclear weapons'. The left blamed him for making this aspiration unacceptable to the Soviets by his insistence on retaining his Strategic Defense Initiative. (Howard, 1988, p. 479)

Still others objected to what they perceived as a cavalier approach by the superpowers to such important nuclear arms control issues. West European capitals 'did not disguise their anger' when the news from Reykjavik indicated that President Reagan, without Allied consultation, proposed to eliminate the US arsenal of ballistic missiles, as these were considered critical to the nuclear umbrella protecting Western Europe (Palmer, 1988, p. 154). Some American observers viewed the dismay over Reykjavik as another example of European inconsistency: criticising their American ally when he does not negotiate with the Soviets and likewise criticising him when he does.[21]

> Ironically, the shock in Western Europe at Reagan's proposal [at Reykjavik to eliminate nuclear weapons] ultimately deprived him of the credit he deserved for boldness in US–Soviet nuclear negotiations, which the allies had long urged upon him and his predecessors. (Hunter, 1988, p. 152)

Despite the gloomy post-mortem on Reykjavik found throughout Western Europe, US Administration officials were impressed with the progress made on a variety of arms control issues. Chief arms control negotiator Paul Nitze said that even though the press built up Reykjavik as a disaster, it 'was a tremendous success' (Nitze, 1990). Ken Adelman, director of the US Arms Control and Disarmament Agency recounted that 'in this intense and serious effort of bargaining, our two countries reduced differences in virtually every aspect of nuclear arms control' (Adelman, 1986, p. 1).

The pessimistic British and German assessment of Reykjavik's accomplishments on arms controls issues was quite similar to that found after Geneva (Tables 6.3 and 6.6). In these two countries sizable majorities of about seven in ten did not think the Reykjavik summit had accomplished much in resolving arms control issues. The French, however, viewed the Reykjavik summit somewhat more favourably than they did Geneva on this issue. A large plurality (46 per cent) in France said Reykjavik did help to resolve arms control issues compared to only 25 per cent after Geneva.

A battery of arms control questions asked after the Reykjavik summit indicate some Western Europeans held somewhat contradictory views on the nuances of arms control issues. Among those who were familiar with the summit, half or more in Britain (50 per cent), France (66 per cent), and West Germany (67 per cent) agreed that the USA and Soviet Union should have agreed to eliminate all strategic nuclear forces during the next ten years while allowing SDI research

Table 6.6 Nuclear arms control accomplishments at Reykjavik, October 1986 (per cent)

	Britain	France	West Germany
Great deal	6	13	3
Fair amount	21	33	11
Subtotal	27	46	14
Not very much	45	18	48
Nothing at all	23	13	22
Subtotal	68	31	70
Don't know/not asked[a]	5	23	16
Total	100	100	100

[a] Those who said they had heard nothing at all about the summit were not asked this question.

Question: In particular, how much do you think this meeting accomplished in helping to resolve nuclear arms control issues – a great deal, fair amount, not very much, or nothing at all?

Source: October 1986 Post-Reykjavik Summit Telephone Survey I.

and development. On the other hand, about half or more in Britain (51 per cent), France (47 per cent) and West Germany (56 per cent) agreed that the Soviet Union was right to take the position at Reykjavik that agreements on all nuclear arms control issues could only be reached if the USA limited SDI research to the laboratory. West European publics were clear, however, on their position toward the INF missiles. Among those who were familiar with the summit, vast majorities of three in four or more in each country agreed that the superpowers should have reached an agreement at Reykjavik on limiting INF nuclear missiles in Europe despite their differences on SDI.[22] After the Reykjavik summit, Britains (56 per cent) and West Germans (68 per cent), by even wider margins than immediately after Geneva, said that the USA should give up SDI if that were necessary in order to reach any nuclear arms control agreement with the Soviets. Even the French, previously supportive of SDI, were predominantly (47 per cent) in favour of trading SDI for an arms control agreement.[23]

Continued US insistence on pursuing SDI research combined with Gorbachev's rising popularity as an arms control advocate began to take its toll on West European perceptions, especially among the British and Germans, of US resolve to reach an agreement. After the Reykjavik summit, the prevailing view in Britain (46 to 20 per cent) and Germany (42 to 18 per cent), both INF basing countries, was that the Soviet Union, not the United States, was making a greater effort to bring about a nuclear arms control agreement. In France, a plurality believed the USA (35 per cent) was making a greater effort on arms control than the Soviet Union (20 per cent). Furthermore, among those that had heard at least something about the summit, a greater number in Britain (35 to 9 per cent) and Germany (43 to 6 per cent) blamed President Reagan, rather than Mr Gorbachev, for not accomplishing more at the meeting. In France, an almost equal number blamed Reagan (12 per cent) as blamed Gorbachev (15 per cent). However, among those familiar with the Reykjavik meeting, the prevailing view in Britain (51 per cent) and France (60 per cent) held *both* leaders responsible for not accomplishing more at the Reykjavik meeting.[24] A second telephone survey conducted three weeks after Reykjavik showed almost no change in the assessment of blame between Reagan and Gorbachev for the lack of achievements at the summit. These survey data suggest that the competing public diplomacy efforts of the superpowers post-summit to assign blame to each other for the dismal results of Reykjavik did not resonate throughout the West European publics.

Washington Summit: The INF Treaty

Given the dour mood cast over superpower relations in the wake of Reykjavik, few Western Europeans thought the USA and Soviet Union would achieve an arms control agreement by the end of 1987. As late as July 1987, majorities in Britain (75 per cent), France (61 per cent), and West Germany (72 per cent) said it was unlikely that the USA and Soviet Union would sign an agreement eliminating all intermediate-range nuclear missiles in Europe before the end of the year.[25] Although West Europeans were not hopeful of an arms control agreement, in February 1987 three-quarters or more in Britain (84 per cent), France (73 per cent), Italy (87 per cent), and West Germany (77 per cent) thought it important that the superpowers hold a summit meeting during 1987.[26]

Despite the fact that superpower arms control efforts ran aground at Reykjavik, both superpowers, for their own different reasons, were determined to reach agreement on the INF issue. Numerous rounds of consultations and exchanges took place during 1987 with the Soviets eventually dropping their insistence that an INF Treaty be linked to a limitation of SDI. This, in addition to other accommodations by the respective superpowers, paved the way for the historic treaty signing summit in Washington in December 1987. In the run-up to the Washington summit, and the impending INF Treaty, a substantial number of European arms control elites cautioned that the elimination of INF missiles could signal a dangerous decoupling of US and West European security interests (Gordon, 1987, p. 175). This was not, however, the prevailing view among the West European public immediately after the Washington summit. As Table 6.7 shows, majorities in Britain (60 per cent), Italy (69 per cent), the Netherlands (73 per cent) and West Germany (74 per cent), and large pluralities in Belgium (53 per cent) and France (48 per cent) said that even after the elimination of US intermediate range nuclear weapons in Europe, the USA would be just as committed to the defence of Western Europe. Furthermore, majorities in Britain (59 per cent), France (61 per cent), Italy (67 per cent), the Netherlands (57 per cent), and West Germany (56 per cent) had at least a fair amount of confidence that the USA would do whatever is necessary to defend their country in case of an attack. The Belgians, by contrast, were evenly divided (46 to 44 per cent) on this question.

The INF Treaty signed at the Washington summit culminated almost ten years of superpower confrontation over intermediate-range

Table 6.7 US Defence commitment to Western Europe in wake of INF Treaty, December 1987

	Belgium	Britain	France	Italy	Netherlands	West Germany
USA less committed	27	24	31	19	19	15
USA just as committed	53	60	48	69	73	74
Don't know	20	15	21	14	8	11
Total	100	100	100	100	100	100

Question: Some people say that the elimination of US intermediate-range nuclear missiles now in Western Europe will mean that the USA is less committed to the defence of Western Europe. Others say that the USA will be just as committed to the defence of Western Europe. Which view is closer to your own?

Source: December 1987 Post-Washington Summit Telephone Survey.

nuclear missiles in Western Europe and the Soviet Union (see Chapter 3 for full details on the INF issue). The Treaty represented the first time an entire class of nuclear weapons would be destroyed. Given West European opposition to nuclear weapons it was not surprising that the INF Treaty met with near unanimous approval in Italy, the Netherlands and West Germany, as well as receiving substantial support in Belgium, Britain and France where at least eight in ten in each country supported the Treaty. As shown in Table 6.8, support for the Treaty was quite enthusiastic as large majorities exceeding 70 per cent in Italy, the Netherlands and West Germany, and exceeding 60 per cent in Britain said they strongly favoured the treaty. Virtually no one in the six countries strongly opposed the INF Treaty.

Although the West European publics had expressed a willingness to give up SDI for an arms control agreement, they acknowledged its value as a bargaining chip in superpower negotiations. A pre-Washington summit telephone survey indicated the prevailing view in Britain (55 to 18 per cent), France (45 to 7 per cent), and, by a slim margin, West Germany (37 to 32 per cent) was that the US decision to undertake research on a defense against nuclear missiles – the so-called Strategic Defense Initiative – made the Soviet Union more, rather than less, willing to negotiate reductions in nuclear missiles. Additionally, Western Europeans, ranging from about half in France (49 per cent) to a majority in Britain (56 per cent), credited NATO resolve to deploy

Table 6.8 West European support for INF Treaty, December 1987 (per cent)

	Belgium	Britain	France	Italy	Netherlands	West Germany
Strongly favour	26	65	34	79	76	77
Somewhat favour	53	23	44	18	21	19
Subtotal	79	88	78	97	97	96
Somewhat oppose	9	6	10	1	1	2
Strongly oppose	3	2	4	2	0	0
Subtotal	12	8	14	3	1	2
Don't know	9	4	8	0	2	2
Total	100	100	100	100	100	100

Question: At the summit, President Reagan and Soviet leader Gorbachev signed an agreement to eliminate all US and Soviet intermediate range nuclear missiles. Do you strongly favour, somewhat favour, somewhat oppose, or strongly oppose this agreement?

Source: December 1987 Post-Washington Summit Telephone Survey.

their own intermediate-range nuclear weapons with bringing the Soviets to the bargaining table. Although Western Europeans acknowledged the role played by President Reagan's pursuit of SDI and NATO's INF deployment in bringing the Soviets to the negotiating table, a majority in Britain and West Germany, and a plurality in France credited Gorbachev rather than Reagan for arms control progress, as illustrated in Table 6.9.

Much like the Geneva and Moscow summits, the Washington meeting was generally recognised by West European publics as having reduced East–West tensions but not with having helped to resolve the Afghanistan issue or human rights violations in the Soviet Union (Table 6.10). Except in France, at least half or more said the Washington summit led to a reduction in East–West tensions. By contrast, except in Italy, only one in four or less said they thought much was accomplished at the Washington meeting in resolving the war in Afghanistan or Soviet human rights abuses.[27]

Although large proportions, ranging from 52 per cent in France to 82 per cent in Italy, expressed confidence that the Soviet Union would

Table 6.9 Credit for progress on arms control negotiations, November 1987 (per cent)

	Britain	France	West Germany
President Reagan	18	25	17
Mr Gorbachev	61	38	61
Don't know	21	37	22
Total	100	100	100

Question: Who would you say deserves more credit for the recent progress in arms control negotiations – President Reagan or Soviet leader Gorbachev?
Source: November 1987 Pre-Washington Summit Telephone Survey.

Table 6.10 Washington summit accomplishments, December 1987 (per cent saying great deal/fair amount was accomplished)

	Belgium	Britain	France	Italy	Netherlands	West Germany
Summit issues						
Reducing East–West tensions	55	71	42	83	60	67
Resolving Afghanistan issue	16	11	7	36	10	11
Resolving Soviet human rights issues	25	20	13	50	19	14

Question: In general, how much do you think the Washington summit accomplished in [reducing East–West tensions, resolving the issue of the Soviet war in Afghanistan, resolving human rights issues in the Soviet Union] – a great deal, fair amount, not very much or nothing at all? Each item was asked separately.
Source: December 1987 Post-Washington Summit Telephone Survey.

observe the conditions of the freshly-signed INF Treaty, majorities in Britain (67 per cent), France (65 per cent), the Netherlands (55 per cent), and West Germany (59 per cent) and half in Italy (50 per cent) said NATO should not continue to proceed with the elimination of their INF missiles if Soviet violations were observed. The Belgians were closely split (45 to 41 per cent) over this issue.[28]

President Reagan intended the Washington summit not only as a treaty-signing ceremony, but as a prelude to a START (Strategic Arms Reduction Talks) agreement to be concluded at the final Reagan–Gorbachev summit in Moscow the following spring (Talbott, 1989). The long sought-after START agreement would cut the superpower nuclear arsenals by 50 per cent. In the euphoric aftermath of the Washington summit and the overwhelming European public support for the INF Treaty, anticipation among Western Europeans for a START agreement ran high. In December 1987, majorities in Belgium (56 per cent), Britain (71 per cent), Italy (69 per cent), the Netherlands (61 per cent), and West Germany (62 per cent) and a large plurality in France (46 per cent) thought, in the wake of the Washington summit, that it was at least fairly likely that the Soviet Union and United States would reach an agreement in the next year to make major cuts in their strategic nuclear arsenal.[29] A March 1988 pre-Moscow summit telephone survey indicated that pluralities in Britain (44 per cent), France (40 per cent), and West Germany (49 per cent) said reducing US and Soviet strategic nuclear weapons, rather than reducing conventional or short-range nuclear forces, would do the most to enhance the peace and security of Europe. Support for further bilateral nuclear arms reductions was found in a commercial survey in January 1988. Sizeable numbers in Britain (29 per cent), France (19 per cent), and West Germany (39 per cent) chose reduction of strategic and tactical nuclear weapons as the one most important issue to address after the Washington summit.[30] Regardless of the momentum provided by the INF Treaty, the final Reagan–Gorbachev summit in Moscow would not produce the strategic arms control agreement West Europeans had predicted and desired.

In the run-up to the Washington summit, Western Europeans were sceptical that an arms control agreement would be reached, but thought it important for the summit to be held. Similar to the Geneva summit, Western Europeans did not think the Washington summit served to accomplish much in resolving specific international problems. However, majorities in five countries once again thought the summit helped reduce general East–West tensions.

Moscow Summit: Confirmation of US–Soviet Goodwill

Although the Moscow summit did not result in the arms control breakthrough many had hoped for, it did enhance the West European publics' image of a continuing good relationship between the superpowers, epitomised by Ronald Reagan and Mikhail Gorbachev strolling arm-in-arm through Moscow's Red Square. West European reaction to the Moscow summit generally mirrored that which followed the previous Reagan–Gorbachev meetings. As Table 6.11 indicates, more of the public in Britain, France and West Germany credited the summit with reducing East–West tensions than with resolving human rights problems in the Soviet Union or, to an even lesser degree, with resolving regional conflicts.

Acknowledging that a START agreement was well beyond the scope of the Moscow summit, President Reagan placed a great deal of emphasis on human rights abuses in the Soviet Union. The major West European press praised President Reagan's efforts at the summit for producing a better environment for superpower relations, and most of the press commentary approved of President Reagan's stress on human rights, noting that human rights is an important issue for building better East–West relations (Ederma, 1988b). The level of West European public support for President Reagan's outspokenness on Soviet human rights violations at the summit varied by country. A large majority in West Germany (74 per cent) and half in France (52 per cent) said it was appropriate for Reagan to criticise the Soviet Union over human rights abuses during the Moscow summit. However, about half in Britain (53 per cent) said such criticism was inappropriate.[31]

Table 6.11 Moscow summit accomplishments, June 1988 (per cent saying great deal/fair amount was accomplished)

	Britain	France	West Germany
Reducing East–West tensions	77	38	53
Resolving regional conflicts	19	9	7
Improving respect for individual rights in the Soviet Union	43	27	26

Question: In general, how much do you think the Moscow summit between Reagan and Gorbachev accomplished in [reducing East–West tensions; resolving regional conflicts such as in Angola and Central American; improving respect for individual freedoms in the Soviet Union] – a great deal, fair amount, not very much or nothing at all? Each item was asked separately.

Source: June 1988 Post-Moscow Summit Telephone Survey.

CONCLUSION

Although Western Europeans generally believe it is important that the two superpowers meet and discuss world problems they were not convinced their own interests were protected by the USA at the Reykjavik, Washington, and Moscow summits. For example, as Table 6.12 shows, only 40 per cent or less in six West European countries thought the USA protected their countries' interests even during the highly successful Washington summit which concluded the widely endorsed INF Treaty. The series of Reagan–Gorbachev meetings somewhat improved the outlook among the British and West Germans that the USA is protecting West European interests, but the French remain pessimistic. Between the 1986 Reykjavik and the 1988 Moscow summits, the proportion of British who said the United States protected their interests increased from 35 per cent to 47 per cent and

Table 6.12 USA protects West European interests at the summits, 1986–88 (per cent saying West European interests protected great deal/fair amount)

	Reykjavik Oct. 1986	Washington Dec. 1987	Moscow June 1988
Belgium	N/A[a]	17	N/A
Britain	35	31	47
France	21	16	15
Italy	N/A	40	N/A
Netherlands	N/A	34	N/A
West Germany	16	28	39

[a] (N/A) question not asked.

Question: October 1986: How much do you think the United States protected West European interests in negotiating with the Soviet Union at Reykjavik? Question December 1987: How much do you think the United States protected [survey country] interests in negotiating with the Soviet Union at the Washington summit? Question June 1988: How much do you think the United States is protecting [survey country] interests during its current arms control negotiations with the Soviet Union?

Sources: October 1986 Post-Reykjavik Summit Telephone Survey I, December 1987 Post-Washington Summit Telephone Survey, June 1988 Post-Moscow Summit Telephone Survey.

the number in West Germany more than doubled from 16 percent to 39 per cent. During this same time period, however, the number in France who said the USA protected their interests at the summits actually declined from 21 to 15 per cent.

The ebb and flow of US–Soviet relations during the Reagan years was quite clearly reflected in the events surrounding the four superpower summits. The successful US–Soviet summits in Washington and Moscow vastly improved the superpower relations in the eyes of the West European public. These improved relations were welcomed by Western Europeans without concern that an improved superpower relationship would jeopardize Allied security interests. For example, after the Moscow summit, only small minorities thought this new superpower relationship would pose a threat to the interests of their own country. By contrast, vast majorities in Britain (72 per cent), France (68 per cent), and West Germany (83 per cent) were unconcerned that the Soviet Union and the United States would become so close that their own country's interests would be damaged. Half or more, ranging from 51 per cent in France to 63 per cent in Great Britain, also said that the benefit of good US–Soviet relations is a general reduction in international tensions. Only ten per cent or less said there was little benefit from improved superpower relations.[32]

During the 1980s West Europeans used the summits as indicators of superpower relations. The first Reagan–Gorbachev summit in Geneva in 1985 was considered a major breakthrough in superpower relations as it was the first such meeting in six years. This meeting was followed by the encounter at Reykjavik in 1986, widely perceived as unsuccessful, where dramatic arms control possibilities were dashed over the issue of SDI. However, by December of the following year the two powers signed the historic INF Treaty at the Washington summit. The two leaders met one last time in a summit setting in Moscow in 1988, a summit which was viewed as a goodwill meeting. Both leaders used these summits to pursue foreign policy objectives as well as to hone their respective images among both their domestic population and the international community. Western Europeans clearly endorsed the superpower summitry during the Reagan years as a vehicle to improve US–Soviet relations, but they generally perceived the summits as reducing overall East–West tensions rather than resolving specific issues which divide the two superpowers.

7 US Public Diplomacy Efforts in Western Europe

During the 1980s the United States was alarmed that developments in Western Europe, coupled with an intensive Soviet propaganda campaign, would lead to the unravelling of NATO and a deterioration of the special American relationship with the Allies. Large demonstrations against INF deployment, opposition to US policies in Central America, the rise of the Green Party in West Germany, the election of Socialist governments in Greece and Spain, and a new and improved Soviet image were viewed by the USA as indications that the Western Alliance was being severely tested. The US foreign policy community in general, and the Reagan White House in particular, were especially sensitive about the attitudes and actions of Western Europe's younger generation. In response, the Reagan Administration – which keenly appreciated the value of public relations – embarked on a massive public diplomacy campaign aimed principally at Western Europe to stem the perceived tide of anti-Americanism and neutralism. This chapter focuses on US efforts to 'tell America's story' in Western Europe and thereby influence public opinion.

IMPORTANCE OF PUBLIC DIPLOMACY

Public diplomacy is a familiar tool used by governments to improve the understanding of their society and its policies in other countries within the international community. In the post-war era, the United States relied on the traditional methods of international public diplomacy in Western Europe which included providing information to members of the foreign press and developing cultural and student exchanges. While these efforts met with some success, they were primarily targeted to an elite audience within each country.

With a growing recognition of the role played by foreign public opinion on the outcome of US policies, the Reagan Administration emphasised the need for American public diplomacy efforts to reach wider audiences. With this in mind, the White House carefully orchestrated media appearances in Europe for key Administration officials including the President and Vice President. Furthermore, in an attempt to influence broad public opinion throughout Western Europe, two new communications channels were opened to Western Europe by the US Government during the Reagan years: a special Voice of America service in Western Europe and Worldnet television. The commitment to a massive public diplomacy effort was further indicated by the almost doubling of the US Information Agency's budget during the Reagan years. In his final budgetary testimony before the House Appropriations Committee in 1988, the USIA Director Charles Z. Wick, then near the end of almost 8 years in office, said that one of his major contributions to public diplomacy during his tenure was the 'increased recognition of public diplomacy as an integral component of this country's foreign policy effort'.[1] Organisationally, the Reagan White House placed a renewed emphasis on public diplomacy. National Security Decision Directive 77 (NSDD-77) established a special planning group within the National Security Council responsible for the 'overall planning, direction, coordination and monitoring of implementation of public diplomacy activities'.[2] The directive defined public diplomacy as comprised of 'those actions of the US Government designed to generate support for our national security objectives'. The White House also formed an Office of Planning and Evaluation which kept the President abreast of trends in foreign public opinion (Wirthlin, 1990).

The massive Soviet propaganda effort (as described in Chapter 5) mounted in Western Europe during the first half of the 1980s, presented a critical challenge to the USA to develop an information campaign that could counteract the Soviets. In the second half of the 1980s, the US Government was also concerned that the positive image of Gorbachev found in both the media coverage and wider public opinion could serve to undermine support for the Western Alliance. Table 7.1 indicates that, at least from the reading of public opinion tea leaves, there was some justification for thinking that Gorbachev was the benefactor of positive European press coverage. Majorities in the three of the four major countries said media coverage of Gorbachev was positive. In all four countries more said press coverage of Gorbachev was positive than thought so of the media's treatment of Reagan.

The USIA, which states as its primary goal to 'strengthen foreign understanding and support for United States policies and actions', is a

Table 7.1 Perception of media coverage of Gorbachev and Reagan, September 1987 (per cent)

	Britain		France		Italy		West Germany	
	Gorbachev	Reagan	Gorbachev	Reagan	Gorbachev	Reagan	Gorbachev	Reagan
Very positive	13	14	4	3	11	8	10	11
Fairly positive	63	46	44	35	68	44	73	47
Positive	76	60	48	38	79	52	83	58
Fairly negative	10	24	8	21	7	34	6	29
Very negative	2	5	1	2	1	3	1	2
Negative	12	29	9	23	8	37	7	31
Don't know	13	11	42	40	13	12	11	11
Total	101	100	99	101	100	101	101	100

Question: Thinking now about recent coverage of Gorbachev/Reagan by survey country media, would you say that coverage has been generally very positive, fairly positive, fairly negative, or very negative?

Source: September 1987 Security Survey.

key player in implementing US public diplomacy strategies.[3] Although public relations and organised information campaigns to strengthen international understanding cannot singlehandedly overcome unpopular foreign policies, it is critical 'to worry about how you present the issues' (Nitze, 1990). The impact of the media on public opinion and the importance of a public diplomacy strategy to influence the media was appreciated by the Reagan Administration.[4] Their successful use of the media to heighten domestic popularity was applied to the foreign media as well, in hopes of influencing foreign public opinion. President Reagan's carefully choreographed appearances at superpower summits and European meetings and his dramatic speeches before the British Houses of Parliament in June 1982 and at Normandy in June 1984 on the 40th anniversary of the Allied landings were tailored for maximum media exposure. The Reagan White House expended great effort in choosing appropriate sites which could best portray the desired image of the President to the media.[5]

The objectives of some of the major public diplomacy campaigns during the Reagan years included the effort to convince Europeans that the USA was truly committed to the negotiations component of the 'dual track' decision of INF deployment which would remove an entire class of nuclear weapons from the face of the earth (Thompson, 1987). They also included stressing the importance of NATO unity, the advantages of the Strategic Defense Initiative, and the need to respond collectively to states that support terrorism, especially Libya.

One of the most intensive American public diplomacy efforts during the Reagan years was the information campaign designed to influence West European public opinion to support the INF deployment. Although the White House public opinion experts recognised that the anti-INF demonstrators were a small minority whose neutralist attitudes did not reflect the attitudes of the general public, policymakers were concerned that these attitudes would catch fire (Nitze, 1990; Wirthlin, 1990). The fundamental themes used during this campaign emphasised that the INF deployment decision was a NATO decision which was of equal advantage for both Americans and Western Europeans and that the negotiations track would be aggressively pursued to eventually eliminate an entire class of nuclear weapons. These themes were reiterated by well-publicised speeches by key US government officials, such as Vice President Bush's tour through the NATO capitals in 1983. Prior to this tour, as well as before several Presidential visits, the White House digested reams of

European public opinion data in search of themes that would reach the desired audiences.

However, the effect of US communication efforts directly with the public was rather limited. As Chapter 3 demonstrates, public diplomacy efforts did not have much impact on the widespread anti-nuclear sentiments in Europe. The actual deployment of the missiles took the wind out of the demonstrators' sail because once the missiles were in place the controversy was all but over, and media coverage, the lifeblood of any demonstration movement, quickly evaporated. In this case at least, the events were clearly more influential than the public diplomacy campaigns (Nitze, 1990).

PUBLIC DIPLOMACY OVER THE RADIO

Responding to White House concerns that anti-Americanism was growing among the post-World War II generation of Western Europeans (a concern which was partly based on a perceived anti-American bias in West European newscasts) the US's Voice of America started an English-language West European broadcasting service. On 15 October 1985,

> the Voice of America resumed broadcasting to Western Europe for the first time in 25 years. VOA Europe broadcast[ed] 24 hours a day, seven days a week, in English to a network of radio stations and community cable systems in Western Europe. The service combine[d] the major programs produced for worldwide broadcast and programming presented by VOA Europe hosts.[6]

The programming was a fast-paced format focussing primarily on popular American music, newsbriefs, and sports and weather reports. The delivery system consisted of a patchwork of FM cable, medium wave transmission and short wave broadcasts which relied primarily on feed service rather than direct broadcast.

As displayed in Table 7.2, data from audience listenership studies in each of six cities during 1988–89 indicate that the proportion of the population that listens to VOA Europe at least once a week is quite small. The relatively large listening audience in Geneva is due, in part, to the sizable foreign population residing in and visiting Geneva. Although American (and other countries') foreign radio broadcasts seldom reach wide mass audiences, they can have an impact if they reach a selected 'elite' listenership. In general, listening rates to VOA

US Public Diplomacy Efforts in Western Europe

Table 7.2 Selected VOA Europe 1988–89 listenership rates (per cent)[a]

City	Age 14 and older	Age 14–24	Age 25 and older
Amsterdam	1.9	2.3	1.8
Geneva	10.5	12.0	10.1
Munich	2.7	3.8	2.4
Oslo	3.2	3.9	3.1
Toulouse	2.4	6.1	1.4
Milan	2.1	3.5	1.4

[a] Audience levels based on prompted and unprompted questions.

Source: Listening to VOA Europe in Oslo, Norway, R-11-89; Listening to VOA Europe in Milan, Italy, R-4-90.

Europe broadcasts are higher among younger listeners, students, people with higher education, and English speakers. As Table 7.2 illustrates, listener rates are higher among people aged 14 to 24 as compared to the those over 24 years of age. This younger audience – the younger, better-educated successor generation – is the intended market. The objective of VOA Europe is to 'reach Europeans too young to have experienced World War II or the postwar reconstruction' (Gibson, 1988, p. 1).

The USA has a legitimate interest in maintaining an international broadcasting network;

> as a superpower with major involvements in global security, trade and culture, the United States wants to be sure that the public record of its activities remains as accurate as possible and that U.S. positions on democracy, human rights, and political economy receive fair international coverage. (Elliot, 1989, p. 114)

However, the utility of VOA Europe as an effective public diplomacy tool in reaching the West European successor generation was debated from the start.

Since its inception VOA Europe, unlike its sister VOA service to Eastern Europe and the Soviet Union, has achieved limited, if any, success in meeting its objectives of providing an effective alternative source of news regarding US issues which in turn would promote positive American attitudes among the younger generation. Unlike those in many Third World nations and closed societies which must rely on international broadcasts for accurate information about world events and even developments within their own country, Western

Europeans enjoy a saturated media market. Comprehensive international news coverage and a variety of entertainment programmes are readily available to any Western European listener. Given this media environment, the addition of an American, English-language broadcast station to an already established market should not be expected to reach much of an audience. A further question arises as to how much of an influence VOA Europe's programming content of popular entertainment and newsbriefs can have on successor generation attitudes toward the USA generally and toward its specific foreign policies. Also the English language nature of the broadcast and the mixed delivery system can reduce its appeal. All of these factors make it quite difficult for the USA to use radio as an effective channel for public diplomacy in Western Europe. Furthermore, as Chapter 4 clearly demonstrates, the original stimulus for the radio service, the Reagan Administration perception that anti-Americanism was sweeping the Continent, was off the mark. The recognition of this and the new opportunities in Eastern Europe have led VOA Europe to attempt to broaden its mission for the 1990s. For example, in Spring 1990 VOA Europe established its first Eastern Europe radio affiliate in Budapest, Hungary called 'Radio Bridge'. This arrangement will allow Hungarian radio to broadcast VOA Europe programming.[7]

WORLDNET: TELE-DIPLOMACY

Television provides an innovative medium to reach potentially millions of viewers throughout Western Europe. During the Reagan Administration, Charles Z. Wick, USIA Director and a personal friend of Reagan, embarked on an aggressive programme to develop a worldwide television network (Worldnet) 'to bring the latest news and information about the United States to an international audience'.[8] Worldnet was originally designed to deliver two types of broadcasts: an interactive interview format which would address current US policies, and more traditional news and entertainment programs produced by USIA or private organizations. Interactive broadcasts began first followed by daily Worldnet programming service to Europe in April 1985. This service was expanded to four hours daily in April 1987.

The interactive programmes, where foreign journalists could question US policymakers in Washington via satellite, were designed to provide US Government positions on topical issues which the foreign television stations would then replay on their own local newscasts, and to generate stories in the local papers. This public diplomacy tool counted on the 'multiplier effect' to disseminate the desired information to wider public audiences. After the US invasion of Grenada in 1983, the US Ambassador to the United Nations Jeanne Kirkpatrick appeared on the newly established Worldnet interactive satellite television program to present the US policy to foreign journalists assembled at American embassies in Western Europe. This presentation was considered by the Administration as a highly successful public diplomacy tool in turning around perceived negative opinion of the US action in Grenada and gave the fledgling television service newfound credibility within the Administration.

The interactive programmes constitute the core of Worldnet service. US embassy personnel have come to rely on Worldnet programming and consider Worldnet interactives as an effective way to disseminate US Government policies and positions to local journalists and television stations. As Table 7.3 shows, a large number of interactive programmes have been requested by USIA Posts overseas in their annual country plans.

The daily programmes of sports and information, which included the commercially produced George Michael Sports Machine as well as in-house productions such as 'America Today', were designed to reach the mass audiences directly to portray the desired image of the United States and American life. To encourage local stations to carry the programming, USIA provided the Worldnet broadcast at no cost. However, as an effective public diplomacy tool in the age of television, daily Worldnet programming had a difficult time getting off the ground. Initially, programming was limited to about five hours a

Table 7.3 WORLDNET interactive programs requested and produced and broadcast to Western Europe, fiscal years 1986–90

	Requested	Produced and Broadcast
FY 86	N/A	85
FY 87	185	133
FY 88	386	158
FY 89	426	141
FY 90	396	110

Source: USIA Television and Film Service.

day, and cable access was not available to all European viewers. In 1988, it was estimated that Worldnet was available to approximately 5 million cable households.[9] Of course availability and actual viewing are much different. In addition to the technical difficulties of starting up a large scale satellite television network, congressional support for Worldnet's daily programming was lukewarm in some key quarters.

Overzealous estimates of West European Worldnet viewers by USIA led to a growing concern on Capitol Hill that Worldnet was not reaching the number of viewers claimed and that the cost was too high, taking money away from already established programmes. On 1 October 1988, 'Worldnet suspended its program service pursuant to legislation (PL 100–204) that required the shutdown unless research showed an average daily audience of two million for non-interactive programs in Europe'. This shutdown of daily programming occurred because a USIA-commissioned audience survey found approximately 234,000 regular viewers.[10]

Prior to October 1988,

> Worldnet experimented with several types of programs for daily broadcast. 'America Today' was an Agency-produced magazine format program of news, public affairs, and features on American life. 'Hour USA' was a collection of programs from the private sector on the arts, science, English teaching, sports, and entertainment. 'Newsfile', a televised newsclip service, was translated into Spanish, Portuguese, French, and Arabic for USIA's posts to distribute to local television stations.[11]

The congressional restraints on Worldnet programming were partially lifted approximately one year after their initial application. In the wake of the congressional action over the past several years regarding Worldnet's ability to provide programming, the 1990 strategic objectives and priorities of Worldnet included:

- regaining ground in satellite television programme delivery lost to other countries during the congressional ban;
- positioning USIA television service as a subtle US Government satellite tv programme 'syndicator' (as distinguished from CNN's commercial TV orientation), emphasising more US Government policies, bilateral relationships, 'public service' programming;
- reaching two distinct audiences: (a) Post-identified elites (chiefly via interactive teleconferences) and (b) Mass-audiences through broadcast placement and home video distribution.[12]

Just as VOA Europe has retooled its operation to seize the opportunity to enter the East European market, so too has Worldnet. Worldnet is working to provide broadcasts and equipment to Eastern Europe. For example, Worldnet contributed programming to a newly formatted television station in Czechoslovakia which started broadcasting in May 1990. In conjunction with President Bush's 1989 trip to Hungary, Worldnet officials explored 'ways of exchanging features, reports and other TV programs'.[13]

THE WEST EUROPEAN AUDIENCE

In order to conduct large scale public diplomacy campaigns that directly address foreign publics, the US Government must rely on the numerous media outlets in Western Europe. Therefore, it is important to identify the medium which is relied upon most frequently for information on topics related to US policies and interests. Western Europeans enjoy a media-rich environment which has a wide range of news outlets ranging from international radio and television broadcasts to the dozens of newspapers which cover the ideological spectrum.

Not surprisingly Western Europeans primarily rely on television for information on foreign affairs. This is demonstrated by abundant recent survey data. Table 7.4 shows that for information on relations between the USA and the survey country, more respondents in each of the five countries where this question was asked in October 1987 said television was their primary source. Newspapers were a strong second as a source of information. Reliance on foreign radio and satellite television broadcasts was very infrequent; less than 1 per cent of the public primarily rely on these sources for information.

This same media usage pattern applies to sources of information on international affairs and arms control issues (Table 7.5). Several surveys in the 1980s specifically asked the public separately which medium they relied on the most for information about arms control issues and international affairs. Television again ranked at the top.

The better-educated target groups for elite-oriented US public diplomacy efforts are more likely to rely on the print media for information on their country's relations with the United States. A 1987 survey found that a larger proportion of the better-educated were less reliant on television and more reliant on newspapers for foreign affairs information than the lesser-educated (Table 7.6). For example,

Table 7.4 Primary source of information on US–European relations, October 1987 (per cent)

	Britain	France	Italy	Spain	West Germany
Television	70	43	53	44	46
Newspapers	36	14	30	24	25
Domestic Magazines	1	6	6	1	10
Foreign Magazines	1	1	—[a]	—	1
Domestic Radio	3	9	3	10	4
Foreign Radio	—	1	—	—	—
Foreign Satellite TV	—	1	—	—	1
Friends/Relatives	2	4	3	3	9
Political/Union leaders	—	1	1	—	2
Don't know	3	21	3	18	3
Total	116[b]	101	99	100	101

[a] (—) indicates less than one per cent.
[b] British responses exceed 100 per cent due to multiple responses.

Question: Here is a card on which are listed some sources of information about relations between (survey country) and the United States. Which one of the following do you rely on most for information about our country's relations with the United States?

Source: September—October 1987 American Image Survey.

Table 7.5 Source of information on arms control and international affairs, 1986–87 (per cent)

	Britain			France			West Germany		
	Nov. 1986	May 1987	Sep. 1987	Nov. 1986	May 1987	Sep. 1987	Nov. 1986	May 1987	Sep. 1987
Television	74	53	59	53	55	61	72	43	50
Newspapers	60	37	34	21	23	18	50	42	41
Radio	17	5	5	13	13	13	30	9	6
Magazines	9	1	1	10	6	6	16	4	1
Don't know	2	5	1	3	3	2	2	3	2
Total	155[a]	101	100	100	100	100	170[a]	101	100

[a] Totals exceed 100 per cent due to multiple responses.

Questions: November 1986 and May 1987 – From which medium – newspapers, radio, television, or magazines – do you get most of your information on arms control?
September 1987 – From which medium – newspapers, radio, television, or magazines – do you get most of your information on international affairs?

Sources: October–November 1986 Post-Reykjavik Summit Telephone Survey II; May 1987 INF Telephone Survey; September 1987 Reagan–Gorbachev Telephone Survey.

Table 7.6 Media habits and education level (per cent)

Education	Britain		France		Italy		Spain	
	Less	Better	Less	Better	Less	Better	Less	Better
Television	70	55	48	19	53	29	46	15
Newspapers	33	43	12	24	29	45	22	53
Domestic Magazines	5	7	5	13	5	15	1	7
Foreign Magazines	2	3	1	2	—[a]	1	—	1
Domestic Radio	2	7	8	11	3	2	10	12
Foreign Radio	1	1	—	1	—	1	—	—
Foreign TV	—	1	—	—	—	—	—	—

[a] (—) indicates less than one per cent.

Question: Here is a card on which are listed some sources of information about relations between [survey country name] and the United States. Which one of the following do you rely on most for information about our country's relations with the United States?

Source: September–October 1987 American Image Survey.

in Britain, the better-educated rely less on television (55 per cent) and more on the press (43 per cent) for information on US–British relations than do the less-educated public. The vast majority of the less-educated public (70 per cent) depend on television while only a third (33 per cent) rely on newspapers. Preferences for individual newspapers also reflect education levels in Britain. The *Guardian* (16 per cent) is the most popular source of information on US–British relations among the better-educated who rely on newspapers. The other serious dailies follow. By contrast, the less-educated public rely less frequently on the serious press than they do on the numerous tabloids (recognised for page three photographs and in-depth sports reporting).

As Table 7.6 shows, a larger number of the less-educated as compared to the better-educated in France (48 to 19 per cent), Italy (53 to 29 per cent), and Spain (46 to 15 per cent) rely on television for international news. Correspondingly, as was the case in Britain, a larger proportion of the better-educated in each of these three countries said they rely on newspapers and magazines than did the less-educated.

Since a primary goal of US public diplomacy strategies targeted to wider public audiences is to counteract the basis for anti-American attitudes, an examination of media usage habits by respondents' attitudes toward the United States may be revealing. Among the

Table 7.7 Sources of information by attitudes toward the US, October 1987 (per cent)

	Britain		France		Italy	
	Pro-American	Anti-American	Pro-American	Anti-American	Pro-American	Anti-American
Television	70	70	43	35	56	42
Newspaper	36	38	14	19	29	34
Domestic Magazines	1	—[a]	7	7	4	10
Foreign Magazines	—	1	2	2	—	—
Domestic Radio	3	2	8	9	3	3
Foreign TV	—	—	—	—	—	—
Foreign Radio	—	—	—	1	—	—
Other	3	2	3	7	4	10

[a] (—) indicates less than one percent.
Source: September–October 1987 American Image Survey.

three countries where data on this issue are available, two somewhat different media habits are exhibited by those holding anti- and pro-American attitudes. As Table 7.7 indicates, this occurs in both France and Italy, where a slightly larger proportion of the pro-American publics rely more on television for news on relations between their country and the United States. Correspondingly, slightly more of those with anti-American attitudes primarily rely on newspapers. Media habits in Britain are almost identical between those who say they are anti- and pro-American. Both groups rely to the same extent on television (70 per cent) and newspapers (36 to 38 per cent).

FUTURE PUBLIC DIPLOMACY STRATEGIES

The US Government can selectively use the ever-expanding television market for public diplomacy efforts to reach wide West European audiences effectively. But it must balance its own programming objectives with the fact that substantial amounts of American programming are already available throughout Western Europe and will surely increase with rapidly expanding new satellite technology. The opportunities now making themselves available in Eastern Europe present new challenges for US public diplomacy efforts to present the story of American democracy.

8 Combating International Terrorism

Throughout much of the 1970s and 1980s, many West European governments struggled against indigenous terrorist groups. These groups tended to be small, close-knit organisations espousing some form of revolutionary ideology, with little public support.[1] Some of the major terrorist groups included the West German Red Army Faction, the French Action Directe, the Italian Red Brigades, and the Greek 17 November. Other West European countries such as Spain and Turkey experienced terrorism in the form of ethnic separatist movements. In Great Britain, the Irish Republican Army has used various methods – many of them violent – in its effort to drive the British out of Northern Ireland. In most cases, the governments were successful in mounting intensive anti-terrorist efforts which dramatically curtailed terrorist activities. A key ingredient in the fight against indigenous terrorist groups was 'more efficient police work and a greater public readiness to provide information to the police'.[2] For the most part, West European governments took full responsibility for combating the problem. The US role was generally limited to providing intelligence in so far as these groups targeted US military and NATO facilities.

The role of the United States and its relations with Western Europe capitals in combating terrorism changed, however, with the advent of terrorist attacks against American and West European civilians sponsored by outside nations, especially from Middle Eastern countries such as Iran, Libya and Syria. The 1980s recorded a large increase in the number of anti-US attacks in Western Europe, primarily from Middle Eastern groups. A particularly large increase in the number of anti-US bombings occurred between 1981 and 1982 when anti-US incidents rose from approximately 40 to almost 120. From 1983 through 1987, the number of bombing incidents against USA targets ranged between 25 and 60 per year.[3] Libya in particular was singled out as fomenting terrorist attacks against American and West European targets, mostly on West European soil. Although Libya was not the most frequently chosen supporter of terrorism, as early as 1981 a substantial number in Britain (25 per cent), France (25 per cent), and West Germany (34 per cent) said Libya actively promoted terrorism in other countries. As Table 8.1 indicates, the British and French most frequently picked the Soviet Union while the West Germans said the PLO.

Table 8.1 Countries and organizations which promote international terrorism, February 1981 (per cent)

	Britain	France	West Germany
USSR	46	33	43
Cuba	34	26	41
USA	18	19	12
Libya	25	25	34
PLO	34	27	52
Israel	14	12	11
None of these	1	1	14
Don't know	25	47	8
Total	197[a]	190	215

[a] Totals exceed 100 per cent due to multiple responses allowed.

Question: Which of the following would you say actively promotes and supports terrorist activities in other countries?
Source: February 1981 International Issues Survey.

Libyan strongman Colonel Qaddafi, who came to power in 1969, had long irritated Western leaders by directing military forays into neighbouring Chad, hosting Soviet troops, and using Libyan embassies as sources of terrorist activities. Britain was especially critical of Libya and, indeed, broke diplomatic relations in 1984 following the fatal shooting of a British policewoman by a Libyan diplomat from inside Libya's London embassy. The United States, which had been calling on its European Allies to join it in isolating Libya, hoped to no avail that Britain's breaking of diplomatic relations with Libya in 1984 would encourage other West European countries to take action as well. Allied patience with Qaddafi began to wear thin after it was believed that Libya sponsored the spectacular terrorist attacks on the Vienna and Rome airports on 3 December 1985 in which 18 people were killed and over 100 injured.

Debating the appropriate response to Libyan-sponsored terrorism created friction for the US–West European Alliance. The USA called for stringent diplomatic and economic sanctions against Libya. Most

West European governments, however, were hesitant to risk terrorist retaliation as well as their economic ties with Libya. This was especially the case in France, Italy and West Germany, which relied more heavily on imported Libyan oil. Several West European nations were also concerned for the safety of their own nationals working in Libya. Following the US pressures earlier in the 1980s for economic sanctions against the Soviet Union, West European capitals resented what they considered yet another US call for economic sanctions. West European governments have traditionally opposed such retaliations as ineffective and were not eager to co-operate with the US request.[4] Furthermore, West European publics generally did not favour economic sanctions to combat international terrorism (Table 8.2).

Occasional finger-pointing broke out among the West European capitals as to who failed to do their fair share to curtail international terrorism. The British urged the EC to take a stronger stand against Qaddafi. At other times, France was criticised for refusing to extradite known terrorists, as was Greece for lax airport security which allowed Middle East terrorists greater freedom of movement throughout Western Europe.

Table 8.2 Attitudes on actions against countries which harbor or support terrorists, April 1985 (per cent)

	Britain	France	Italy	West Germany
Do nothing	4	2	3	7
Use diplomatic pressure	62	41	62	56
Use economic sanctions	36	23	18	36
Retaliate by using military force against terrorists who have taken refuge in other countries	13	9	12	8
Try to prevent terrorist attacks by striking against suspected terrorists in other countries	13	45	35	11
Don't know	9	19	5	4
Total	137[a]	139	135	122

a Totals exceed 100 per cent due to multiple responses.

Question: What actions on this list (Show Card) should the [Survey Country] government take against other countries that harbor or support terrorists?

Source: March–April 1985 Terrorism Survey.

WEST EUROPEAN PUBLIC REACTION TO TERRORISM

Overwhelmingly, Western Europeans did not perceive terrorism as justified. However, in the Spring of 1985, as international terrorism continued to attract worldwide attention, a substantial number, reaching 65 per cent in France, were not hopeful that international terrorism could be fought successfully.[5] Furthermore, West European publics were not in favour of strong action against nations supporting terrorism. As Table 8.2 demonstrates, more of the British (62 per cent), West Germans (56 per cent), and Italians (62 per cent) supported using the less controversial 'diplomatic pressure' against terrorist-supporting nations than any military solutions. French attitudes were somewhat different: about the same number supported diplomatic pressure (41 per cent) as endorsed preventing terrorist attacks by pre-emptive military action against countries that harbour or support terrorists (45 per cent).[6]

When asked how their own country should respond to a terrorist attack, the public in each of these four countries was generally supportive of the following policies:

1. sharing intelligence and co-ordinating anti-terrorist policies with other countries;
2. increasing intelligence gathering expenditures (except among the French);
3. broadening police powers to search out terrorists; and
4. imposing the death penalty on terrorists.

In each country, the public generally disapproved of capitulating to terrorist demands or reducing penalties for terrorists who provide information on other terrorists.[7]

Although West Europeans did not consider terrorism as important as economic problems during the 1980s, terrorism was considered a salient issue and a serious threat. When asked in March–April 1985 majorities in Britain (64 per cent), France (59 per cent), Germany (59 per cent), and Italy (80 per cent) said they had heard or read at least a 'fair amount' about terrorism in Western Europe. While most people did not feel personally threatened by terrorism, large numbers believed terrorism was a threat to their country's political system. The perception of this threat appeared most acutely in Britain and Italy, where it was the majority view. In Britain, this concern most certainly reflected the decades old conflict between the government and the Irish

Republican Army (IRA) in Northern Ireland. A June 1986 survey found that terrorism was considered at least a moderate threat to the people living in their country by large majorities in Britain (81 per cent), France (86 per cent), Italy (95 per cent), Portugal (77 per cent), Spain (92 per cent), and West Germany (73 per cent). A sizeable number of people, ranging from 36 per cent in Britain to 79 per cent in Spain, said terrorism was a 'great threat'.[8] USIA annual Economic Summit surveys asked respondents to name the most important problem(s) facing their country. Survey results over the past 10 years indicate that economic problems are by far the most frequently mentioned, with terrorism seldom mentioned as the country's major problem. However, providing the respondent with a list of problems, in contrast to an open-ended question, can result in a wider level of registered concern over terrorism. For example, the USIA June–July 1984 Central American Issues Survey in Britain, Italy, the Netherlands and Spain, asked respondents to identify the two problems which worry them the most, from a predetermined list of six items. Asked in this manner, sizeable numbers – 41 per cent in Britain, 59 per cent in Italy, 29 per cent in the Netherlands, and 60 per cent in Spain – identified 'international terrorism' as an important problem.

WHAT TO DO ABOUT LIBYA?

In Spring 1985, Libya and Iran were the countries most frequently identified by Western Europeans as supporting terrorism in other nations (Table 8.3). Furthermore, following the December 1985 terrorist attacks at the Rome and Vienna airport, a *New York Times* poll on terrorism conducted in February 1986 found that majorities in Britain (65 per cent), France (64 per cent), and West Germany (58 per cent) identified Libya as being involved 'in the planning and financing of international terrorist activities such as airplane hijackings, bomb attacks and so on'. Iran was also frequently identified by the British (37 per cent), French (62 per cent), and West Germans (30 per cent) as supporting terrorism.[9]

In 1985, slightly more than one-third of the British (37 per cent) identified the United States as actively promoting and supporting terrorist activities in other countries. This sentiment was driven, in part, by the British perception that US groups provided financial assistance to the IRA. However, by June of 1986 the percentage of British who said the USA supported terrorism dropped to 19 per cent.

Table 8.3 Nations supporting terrorism in other countries, March–April 1985 (per cent)

	Britain	France	Italy	West Germany
USSR	32	41	34	38
USA	37	25	28	12
Cuba	35	26	21	34
Israel	21	24	22	15
Libya/Qaddafi	67	50	44	51
Iran	48	53	37	41
Syria	18	32	15	31
Saudi Arabia	9	17	15	20
Don't know	10	24	20	24
Total	277[a]	292	236	266

[a] Totals exceed 100 per cent due to multiple responses.

The Soviet Union was identified in 1985 by a third or more in Britain (32 per cent), France (41 per cent), Italy (34 per cent), and West Germany (38 per cent) as actively supporting terrorism.[10]

Libya's image among Western Europeans as a terrorist-supporting nation was reinforced as Libya's leader Colonel Qaddafi became more visible and provocative in the mid-1980s. As well, American relations with Libya continued to deteriorate. Since 1974, Colonel Qaddafi had claimed the Gulf of Sirte as Libyan territory, not international waters, and drew a 'line of death' which he dared the United States to cross. Few nations in the international community accepted Libya's claim that the Gulf of Sirte was not in international waters. The US Navy carried out exercises in the area during the early and mid-1980s, in part to ensure that the Gulf remained as international waters. During the summer of 1981 when the American Sixth Fleet was conducting such exercises in the Mediterranean, two Libyan Su–22 jets engaged two American F–14 Tomcats. During the ensuing dogfight, the Libyan fighter planes were shot down by the US fighters. A second encounter occurred in March 1986 when US naval ships exchanged fire with Libya after being fired upon in the Gulf of Sirte.

US–Libyan tensions further mounted when, on 5 April 1986, a West Berlin nightclub frequented by US servicemen was bombed. One US serviceman, Sgt Kenneth Ford, and a young Turkish woman were killed, and several hundred others were wounded. The United States blamed Libya and immediately set out to present a united Allied front against Qaddafi. President Reagan charged that

> [o]n March 25 . . . orders were sent from Tripoli to the Libyan's People Bureau in East Berlin to conduct a terrorist attack against Americans, to cause maximum and indiscriminate casualties. Libya's agents then planted the bomb.[11]

The Reagan Administration was in a difficult public diplomacy position. On the one hand, it wanted to publicly provide all the accumulated evidence of Libya's responsibility for the terrorist attack to garner West European public support to enact measures against Libya. But, on the other hand, the Administration did not want to reveal all of its sensitive intelligence-gathering methods and sources.

US actions and rhetoric following the Berlin bombing led the West European press to believe the USA was leaning toward military retaliation against Libya. President Reagan's characterisation of Qaddafi as the 'mad dog of the Middle East' provided journalists with sensational copy. Commenting on the US rhetoric, Britain's independent *Financial Times* wrote 'The [Reagan] Administration's finger-pointing at Colonel Qaddafi roused speculation that it might be preparing US and international opinion for tough US military retaliation against Libya . . .'.[12] Additionally, the West European press, especially in Great Britain, devoted front page coverage to developments implying an eventual US military strike. As early as 11 April 1986, France's *Antenne-2* television predicted an 'imminent US attack against Libya. It's only a question of hours or days'.[13] On the day before the attack, *The Times* of London ran a photograph of American F–111 fighter bombers arriving at British bases in Oxfordshire and Suffolk. The European press provided further evidence of US intentions with the news that the US carrier *Coral Sea* changed its course to join the USS *America* in the Mediterranean, placing it within striking distance of Tripoli.

Tensions between the USA and West European governments reached fever pitch immediately preceding the eventual US raid on Libya in mid-April. The United States was discouraged that the European Community would not enact retaliatory economic sanctions against Libya to help stem terrorist acts. EC leaders failed to adopt the economic sanctions requested by the USA at their early April 1986 meeting in The Hague. During this meeting, in an attempt to head off US military action, EC ministers could only muster support for a forced reduction in Libyan diplomatic and consular staff allowed in each country and an affirmation of the previously-endorsed EC ban on military sales to Libya. Some, including Britain's Foreign Secretary Sir Geoffrey Howe, believed that this lack of firm action on the part of the European Allies would allow the USA no other choice but to take unilateral military action against Libya.[14] Several major West European newspapers chided European governments for not acting more decisively toward Libya. For example, West Germany's conservative *Frankfurter Allgemeine* accused European governments of 'cringing before Qaddafi'.[15] Spain, Cyprus and Greece were reported to have denied the USA permission to use its bases to launch an attack against Libya. (It became known after the raid that France and Spain had denied an American request for fly-over privileges to reach Libya.)

West European Reaction to the US Bombing of Libya

In general, Western Europeans overwhelmingly disapproved of their own governments using military action to resolve foreign policy problems, including international terrorism. However, there appears to be some limited feeling among Western Europeans that action by others to combat international terrorism is preferable to their own country doing so. A telephone survey in Britain, France and West Germany immediately prior to the US air strike found virtually no public support (3 per cent of the public or less) for their own government taking retaliatory military action against countries that harbour or support terrorists. However, a larger number in Britain (36 per cent), France (51 per cent) and West Germany (20 per cent) said they would approve of military action by the United States or other major powers against clearly identified terrorist targets in terrorist-sponsoring countries if diplomatic and economic sanctions failed. As for economic sanctions, most people in Britain (62 per cent), France (66 per cent) and West Germany (53 per cent) believed the US application of such sanctions against Libya for the 1985 Rome and Vienna airport attacks was justified. But fewer British (44 per cent) and Germans (35 per cent) believed that their own country should have also imposed economic sanctions. A majority of French people (65 per cent) said their country should also have imposed sanctions.[16]

A week before the actual US air strike, only in France, of the three surveyed countries, did more of the public (45 to 36 per cent) say they would approve of US military action against Libya if there were reasonably good evidence that Libya was behind a new terrorist attack (Table 8.4). In this case, a 'new terrorist attack' referred to an attack subsequent to the Rome and Vienna airport bombings in December 1985. French support for action against Libya may, in part, be explained by their long military involvement against Libya in Chad. The West Germans (78 per cent) widely opposed such action and in Britain opponents outnumbered supporters (47 to 37 per cent).

On 15 April 1986, 18 American F–111 fighter bombers left their bases in Britain to strike terrorist-related targets in Tripoli, Libya. Denied Allied permission to pass through French or Spanish air space, the F–111s had to fly around the Iberian Peninsula and on through the Straits of Gibraltar to reach their targets in Tripoli, Libya; an indirect route that required numerous in-flight refuelings. Some hours after the American F–111s took off from England, the USA sent 15 American A6 and A7 aircraft from the carriers *America* and *Coral Sea* of the US Mediterranean Sixth Fleet to attack military barracks and an air base near Benghazi, east of Tripoli. In Tripoli, Colonel Qaddafi's headquarters was severely damaged as were several near-by West European embassies.[17] It was widely reported that Qaddafi himself narrowly escaped the bombing. Western journalists in Libya provided worldwide media with dramatic pictures and reports of the damage. Many of the West European tabloids prominently displayed photographs of fatally injured civilians.

The US air strike against Libya dominated West European media for more than a week, while commentators throughout Western Europe debated the political, social and economic implications of the action. The major West European newspapers monitored in 15 countries 'overwhelmingly condemned the US air strike against Libya as a deplorable act that w[ould] not stop terrorism' (Ederma, 1986a, p. 1). The West European press generally said the 'US attack could divide NATO and create opportunities for Soviet exploitation' (Ederma, 1986a, p. 1). At the same time, the papers widely assailed the European Community's failure to take more decisive action against Libya. The press was particularly critical of the US action because of the numerous civilian casualties. London's *Financial Times*, typical of the critical press commentary, wrote:

[t]he bombing was futile, deplorable and almost certainly counter-productive. It is unlikely to halt Libyan-sponsored terrorism and will leave in its wake significant political damage. European allies are left looking disunited, ineffective and foolish.

Only a small minority of the major newspapers, primarily the conservative press, applauded the US action as the only way to deal with internationally-sponsored terrorism (Ederma, 1986a). For example, Britain's weekly magazine *The Economist* editorialised that

> ... the time had arrived to use some kind of force against Col. Qaddafi. Unless this week's bombing causes him to stop sponsoring terrorists, the time will come when it will be right to use more force, and if necessary, to overthrow him.[18]

Most major West European news media were not convinced that the US attack on Libya would lead to a reduction of future terrorist attacks. Norway's independent *Dagbladet*, for example, commented immediately prior to the raid that '[a] punitive attack on Libya will not eliminate terrorism, instead perhaps increase it ...'. Likewise, West Germany's *TV-Two* held that the 'attack will certainly not help to fight international terrorism'.[19]

The major West European papers noted the tension within the Alliance created by the US air strike. An editorial in West Germany's conservative *Die Welt* maintained (before the raid) 'It is becoming increasingly clear and depressing that actions by terrorists give rise to disruption and disharmony in the Alliance'.[20] Furthermore, the diplomatic correspondent for Britain's conservative *Daily Telegraph* reported that 'Britain stood alone in Europe ... in condoning America's raid on Libya as NATO appeared to be heading for one of its severest crises'.[21] The editor of Germany's left-of-centre *Stern* blamed the US for discord within the Alliance, writing '... Mr Reagan, by his Libyan foolishness, has shaken the foundation of the Western Alliance ... Ronald Reagan, not Mikhail Gorbachev, is the man people have to be afraid of these days'.[22] Other media outlets blamed European failure to act against Libya for the US military action. In criticising the EC for not standing up to Qaddafi, France's right-of-centre *Quotidien* was particularly harsh, calling the EC '... a market for vegetables, a collapsed souffle, a flabby body totally void of ambition, virtue, loyalty to history, spirit and intelligence ...'.[23] Likewise, Spain's moderate-left *Diario 16* criticised the EC's lack of conviction in fighting terrorism and charged that EC ministers 'left the

United States out on a limb . . . Europe turned her back on the Libya–US conflict . . . . As nearly always, the EEC preferred to blindfold itself and wallow in impotence'.[24]

West European Government Reaction to the US Air Strike

While West European leaders may have privately applauded the US action, no major West European country except Britain publicly endorsed the US air strike.[25] *The Times* of London reported from the United Nations that '. . . America's European allies seemed more disturbed by the raid than a good portion of the Third World, where diplomats said Libya's isolation was glaringly apparent'.[26] President Reagan thanked the few co-operative Allies during a speech immediately after the US bombing:

> To our friends and allies in Europe who co-operated in today's mission, I would only say you have the primary gratitude of the American people. Europeans who remember history understand better than most that there is no security, no safety, in the appeasement of evil. It must be the core of Western policy that there be no sanctuary for terror, and to sustain such a policy, free men and free nations must unite and work together.[27]

The only West European government leader who actively supported the American action was Britain's Mrs Thatcher. She maintained that the USA had not only been right 'to bomb Libyan targets, but they had a duty to do so'.[28] Thatcher continued to support the US decision to retaliate against Libya despite heated criticism from the opposition Labour and Liberal Parties as well as the British public. A MORI poll conducted hours after the air strike found that a large majority (71 per cent) of the British believed that 'Mrs Thatcher was wrong to give President Reagan permission for American bombers to fly from British bases to participate in the attack on Libya'. This attitude was confirmed by a Gallup poll conducted in Britain at the same time which found that 69 per cent thought it was wrong for the British government to allow American use of its bases.[29]

West European Public Opinion and the US Strike

The US military action against Libya touched off numerous, but short-lived, anti-US demonstrations in the streets of Bonn, London and Rome. Among the countries in which survey data were available immediately after the bombing, majorities in Britain, the Netherlands, and West Germany, and half in Switzerland opposed the raid. The French were the most supportive of the strike despite the fact that the French government refused fly-over rights for the US aircraft. British, French and West German public approval levels of the US air strike did not vary significantly from their levels of support for military retaliation recorded before the strike (Tables 8.4 and 8.5). A separate telephone survey conducted in the Netherlands immediately after the raid found little Dutch support for the action. Only 22 per cent said the US action against Libya was a good thing, and many fewer (3 per cent) believed the attack would reduce the likelihood of future Libyan terrorism.[30] The opinion in Switzerland, which mirrored that of most other West European publics, was predominantly (53 per cent to 35 per cent) opposed to the US bombing.[31]

A telephone survey in Britain, France and West Germany asked those who disapproved of the US air strike to explain their opposition. Disapprovers in France and Germany most frequently gave as their reasons that innocent civilians were killed and that they were against the use of military force to combat terrorism. The British public that opposed the US action primarily did so because they said civilians were injured and that they supported other methods to combat terrorism, such as economic sanctions.[32]

Vast majorities in Britain (77 per cent) and West Germany (76 per cent) thought President Reagan acted too quickly to employ US forces

Table 8.4   Pre-raid support for US military action against Libya, April 1986 (per cent)

	Britain	France	West Germany
Approve	37	45	17
Disapprove	47	36	78
Don't know	16	19	5
Total	100	100	100

Question: If there is reasonably good evidence that Libya was behind a new terrorist attack, would you approve or disapprove of a U.S. military action against Libya? The term 'new attack' refers to an attack since the Rome and Vienna airport attack.

Source: April 1986 Pre-Libya Raid Telephone Survey.

Table 8.5 Support for US military action against Libya, April 1986 (per cent)

	Britain	France	West Germany
Strongly approve	14	27	7
Somewhat approve	16	24	19
Subtotal	30	51	26
Somewhat disapprove	17	23	39
Strongly disapprove	43	15	31
Subtotal	60	38	70
Don't know	10	11	5
Total	100	100	100

Question: Now, thinking about the recent US air strike against terrorist-related targets in Libya, do you strongly approve, somewhat approve, somewhat disapprove or strongly disapprove of the US air strike?

Source: April 1986 Post-Libya Raid Telephone Survey.

to solve foreign policy problems. The French were evenly divided on this question (47 to 47 per cent) (Table 8.6). Furthermore, the number believing that US policies risked war rather than promoted peace jumped substantially between March 1986 and June 1986 in Britain, France, Italy and West Germany (Table A.2 in Appendix 3).

Analysis of post-bombing surveys indicated that those who were convinced of Libya's responsibility were more likely to support the US military action.[33] However, not all West Europeans were convinced Libya was responsible for the terrorist attack. An April 1986 post-raid telephone survey showed only 52 per cent in Britain, 38 per cent in France, and 43 per cent in Germany believed Libya was responsible. In addition, immediately after the air strike, Western Europeans were quite divided as to the long term impact the US air strike would have on future Libyan-sponsored terrorist attacks.[34] The prevailing opinion among the British (39 per cent) was that the strike would increase Libyan-sponsored terrorism; among the French (34 per cent) that it would reduce the likelihood; and among the Germans (41 per cent) that US action would have no long-term impact. Asked in an April 1986 telephone survey (after the air strike), majorities in Britain and

Table 8.6 President Reagan too quick to employ US forces, April 1986 (per cent)

	Britain (508)	France (503)	West Germany (502)
Yes, wise use	18	47	21
No, too quick	77	47	76
Don't know	5	6	3
Total	100	100	100

Question: Do you think US President Reagan makes wise use of military forces to solve foreign policy problems or do you think he is too quick to employ US forces?

Source: Newsweek, 28 April 1986, p. 22. Telephone poll conducted by Gallup, 17–18 April 1986.

France and half in Germany said they would approve expelling all Libyan officials from their country if a new Libyan-sponsored terrorist attack were to have occurred. Only in France did a majority (56 per cent) say they would approve of another US military strike against Libya if there were reasonably good evidence that Libya was behind a new terrorist attack. Support for a new US strike was limited to a only a minority of 34 per cent in Britain and 19 per cent in Germany. Even fewer in all three countries ranging from 3 per cent in Germany to 34 per cent in France would approve of their own government using military force against Libya. The survey also showed that the number of British, French, and Germans who believed terrorism could be fought successfully increased since early April before the air raid. However, large majorities in Britain (83 per cent), France (88 per cent), and West Germany (65 per cent) (perhaps fearing retaliation) said that Libyan-sponsored terrorism remained a threat to their fellow countrymen.[35]

Several months after the US air strike, a June 1986 survey again asked West European publics if they would approve another US air strike if reasonably good evidence suggested Libya was behind a new terrorist attack. Slightly more than four in ten in each of Britain, France, Italy and Portugal indicated their approval of such US military action. Fewer in Germany (32 per cent) and Spain (18 per cent) said they would approve of additional US military action against Libya. This survey also found that those who opposed military action most frequently said it was because innocent civilians would be injured or killed. Although the West European public generally opposed the US military action against Libya, majorities in Britain, France, Germany, Italy and Portugal, and half in Spain thought that their country should not change its relationship with the United States as a result of the US action against Libya. The only sizeable public support for their country distancing itself from the United States because of the US action was found in Britain (24 per cent) and Italy (20 per cent).[36]

The June 1986 survey found that a greater number in each of Britain (64 to 25 per cent), France (58 to 16 per cent), and West Germany (41 to 31 per cent) held the opinion that their government *should* impose economic sanctions against Libya. By contrast, the prevailing opinion in Italy (45 per cent), Portugal (56 per cent) and Spain (40 per cent) was that their country *should not* impose economic sanctions against Libya.[37] Despite the lack of consensus across West Europe on the appropriate response to international terrorism, a substantial number surveyed in Britain (58 per cent), Germany (54 per cent), Italy (77 per cent), Portugal (58 per cent) and Spain (58 per cent) said their government should be doing more to protect its citizens against international terrorism.[38]

A US Government report issued in 1988 presented evidence showing that in the months following the US air strike, Libyan leader Qaddafi greatly reduced his visibility, and 'detectable Libyan involvement in terrorist activity dropped significantly through 1987'.[39] However, the West European public gave little credit to the US military action for the subsequent reduction in Libyan-sponsored terrorism. When asked in June 1986 whether the US air strike against Libya had reduced, increased, or had no impact on Libyan-sponsored attacks, only about one-third in Britain and Italy, one-quarter in Portugal, Spain and West Germany, and less than one-fifth in France said it had reduced such attacks. A plurality in each of the six countries except Italy said Libyan-sponsored terrorist activity would likely stay about the same. As many Italians (33 per cent) said the air strike would decrease Libyan attacks as said it would have no impact.[40]

West European press reaction to the decline in Libyan-sponsored terrorist activities closely resembled that of the public. West European media commentary from late April to July 1986 gave little credit to the US air strike for the relative decline in Libyan-sponsored terrorism during this period (Ederma, 1986b). Only a handful of major West European newspapers noted the decline in Libyan-sponsored terrorism. One of these papers, Italy's leftist *La Repubblica*, said: 'How can we deny the existence of a link between the US attack and the subsequent calm in the Mediterranean' (Ederma, 1986b, p. 2).

Support for military action by European governments against terrorist-supporting countries remained low a year after the US bombing. Table 8.7 indicates that only one in four or less supported taking military actions against terrorist targets in these countries. Large majorities in all four of the major West European countries said they would approve of their country stopping all arms exports to terrorist-supporting governments. This action received the most public support compared to the other potential actions against terrorist-supporting countries.[41]

Table 8.7 Actions against terrorist supporting countries, April 1987 (per cent)

	Britain	France	Italy	West Germany
Stop all arms exports	74	64	77	66
Stop airline flights	37	12	11	22
Stop all trade	50	23	27	33
Eliminate investments	47	24	31	37
Expel their diplomats	49	30	26	26
Break diplomatic relations	46	18	28	27
Take military action	26	27	11	10
None of these	3	1	3	7
All of these	—[a]	8	5	—
Don't know	—	7	—	10
Total	332[b]	213	219	238

[a] (—) indicated less than 1 per cent.
[b] Totals exceed 100 per cent due to multiple responses.

Question: Here are a number of specific actions our government could take against countries that sponsor terrorism. Of which of these actions would you approve?
Source: April 1987 Venice Economic Summit Survey.

THE IRAN–CONTRA ISSUE

In the wake of the US air strike, Libyan-sponsored terrorism in Western Europe greatly diminished. However, this was not the only terrorism in the Middle East which continued to embroil the US–West European Alliance. Americans and West Europeans were targets for terrorist hijackings, killings and kidnappings in the Middle East, especially in war-torn Lebanon. Fundamentalist Islamic groups, believed to have been supported by Iran and Syria, carried out a number of spectacular terrorist activities against American and West European targets in Lebanon. In 1984 the US Embassy annex in Beirut was bombed and, in a separate incident, CIA Beirut station chief William Buckley was kidnapped. In 1985 an American airliner, TWA Flight 847, was hijacked during which time an American Navy diver was killed. Also in 1985 terrorists from the Palestine Liberation Front hijacked the Italian cruise ship *Achille Lauro* in the Mediterranean and killed one American tourist on board. The ensuing events strained US–Italian relations. The cruise ship hijackers and their leader Abu al Abbas were apprehended at a NATO air base in Italy after US military aircraft intercepted an Egyptian provided aircraft flying them to a safe haven. Although the Italian authorities took the hijackers into custody, they quickly released Abu al Abbas.[42] The release met with strong US disapproval.

As Western journalists, businessmen, academics and American and European members of the UN Peace Keeping Forces were kidnapped and killed, the Western Allies devoted a great deal of effort in discussing appropriate responses to this brand of terrorism. In fact, terrorism was a major topic at the 1986 Annual Economic Summit, held that summer in Tokyo, in part to help relieve Allied differences over the US action against Libya. Despite efforts to increase US and West European co-ordination and co-operation in combating international terrorism, each government primarily tried independently to retrieve its own citizens held hostage with little apparent Allied co-ordination. One of the most divisive terrorist-related issues for the Alliance was whether governments should negotiate with terrorists or their sponsors for the release of hostages. France and West Germany used thinly-disguised negotiating strategies with Iran and other groups to help free some of their citizens held hostage in Lebanon.[43] The West European publics were predominantly opposed to their own governments negotiating for the release of hostages so that future terrorist actions would be discouraged. A survey in April 1987 indicated that the prevailing view in Britain (58 per cent), France (49 per cent) and Italy (56 per cent) opposed negotiations. By contrast, a majority in West Germany agreed with the view that 'when hostages are taken by terrorists the German government should negotiate with terrorists to gain the release of hostages, even if this may encourage future terrorist attacks' (Table 8.8).

Table 8.8 Should governments negotiate for release of hostages, April 1987 (per cent)

	Britain	France	Italy	West Germany
Should Negotiate	33	34	34	58
Should Not Negotiate	58	49	56	28
Don't know	9	17	10	14
Total	100	100	100	100

Question: When hostages are taken by terrorists, some people say the (Survey Country) government should negotiate with terrorists to gain the release of hostages, even if this may encourage future terrorist attacks. Others say the [Survey Country] government should not negotiate over hostages, in order to discourage future terrorist attacks. Which view is closer to your own?

Source: April 1987 Venice Economic Summit Survey.

During this period, the Reagan Administration 'insisted that it would never deal with terrorists under any circumstances' for the release of American hostages and, on occasion, criticised Allied Governments for doing just that.[44] This policy would later cause the Reagan Administration great discomfort. In late 1986 it was revealed that the USA had not only been negotiating with Iranian officials, but had secretly shipped arms through Israel to Iran (as early as August 1985) in an effort to secure the release of American hostages held in Lebanon. Of particular concern to the USA, especially the American intelligence community, was the retrieval of the CIA's Beirut station chief William Buckley who was kidnapped in 1984 and reportedly killed in captivity.[45] The story became increasingly bizarre as evidence linked American profits from the Iranian arms sales to aid for the US-supported Nicaraguan Contras. The cast of Reagan Administration officials involved and the numerous international connections, including Israel and the Nicaraguan contras, made for dramatic worldwide media coverage. USIA telephone surveys in January and July 1987 indicated that at least three in four in Britain, France and Germany were familiar with the Iran–Contra issue.

The West European press, which was highly critical of the US arms shipments to Iran, gave extensive coverage to the unravelling of the Iran–Contra affair. Even the usually supportive conservative press began to question President Reagan's leadership ability. One observer noted that what saddened the Europeans, especially the President's warmest admirers, was the evidence that the White House, whether with Reagan's knowledge and blessing or not, had done an ignoble deal with terrorists or their sponsors. That was hard to forgive, though it is sensibly placed against the perspective of his general prudence and success. (Johnson, 1989:36)

At the time, the West European press commentary across the political spectrum said President Reagan had suffered a loss of credibility and generally feared that the Iran–Contra issue, which placed the President under extreme domestic political pressure, could weaken US foreign policy and jeopardise chances for a US–Soviet arms control agreement. For example, West Germany's *Frankfurter Allgemeine* commented: 'It is feared that a President who must save his skin in domestic politics could be paralyzed in foreign policy. [There is] concern about the ability of the leading Western power to take effective action in the coming two years' (Ederma, 1986c; 1987).

A December 1986 survey in Britain and Germany found that large majorities exceeding 70 per cent disapproved of President Reagan's dealings with Iran.[46] Furthermore, the effect of the ongoing Iran–Contra issue on US credibility among the West European public was severe. By April 1987, among those at least somewhat familiar with the Iran–Contra issue, majorities in Britain (72 per cent), France (60 per cent), and West Germany (82 per cent) said US credibility had been damaged by the affair (Table 8.9). Similarly, in each of the three countries surveyed, majorities among those familiar with the issue, ranging from 58 per cent in France to 72 per cent in both Britain and Germany, thought 'President Reagan's capacity to lead the Western alliance ha[d] been damaged' by the Iran–Contra episode.[47] US credibility may have been damaged to an even greater extent in the eyes of Allied governments. Various West European capitals expressed their displeasure that the USA provided arms to Iran at the same time the USA was dissuading them from selling their own weapons to Iran.[48]

The USA–West European debate over international terrorism was not resolved by the end of the Reagan Administration as Allied governments continued to deal independently with the issue. The lack of West European public support for aggressive measures against terrorist supporting countries and the damaged credibility of American leadership in the wake of the Iran–Contra issue left the Allies without a co-ordinated policy against international terrorism.

Table 8.9 Iran–Contra issue damages US credibility among informed Western Europeans, April 1987 (per cent)

	Britain (897)[a]	France (372)	West Germany (383)
US credibility damaged	72	60	82
US credibility not damaged	21	22	16
Don't know	7	18	2
Total	100	100	100

[a] The question was asked only of those who said they had 'heard or read at least something' about the issue. Total sample, Britain (1016), France (504), West Germany (493).

Question: Some people say that US credibility has been damaged as a result of the controversy surrounding US–Iranian arms shipments. Others say US credibility has not been damaged. Which view is closer to your own?

Source: July 1987 INF Telephone Survey.

9 US–West European Economic Relations

Economic issues play an increasingly important role in international affairs, especially among the industrialised countries.[1] Within Europe, the 12 member European Community plays a key role: the EC countries have a Common Agricultural Policy; are represented by the EC as one in GATT negotiations; and have a joint mechanism, in which most EC members participate, for stabilising changes in the relative values of their currencies.[2] In addition, the EC's project to make substantial progress toward a common internal market in goods, services, people, and capital by the end of 1992 is bringing about significant changes in many sectors in West European economies. Apart from the many bilateral discussions between the USA and individual EC members, the USA and the EC Commission hold twice-yearly consultations at the cabinet level, and the US President meets every six months with the leader of the country which has assumed the presidency of the EC.

As a result of global economic interdependence, efforts at co-ordinating economic policies have multiplied. Apart from summits, the more formal discussions in international organizations such as the IMF, OECD, or the World Bank, major international negotiations such as GATT, and the more routine discussions such as the periodic US–EC cabinet-level meetings, numerous behind-the-scene consultations of foreign ministers, treasury ministers, central bankers, and many other government officials take place on a regular basis. Recognising the need for top-level involvement the leaders of the seven major industrialised countries (Canada, France, Japan, Italy, the United Kingdom, the United States and West Germany) together with a representative of the European Community hold an Economic Summit each year. The 1991 Summit in London, which focused primarily on economic aid to the Soviet Union and ended with a meeting with Gorbachev, was the seventeenth since the first in 1975.[3] President Reagan attended eight Economic Summits as President. However, despite extensive preparations by officials beginning months before each Economic Summit, few have resulted in important substantive agreements or common policies. Some, in fact, have been marked by conflict among the leaders.

In the early Reagan years, contentious debate occurred at the Summits, and in US–West European relations more generally, over a number of issues. These included the growing US budget deficit, the high real US interest rates, international monetary policy and the overvalued US dollar which reached its postwar high against the German mark and the Japanese yen in February 1985, trade with the Soviet Union, and the different economic approaches between the USA and most European countries (with Mrs Thatcher a major exception on this). During the first Reagan Administration, West European concern over US fiscal and monetary policy and over US efforts to pressure them to go along with US economic sanctions against the Soviets was met by a US leadership 'openly suspicious of co-ordination as a ploy to water down Reaganomics' (Henning, 1987, p. 49). In fact, 'international policy co-operation reached its nadir during the 1981–85 period' (Bergsten, 1988, p.73). As the dollar's value remained very high and the sizeable US trade deficit continued to grow, greater emphasis was put on international economic co-operation during the second Reagan Administration, and some limited success was achieved, particularly in the area of monetary policy. Most important were the Plaza Agreement in September 1985 among the G-5 (Britain, France, Japan, the USA, and West Germany) on pushing down the value of the dollar and the February 1987 Louvre Accord among the G-7 (the G-5 plus Canada and Italy) which attempted to stabilise exchange rates, though in neither case did the agreement go much beyond monetary issues. Therefore, while US–European economic relations have been somewhat better since Fall 1985, conflict over economic issues is far from absent. The degree of broader policy co-ordination beyond handling crises, such as those in the value of the dollar, remains relatively modest.

In the second half of the 1980s, the European Community's 1992 project for developing a freer internal market among the EC's 12 members – the most ambitious effort yet to integrate European economies – further heightened concerns about trade relations and protectionism among the USA, Western Europe and Japan, though US concerns about post-1992 Europe had generally lessened by the early 1990s. In addition, following the beginning of the Uruguay Round of GATT negotiations in 1986 and the July 1987 US proposal for reform of the world's agricultural trade, including the elimination of all subsidies, the US and the EC have periodically had strong disagreements over the issue of free trade in agriculture. Furthermore, in the late 1980s/early 1990s, the vast changes in Eastern Europe and the Soviet Union have greatly altered the nature of the security problem for NATO and even more room for disagreement among the NATO Allies over non-security issues.

International economic issues, because they can directly impact on jobs or other aspects of the domestic economy, frequently have a significant influence on domestic politics, and vice versa. Therefore, international economic issues are more affected by concerns over domestic public opinion than are most other foreign policy questions. Economic issues in most cases play a much greater role in election outcomes than do security issues. As Chapter 3 showed, even during the height of the controversy in Europe over INF deployment, it was not as salient an issue to European publics as were economic problems. Despite the greater importance of international economic issues to domestic politics, much more has been written about European public opinion on security issues than on economic ones. This chapter will examine European attitudes, primarily from the four largest countries, over the past decade on a number of major economic questions, including trade and protectionism, agricultural subsidies and trade, East–West economic relations, and the impact of US economic policies on their economies.[4]

THE HEALTH AND PROBLEMS OF EUROPEAN ECONOMIES

The public in the four largest West European countries were generally pessimistic about their country's economic health in the early to mid-1980s, as Table 9.1 shows. In the second half of the 1980s, the British and Germans have predominantly seen their country's economic health as good. In France, however, optimism remained the minority view throughout the decade. In Italy the large majority were pessimistic in the 1978–85 period; since then the proportion considering Italy's economic health as good increased considerably in 1987 and then dropped in 1988 and 1989.

For a variety of questions, some open-ended and some using lists, about the top economic problems facing their country or about the problems on which they most hoped to see progress made at the next Economic Summit the following results were recorded.

Table 9.1 Perceived economic health of their country, 1977–89 (per cent seeing economic health as very or fairly good)

	1977	1978	1981	1982	1983	1984	1985	1987	1988	1989
Britain	18	41	23	28	36	42	25	53	64	52
France	20	23	40	25	14	15	21	28	29	43
Italy	N/A	13	10	18	10	21	26	62	50	38
W. Germany	47	57	44	27	25	38	41	65	51	83

Question: How would you describe (Survey Country's) economic health at the present time? Would you say it is very good, fairly good, fairly poor, or very poor? Very few said they did not know.

Sources: 1977–89 Economic Summit Surveys.

- *Unemployment*, or the related item of stimulating economic growth, consistently ranked as one of the two top concerns throughout the 1980s in all four major West European countries.
- In Britain, France and Italy, *inflation* ranked as one of the top priorities in the first half of the 1980s and again in the late 1980s; in West Germany inflation was high ranked in 1982, but less so in subsequent surveys.
- *Controlling the value of the dollar and other currencies* was the third or fourth ranking problem in Britain, Italy and West Germany and second ranking in France in March 1984. However, by February 1985, in a survey done about at the time the dollar reached its all-time peak value against most European currencies, this was one of two top-ranked problems for Summit action among all four publics. Then, following the September 1985 Plaza Agreement and the subsequent sizeable drop in the dollar's value, this problem fell to the third or fourth ranked in 1986 and even lower in the late 1980s. In March 1984, this problem was picked by 51 per cent in France, but fewer in Britain (23 per cent), Italy (33 per cent) and West Germany (25 per cent). In February 1985, 41 per cent in West Germany and between 50 and 61 per cent in the other three major countries chose it from a list of five, while by March 1986 the number picking it was at or below the 1984 level once again.
- Throughout the 1980s, the four publics consistently rated both *protectionism* (whether phrased as 'reducing trade protectionism', 'reducing trade barriers', or 'efforts to have freer trade between countries' or as the problems of 'barriers against our exports' or 'influx of foreign imports') and *trade with the Soviet Union* as among the lowest in priority for action by their own government or by the leaders at the Economic Summit.

THE IMPORTANCE AND IMPACT OF THE UNITED STATES ON EUROPEAN ECONOMIES

Throughout the 1980s West European publics have widely recognised the importance of the US economy to their own economy. In 1983 between 67 and 76 per cent in the four major West European countries said their country's economic health was at least fairly dependent on that of the US economy. In 1987 large majorities of 63 to 79 per cent in these four countries believed that the value of the US dollar has at least a fair amount of influence on their country's economic health. In both 1988 and 1989 similar majorities ranging between 60 and 69 per cent in these four countries thought that the economic health of their country depended at least a fair amount on that of the United States; 25 to 30 per cent in each of these countries said that it depended little or not at all on the health of the US economy. In 1989 between 70 and 87 per cent in these four countries called trade with the USA at least fairly important to their country's prosperity.

West European publics predominantly believe that the interests of the USA and their own country are more similar than dissimilar. In May 1989, large majorities in Britain (72–20 per cent) and West Germany (63–27 per cent), a smaller majority in Italy (56–36 per cent) and a large plurality in France (51–33 per cent) said that the interests of the two are similar rather than dissimilar. Few saw the interests of the USA and their country as either *very* similar (between 6 and 16 per cent) or *very* dissimilar (between 3 and 11 per cent).

Given the acknowledged interdependence with the US economy, majorities (ranging from 56 per cent in West Germany to 66 per cent in Italy) said in April 1988 that it is at least fairly important for their country's economic health 'to closely co-ordinate our policies with the United States'. However, willingness to co-ordinate economic policies drops considerably (from 15 to 24 per cent in these four countries) when the factor of self-interest enters into the equation. In April 1987, as Table 9.2 shows, opinion was divided or close to divided in all four major West European countries over whether 'we should co-ordinate our economic policies with the US since this best serves our interests' or 'we should not co-ordinate our economic polices with the USA, since the USA already has too much influence on our economic policies'. Few thought that the US impact was so little that it didn't matter one way or the other.

Similarly, support for co-ordinating with the USA on trade with the USSR when this may mean that their country reduces trade with the Soviets is substantially less than general support for policy co-ordination not linked to their country's self-interest. In fact, as this chapter later discusses in detail, support for co-ordination with the USA on Soviet trade has throughout the 1980s (except for a 1982 survey in Britain) never been the majority view in any of the four major West European countries.

How do Europeans evaluate the way the USA deals with their country and with Western Europe in general on economic matters? First, only a limited minority in the four major West European

Table 9.2 Co-ordination of economic policies with the USA, 1987 (per cent)

	Britain	France	Italy	West Germany
Should co-ordinate	37	35	42	41
Should not co-ordinate	43	33	40	34
Does not matter since the USA has little impact on our economy	13	13	8	9
Don't know	7	19	11	16
Total	100	100	101	100

Question: Here is a card which gives different opinions on economic relations between (Survey Country) and the United States. Please tell me which of the statements comes closest to your opinion. (1) We should co-ordinate our economic policies with the USA since this serves our best interests; (2) We should not co-ordinate our economic policies with the USA, since the USA already has too much influence on our economic policies; (3) It does not matter whether we co-ordinate with the USA or not, since the USA has little impact on our economy.

Source: April 1987 Venice Economic Summit Survey.

countries think that the United States takes the views of Western Europe into account at least a fair amount 'when the USA makes decisions which affect the economic well-being of Western Europe'. Furthermore, as Table 9.3 shows, the number believing this was lower in all four countries in the mid-1980s, after Reagan had been President for four years, than in 1979. In 1985 majorities ranging from 60 per cent in West Germany to 75 per cent in Britain said that the USA takes West Europe's views into account only a little or not at all.

When given three options in 1984 to characterise what 'the USA seeks to do in its economic dealings with Western Europe', more, except in West Germany, chose one of the two negative characterisations – that the USA obtains unfair economic advantages even at the expense of Western Europe or that the USA dominates Western Europe economically – rather than the positive characterisation that the USA co-operates with Western Europe for mutual economic advantage. As Table 9.4 shows, opinion was divided in West Germany over US goals, but half in Britain and majorities in Italy and France chose one of the two negative descriptions. Compared to

Table 9.3 How much the USA takes into account the views of Western Europe on economic decisions important to Europe, 1979–85 (per cent)

	Britain			France			Italy			West Germany		
	1979	1984	1985	1979	1984	1985	1979	1984	1985	1979	1984	1985
Great deal/fair amount A little/	33	25	17	25	14	8	34	34	25	40	23	22
Not at all	46	68	75	50	74	69	44	57	65	43	64	60
Don't know	21	8	8	25	12	22	22	9	10	17	13	18
Total	100	101	100	100	100	99	100	100	100	100	100	100

Question: When the United States makes decisions which affect the well-being of Western Europe, how much do you think that it takes into account the European Community's views – a great deal, a fair amount, a little, or not at all?

Sources: April 1979 Eurobarometer and 1984 and 1985 Economic Summit Surveys.

1979, the number picking one of the two negative statements increased from 28 to 49 per cent in Britain, from 56 to 74 per cent in France, 37 to 56 per cent in Italy, and from 34 to 43 per cent in West Germany.

Indicative of the mistrust many Western Europeans have for US economic goals, in October 1987, when asked whether the phrase 'tries to dominate other countries economically' applied more to the USA, more to the USSR, or equally to both, between 71 and 83 per cent in the four largest West European countries said that it applied more to the USA or to both equally. Those saying that it applied more to the USA numbered 27 per cent in West Germany, 43 per cent in Britain and France, and 48 per cent in Italy. Compared to a 1982 survey, the overall total saying that it applied more to the USA or equally to both stayed the same in France and Italy and increased somewhat in Britain and West Germany; the number saying that it applied more to the USA was little changed between 1982 and 1987.[5]

The British, French, and Germans, in surveys in 1983, 1985, 1986 and 1987, generally had little or no confidence in the ability of the USA to 'provide wise leadership in resolving world economic problems'. In Italy, the public varied between a bare majority having at least a fair amount of confidence and divided opinion. The number having a great deal or fair amount of confidence in the USA ranged from 32 to 39 per cent in Britain, from 29 to 40 per cent in France, from 46 to 55 per cent in Italy, and from 29 to 36 per cent in West Germany. Confidence in US economic leadership was somewhat lower than overall confidence in the US ability to deal responsibly with world affairs, which was discussed in Chapter 4.

West European publics differed in their views on whether the USA was co-operative 'in trying to resolve economic problems with Western Europe and other countries'. In surveys between 1983 and 1988, as Table 9.5 shows, the French consistently viewed the USA as unco-operative, the Germans at times predominantly saw the USA as co-operative and at other times were divided. The Italians ranged from a large plurality seeing the USA as co-operative to a large plurality calling the USA unco-operative, and the British, except in early 1985, predominantly saw the USA as co-operative, though by a smaller margin in 1987 and 1988 than in 1983 and late 1985. With few exceptions, only one in ten or less either called the USA very co-operative or very unco-operative.

When asked about US co-operativeness on particular policy areas in 1983 and 1984, the United States was most consistently seen as unco-operative on *trading with the USSR*, undoubtedly a result of US

Table 9.4 US goals in its economic dealings with Western Europe, 1979–84 (per cent)

	Britain		France		Italy		West Germany	
	1979	1984	1979	1984	1979	1984	1979	1984
Co-operate for mutual advantage	47	35	21	19	43	34	47	42
Obtain unfair advantages at Western Europe's expense	12	25	12	29	11	23	21	30
Dominate West Europe economically	16	24	44	45	26	33	13	13
Don't Know	25	17	24	7	20	10	19	15
Total	100	101	101	100	100	100	100	100

Question: Here are some things people have said the USA seeks to do in it economic dealings with Western Europe. (SHOW CARD.) Which view comes closest to your own? (1) Co-operate with Western Europe for mutual economic advantage; (2) Obtain unfair economic advantages for itself even at the expense of Western Europe; (3) Dominate Western Europe economically.

Sources: April 1979 Eurobarometer and March 1984 London Economic Summit Survey.

Table 9.5 US co-operativeness in resolving economic problems with Western Europe, 1983–88 (per cent)

	Britain						France					
	Apr. 1983	Feb. 1985	Oct. 1985	Mar. 1986	Apr. 1987	Apr. 1988	Apr. 1983	Feb. 1985	Oct. 1985	Mar. 1986	Apr. 1987	Apr. 1988
US Co-operative	57	41	59	53	49	45	18	22	24	31	29	25
US Unco-operative	29	54	32	40	41	39	59	59	57	43	52	56
Don't Know	13	4	10	7	10	16	23	19	19	26	18	20
Total	99	99	101	100	100	100	100	100	100	100	99	101

	Italy						West Germany					
	Apr. 1983	Feb. 1985	Oct. 1985	Mar. 1986	Apr. 1987	Apr. 1988	Apr. 1983	Feb. 1985	Oct. 1985	Mar. 1986	Apr. 1987	Apr. 1988
US Co-operative	36	46	50	42	45	45	39	38	41	35	31	39
US Unco-operative	50	51	34	44	43	42	47	49	46	49	53	40
Don't Know	15	3	16	14	13	13	14	13	14	16	16	21
Total	101	100	100	100	101	100	100	100	101	100	100	100

Question: In trying to resolve economic problems with Western Europe and other countries, is it your impression that the USA has been very co-operative, rather co-operative, rather unco-operative, or very unco-operative?

Sources: October–November 1985 Eurobarometer and 1983, 1985, 1986, 1987, and 1988 Economic Summit Surveys.

pressure in the early 1980s for economic sanctions against the Soviets and more generally for limits on East–West trade. Majorities in France, Italy and West Germany in both years and a large plurality in 1983 and a majority the next year in Britain saw the USA as uncooperative in this policy area. However, by 1984, the USA was also not seen as co-operative in any one of the other three policy areas by any of the four publics. On *dealing with high interest rates*, two publics – the French, whose President Mitterrand was the most outspoken critic of US interest rates, and Italians – rated the USA very negatively in 1983, and the other two – the British and Germans – were both divided. By March 1984, however, many more in all four countries considered the USA as unco-operative. No more than 29 per cent in any of these countries saw the USA as co-operative on interest rates. On *international monetary questions*, the French, by very large margins, and the Italians predominantly saw the USA as unco-operative in both 1983 and 1984. As the dollar continued its overall upward movement, both the British – who moved from a generally favourable view in 1983 to divided opinion in 1984 – and the Germans – who went from a narrow plurality in 1983 calling the USA co-operative to a larger unfavourable plurality in 1984 – had a more negative evaluation by 1984. On *farm trade* the USA, except in Britain in 1983, was predominantly seen as unco-operative. Indicative of the greater specificity of these questions and, therefore higher degree of information required to answer them, sizeable numbers of about one in five in West Germany and three in ten or more in the other three major countries could not answer on each of these four questions.

Throughout the 1978–89 period, Western Europeans were asked about the impact of US economic policies and actions on their country's economy. In most European countries, the most negative results – that is, the largest number calling US policies harmful rather than helpful or of little effect – were in the period between early 1984 and mid-1985 when the news media constantly discussed the overvalued dollar and the inability of the major industrialized countries, with US resistance a primary reason, to agree on bringing its value down (Henning, 1987, pp. 24–32). As Table 9.6 shows, in Britain and West Germany the proportion seeing US policies as harmful was *markedly higher* in this period than earlier or later in the decade. (See Table A.7 in Appendix 3 for full results.)

The British were generally negative on US policies throughout the decade, though the margin of harmful over helpful was much more narrow in the late 1980s than earlier. In France, a plurality considered

Table 9.6 Effects of US policies on their economy, 1982–89 (per cent seeing US economic policies as harmful)

	Apr. 1982	Mar. 1984	May 1984	Oct. 1984	Feb. 1985	Jun. 1985	Oct. 1985	Mar. 1986	Apr. 1987	Apr. 1988	Oct. 1988	May 1989
Britain	32	39	37	57	58	46	38	36	31	33	32	26
France	48	49	N/A	N/A	41	40	37	24	30	38	37	40
Italy	34	35	28	41	34	38	22	38	25	20	19	24
West Germany	29	39	56	41	46	35	26	37	29	25	19	32

Question: Do you think that the economic policies and actions of the United States have been more helpful or more harmful to the economic situation in our country, or have they had little effect on our country?

Sources: Economic Summit Surveys in 1978, 1982, and 1984–89, Eurobarometer surveys in October–November 1984, October–November 1985, and October 1988, May–June 1984 Security Survey, and June–July 1985 Baseline Survey.

US policies as harmful in most surveys. The Germans were consistently negative on US policies through mid-1985, but opinion has fluctuated up and down since then. The Italians, after negative or divided views in most surveys between 1983 and 1986, had a plurality calling US policies helpful in the late 1980s. In all four major countries, as Table 9.7 shows, the margin of those seeing US policies as harmful over those seeing US polices as helpful was considerably greater in the period between early 1982 and mid-1985 than in the period between Fall 1985 and mid-1989 (in Italy, more actually saw US policies as helpful than harmful in the late 1980s). The more negative findings for the first half of the 1980s reflect that this was the low point in economic co-operation among the major industrialised nations.

Results for five other EC countries (Belgium, Greece, Ireland, the Netherlands and Spain) where this question was asked in Fall 1984, Fall 1985 and Fall 1988 parallel those for the four major countries. Again using the net, on average 24 per cent more saw US policies as harmful than helpful in Fall 1984, while by October 1985, shortly after the Plaza Agreement on bringing down the value of the dollar, perceptions of US policies were considerably less negative, with close to equal numbers seeing US policies as helpful or harmful. Results in October 1988 were about the same as those in October 1985. For these five countries, the average number saying US policies were harmful declined from 41 per cent in Fall 1984 to 30 per cent in Fall 1985 to 25 per cent in Fall 1988. (Full results for these five countries are also given in Table A.7 in Appendix 3.)

Similar questions were asked in the four major countries about the effects of the policies of Japan and the European Community. With exceptions in only a few countries in a few surveys, Japanese policies were consistently viewed more negatively than American policies throughout the 1980s. The number seeing Japanese policies as harmful in the 1982–89 period ranged from 43 to 67 per cent in Britain, 34 to 59 per cent in France, 32 to 42 per cent in Italy and 37 to 54 per cent in West Germany. No more than 21 per cent in any of these countries ever saw Japanese policies as helpful, and in most cases this proportion was around one in ten. As Table 9.7 shows, the average net was, except in France, more negative for Japanese than American policies even in the first half of the 1980s. In the period from Fall 1985 to Spring 1989 the gap was much larger in all four countries as the evaluations of US policies on average improved in all four countries while the views on Japanese policies did not improve in three of the countries and did so, but to a lesser degree, in West Germany.

Table 9.7 Perceptions of the effects on their country's economy of US, Japanese, and EC policies, 1982–89 (net per cent helpful minus harmful)

	Effect of US Policies		Effect of Japanese Policies		Effect of EC Policies	
	Apr.–Jun. 1982 1985	Oct.–May 1985 1989	Apr.–Jun. 1982 1985	Oct.–May 1985 1989	Jun. 1985	May 1989
Britain	−35	−15	−43	−40	−25	
France	−34	−18	−34	−31	+15	
Italy	−9	+11	−29	−24	+21	
West Germany	−26	−4	−41	−31	−3	

Question: Do you think that the economic polices and actions of (the United States) (Japan) (European Community) have been more helpful or more harmful to the economic situation in our country, or have they had little effect on our country? This table presents the average net for each period. The net for each survey was derived by subtracting the number calling the policies harmful from the number calling the policies helpful.

Sources: Economic Summit Surveys in 1978, 1982, and 1984–89, Eurobarometer surveys in October–November 1984, October–November 1985, and October 1988, May–June 1984 Security Survey, and June–July 1985 Baseline Survey.

These four publics were also asked about the effects of the policies of the European Community in surveys from 1985 through 1989. During this period, as Table 9.7 shows, EC policies were viewed considerably more positively than those of the USA in France, somewhat more positively in Italy, and slightly more positively in West Germany. However, in Britain, where anti-EC feelings continue to be held by sizeable numbers, the policies of the European Community received substantially lower marks than those of the United States. The number seeing EC policies as harmful ranged from only 10 to 21 per cent in France and 13 to 25 per cent in Italy; in West Germany, somewhat more, from 25 to 38 per cent, held this view. However, in Britain the number seeing EC policies as harmful never fell below 38 per cent and reached as high as 56 per cent.

US policies, in any case, were not apparently seen by most Western Europeans as the principal cause of their country's economic problems. In fact, even in Fall 1984, in a survey done during the period of the 1980s in which US policies were viewed most negatively, out of the ten EC publics only the Greeks most often chose US economic policies from a list of six possible causes. Except in Greece, between 50 and 65 per cent picked either worldwide recession or developments within their own country as the most important cause of their country's economic problems. American economic policies, named by 26 per cent in Greece and between 4 and 19 per cent in the other nine countries, were, except in Greece, either the third or fourth most often named factor of the six on the list. Japanese policies, though broadly seen in a negative light, were chosen by no more than 3 per cent as the principal cause of their economic problems.[6]

PROTECTIONISM

Protectionism, though consistently lower-ranked by the public as a priority issue than unemployment, inflation, and monetary questions, remained a major concern to policy-makers in the 1980s, particularly as the Uruguay Round of GATT negotiations, begun in 1986, dragged on with only limited progress. While US fears appear to have subsided by the early 1990s as it has become clear that US subsidiaries established in Europe will be able to operate freely there, the EC's goal, first announced in 1985, of making significant progress by 1992 in achieving a common market of goods, services, people and capital among its 12 member states also generated substantial concern among

US government officials and business elites. Protectionism in agriculture, the most widely publicized and contentious trade issue between the USA and Western Europe in the second half of the 1980s, will be discussed separately in the following section.

Despite the low priority given by the public to dealing with protectionism and trade questions, the issue of international trade impacts directly on the problem always in the forefront of the public mind, that is, unemployment. In fact, free trade is widely supported in principle by Western Europeans, but, when the protection of jobs or domestic industries is included in the question, the prevailing view favours restrictions on imports – meaning that a substantial number support free trade only in principle but not in practice. This has been illustrated in many surveys in the 1980s. In the four major West European countries, free trade, defined as 'fewer restrictions on the freedom of countries to buy and sell to each other', has predominantly been supported by the publics over restrictions to protect products against foreign competition. When asked this way, in the 1980s majorities in three countries – ranging from 58 to 62 per cent in France, from 60 to 73 per cent in West Germany, and from 62 to 75 per cent in Italy – and large pluralities or majorities in Britain, ranging from 51 to 63 per cent, have favoured free trade. However, even when told that restrictions 'would lead to higher consumer prices for certain products', the publics in all surveys in Britain, France and Italy and in three of five surveys in West Germany favoured restrictions premised on 'protecting jobs in certain industries'. In fact, the opposition to trade restrictions on this question in the 1985–88 period in which it was asked ranged from 28 to 34 per cent in Britain, from 28 to 38 per cent in France, from 31 to 40 per cent in Italy, and from 29 to 42 per cent in West Germany. In sum, as Table 9.8 demonstrates, in each of the four major countries, the average support for free trade in the 1980s was roughly 30 per cent greater for free trade in principle than for free trade when restrictions on imports were linked to protecting jobs in their country.

Similarly, though free trade was supported in principle by sizeable majorities in the four major West European countries in April 1983 and March 1984 surveys, in an October 1983 survey restrictions on free trade were predominantly favoured 'because jobs are being lost to foreign competition'. Altogether, free trade was supported by about 20 per cent fewer in Britain and France and about 40 per cent fewer in Italy and West Germany when the question linked attitudes on free trade to a loss of jobs.[7]

Table 9.8 Support for free trade in the 1980s (average per cent for all times asked)

	Britain	France	Italy	West Germany
Support in principle (1982–84, 1988–89)	56	62	74	68
Support when restrictions linked to protecting jobs (1985–88)	30	33	37	36

Questions: (1) for support in principle – Some countries favour free trade – that is, fewer restrictions on the freedom of countries to buy and sell to each other. Other countries favour restrictions on free trade in order to protect their own products against foreign competition. Which policy do you personally favour?; and (2) for support when restrictions linked to protecting jobs – Some people favour restrictions on foreign imports to protect (Survey Country's) jobs in certain industries. Other oppose restrictions because they would lead to higher consumer prices for certain products. Which view is closer to your own?
Sources: 1982–89 Economic Summit Surveys.

In the 1970s, the USA was, in most surveys in the four major West European countries, seen as more a free trader than protectionist (see Table 9.9). In the 1980s, however, despite the avowed free trade orientation of the Reagan Administration even in the face of a growing US trade deficit, opinion was more mixed:

- In Britain, opinion was divided or close to divided. (In 1989, with the Bush Administration in office, a plurality called the US policy more free trade-oriented.)
- In France a plurality has consistently seen the USA as protectionist.
- In Italy, opinion was close to divided in the 1983–85 period, while a plurality in 1988 and majority in 1989 saw the USA as more free trade-oriented.
- In West Germany, a plurality, except in 1988, has seen the USA as more a free trader.

On a separate and more specific question asked in the 1979–85 period, opinion was close to divided in Britain, France, and West Gemany in 1979 on whether the USA made it easy or difficult for their country to sell its manufactured products in the USA, but in the 1983–85 period,

Table 9.9 US trade policy – free trade or protectionist?, 1976–89 (per cent)

Britain

	Jun. 1976	Mar. 1977	Jun. 1978	Jun. 1979	Apr. 1983	Mar. 1984	Feb. 1985	Apr. 1988	May 1989
Free Trade	37	42	44	43	39	33	34	37	47
Protectionist	25	29	25	26	38	41	38	42	36
Don't Know	38	29	31	31	23	25	28	21	17
Total	100	100	100	100	100	99	100	100	100

France

	Jun. 1976	Mar. 1977	Jun. 1978	Jun. 1979	Apr. 1983	Mar. 1984	Feb. 1985	Apr. 1988	May 1989
Free Trade	33	29	41	46	28	27	25	27	35
Protectionist	32	36	23	26	34	45	41	48	41
Don't Know	35	35	36	28	38	27	34	25	24
Total	100	100	100	100	100	99	100	100	100

Italy

	Jun. 1978	Apr. 1983	Mar. 1984	Feb. 1985	Apr. 1988	May 1989
Free Trade	55	39	44	41	45	56
Protectionist	13	36	40	35	34	30
Don't Know	32	25	16	24	21	15
Total	100	100	100	100	100	101

West Germany

	Jun. 1976	Mar. 1977	Jun. 1978	Jun. 1979	Apr. 1983	Mar. 1984	Feb. 1985	Apr. 1988	May 1989
Free Trade	44	40	42	46	48	47	46	35	50
Protectionist	25	32	30	28	33	39	32	45	35
Don't Know	32	28	28	26	19	14	21	20	14
Total	101	100	100	100	100	100	99	100	99

Question: Which policy do you think the United States generally follows – free trade or restrictions? This question was always preceded in the survey by the following preface: 'Some countries favour free trade, that is, fewer restrictions on the freedom of countries to buy from and sell to each other. Other countries favour restrictions in free trade in order to protect their own products against foreign competition.'

Sources: 1976–89 Economic Summit Surveys.

these three publics predominantly saw the USA as making it difficult for their country's products (see Table 9.10). While the Reagan Administration strongly resisted protectionist measures, its trade image may have been hurt by the overvalued dollar or the more general negative feelings about US policies. In Italy, where the question was not asked in 1979, opinion was close to divided in 1983 and 1985, with a large plurality in 1984 saying the USA made it easy. At the same time, when directly compared to the Japanese in another question, the USA comes out much better than Japan in all four countries on its trading practices. Considerably more – large pluralities in France, Italy and West Germany and a majority in Britain in surveys in 1983, 1984 and 1985 – said that the Japanese make it more difficult than do the Americans for the Europeans to sell them manufactured products.

Western Europeans clearly believe they have a good record on trading practices. Majorities, and usually large majorities, in the four major West European countries have throughout the 1980s seen their own country as a free trader. Furthermore, West Europeans generally do not believe that American complaints that the European market is not as open to American products as is the American market to European products are justified. In 1989, majorities in France (54–17 per cent) and West Germany (58–13 per cent) and pluralities in Britain (37–30 per cent) and Italy (43–27 per cent) felt that such American complaints were not justified.

Western Europeans broadly support free trade in principle, but only minorities favour it in practice when restrictions are seen as a means of protecting jobs in their country. Western Europeans generally give their own country good marks on having free trade practices, but opinion is more mixed on US trade practices. The British, French and Germans, though not the Italians, predominantly think the United States makes it difficult for their products to enter the American market. Most Europeans do not see their market as more closed to American products than is the American market to European products. The Japanese are most widely seen as the biggest culprits on protectionism.

AGRICULTURAL TRADE AND SUBSIDIES

A major international economic issue in the second half of the 1980s, in particular since the Uruguay Round of GATT negotiations began in

Table 9.10 Western European perceptions of US barriers to their country's manufactured products, 1979–85 (views on how USA makes it for their products)

	Britain				Italy			France			West Germany			
	Apr. 1979	Apr. 1983	Mar. 1984	Feb. 1985	Apr. 1983	Mar. 1984	Feb. 1985	Apr. 1979	Apr. 1983	Mar. 1984	Feb. 1985	Apr. 1979	Apr. 1983	Mar. 1984	Feb. 1985
Easy	43	32	32	31	40	28	43	33	19	29	31	36	27	28	24
Difficult	35	46	50	46	41	56	37	37	52	51	46	42	49	56	47
Don't Know	22	22	18	22	19	17	21	31	30	21	23	22	25	17	29
Total	100	100	100	99	100	101	101	101	101	101	100	100	101	101	100

Question: How easy would you say the USA makes it for (Survey Country) to sell its manufactured products in the USA – very easy, fairly easy, fairly difficult, or very difficult?

Sources: 1979 and 1983–85 Economic Summit Surveys.

September 1986, has been agricultural trade. Agriculture has also been a key and tension-producing factor in US–West European relations since the mid-1980s. For all industrialised countries together, subsidies to farmers cost taxpayers and consumers about $250 billion in 1989, with government subsidies equal to $104 billion of this amount and the rest the higher cost of food paid by consumers as a result of the protectionism in agricultural trade. While all the major industrialised countries give some forms of subsidies to their farmers, the subsidies are greater for European than American agriculture, especially the direct export subsidies.[8] As a result of the European Community's Common Agriculture Policy (CAP), the majority of the agricultural support payments in the EC come through higher consumer prices, while in the USA two-thirds of the support to agriculture comes from direct government payments. In mid-1987 President Reagan proposed the total elimination of 'trade-distorting' agricultural subsidies, with export subsidies to be phased out within five years and internal price supports to be phased out within ten, and the removal of non-tariff barriers to market access. He also said that he did not want a short-term deal without a long-term commitment to full elimination. In direct contrast, the European Community, generally supported by Japan, has said it would accept some reduction of agricultural subsidies in the short-term, but has adamantly opposed any agreement for full elimination of subsidies. The USA and the EC have sharply disagreed over agricultural issues throughout in the second half of the 1980s. As the GATT Uruguay Round came closer to its end and no concrete solution was achieved, the conflict over agriculture – which held up progress on other trade areas – became even more difficult. At the Economic Summit in Houston in July 1990, agricultural trade was one of the key issues. A compromise was reached which it was hoped would give impetus to some kind of solution involving progressive, substantial reductions in subsidies, both internal supports and exports subsidies, and increased access to markets for farm producers from other countries. However, in December 1990, when the Uruguay Round was scheduled to end, the GATT negotiations broke down as the US and the EC remained far apart on agriculture. A widely shared desire to re-open these negotiations – which cover a large number of trade areas in addition to agriculture – was aided by the EC's commitment in February 1991 to negotiate large reductions in agricultural subsidies. GATT negotiations resumed in March 1991, but a concrete agreement on agriculture remains problematical given the domestic political pressures in Europe.

In the 24 industrialised countries which are members of the OECD, agriculture represents only about 3 per cent of economic output and 8 per cent of employment; furthermore, the farm population is continuing to decline. Nevertheless, agricultural interests still remain politically powerful, and this is more true in Europe, which, with about one-third more total population than the USA, has over five times as many farmers – 11 million compared to 2 million in the USA.[9] In addition, the agricultural interests have especially strong ties to major Christian Democratic parties, most importantly the CDU/CSU in the FRG, and conservative parties. This residual, though slowly declining, power of Europe's agricultural lobby is the single most important factor in understanding the EC's opposition to elimination, or even substantial reduction, of agricultural subsidies.

However, it is important to recognise that the traditional public sympathy for the farmer in Western Europe also hinders achievement of subsidy-free agriculture by adding clout to well-organised interest groups. In fact, in Spring 1987, a large plurality (50 per cent) in the 12 EC countries together thought that farmers are at a disadvantage compared to the rest of the population: Support for this view ranged from minorities in Britain (31 per cent) and Denmark (29 per cent) to large pluralities in France (45 per cent) and the Netherlands (50 per cent) and majorities in West Germany (58 per cent) and the four southern European EC members – Greece (60 per cent), Italy (55 per cent), Portugal (71 per cent), and Spain (67 per cent).[10] Furthermore, there is clearly no consensus that farmers in Europe have too much control over public policies toward agriculture. In most EC countries opinion was roughly divided in Spring 1987 on whether 'farmers' organizations have far too much influence on political decisions'. Only in the small countries of Ireland and Luxembourg did majorities believe they do.

Western Europeans generally favour *internal price supports* to *farmers*. In both 1987 and 1988 surveys, agricultural subsidies to farmers 'to guarantee them a certain price for their products' were predominantly supported in the four major West European countries. In April 1988, this was by majorities in France (54–36 per cent) and Italy (74–21 per cent) and by pluralities in Britain (52–33 per cent) and West Germany (42–29 per cent). In October 1988, in a slightly different question which asked about support for 'the agricultural policy of the European Community which guarantees farmers a certain price', subsidies were supported by majorities in nine of 11 EC countries surveyed, but opinion was close to divided in the FRG and slightly opposed in Britain. In May 1989, on the same question asked in October 1988, majorities in France (63–21 per cent) and Italy (72–17 per cent) and a large plurality in West Germany (50–35 per cent) supported the EC's agricultural policy, while a plurality (51–40 per cent) were opposed in Britain.[11]

In the Spring 1987 in-depth EC survey on agriculture, subsidies for agriculture were broadly supported in all 12 EC countries. In fact, when given a list of six economic sectors – the steel industry, the car industry, agriculture, the computer industry, shipbuilding, and telecommunications – and asked which ones they thought it would be 'a good thing that they get financial help from public funds', Western Europeans much more frequently named agriculture than any of the other five. For the 12 EC countries together, 59 per cent chose agriculture, while no more than half this number (28 per cent) picked any other sector. In some countries substantial numbers reaching as high as a third to 40 per cent supported subsidies for the steel and shipbuilding industries, but agriculture was most often picked, and usually by a wide margin, in *each* of the 12 countries. Internal price supports were favoured on a number of other questions in this survey as well. Only on one question was support for subsidies the minority view; 62 per cent in the 12 EC countries – including majorities in Britain (60 per cent), France (71 per cent), Italy (62 per cent), and West Germany (70 per cent) – agreed that 'it is no longer possible that we should, as consumers, pay higher prices for food stuffs and at the same time, as taxpayers, pay subsidies for farming'. This, of course, is exactly what happens to Western Europeans as a result of the EC's Common Agricultural Policy, but the EC's Spring 1987 survey shows that only a small minority of Western Europeans have detailed knowledge of how the CAP functions.

Secondly, *import restrictions* are predominantly supported by West Europeans, even at the cost of higher food prices, in order to protect European agriculture. In most surveys in the four major countries in the 1984–88 period, customs duties have generally been supported to protect European farmers, even though respondents were told that this would increase the price of food. When this question was asked to eleven EC publics in October 1985, majorities or pluralities in all but Portugal favoured customs duties.[12] Similarly, in Spring 1987, majorities or pluralities in all 12 EC countries agreed that 'we must protect European agriculture from imports from outside even if the European consumer has to pay more for some food stuffs'.

Thirdly, in 1983 and 1985, when asked about whether their country 'should subsidize our farmers to make it easier for them to sell our country's products outside Europe' or whether 'our farmers should not receive government subsidies even if that means some loss of sales outside Europe', the publics in all four major West European countries supported such *export subsidies*; by large majorities in Italy, by a large plurality in 1983 and a bare majority in 1985 in Britain, and by large pluralities in France and West Germany. In 1985, opposition to the export subsidies, the most controversial aspect of all in US–EC negotiations, totalled about one-third in Britain, France and West Germany and only 17 per cent in Italy.[13] At the same time, when the loss of sales was not included in the question but rather the fact that taxes would have to pay the subsidies was included, support for export subsidies dropped considerably and was the view of only 32 per cent in France and Italy, 40 per cent in West Germany and 45 per cent in Britain.[14]

In sum, internal price supports to farmers and import restrictions on farm products are generally supported by Western Europeans. The evidence is more mixed on the even more controversial issue of export subsidies with support varying greatly depending on how the question is posed. An emphasis on subsidies to prevent loss of sales increases support, while an emphasis on the cost to taxpayers decreases support. Overall, the data suggest that West European publics generally sympathise with farmers and, under most circumstances, are prepared to support agricultural subsidies. In fact, in April 1987 only one in five in the 12 EC countries as a whole believed there to be too much public spending on agriculture by their own government and the EC.

EAST–WEST TRADE

One of the most contentious economic issues between the USA and Western Europe in 1980s, in particular in the first half of the 1980s, was over East–West trade. There were American pressures on Western Europe – strongly resisted by many West European countries – to co-operate in economic sanctions against the Soviet Union twice in the early 1980s: (1) in early 1980 by President Jimmy Carter following the Soviet invasion of Afghanistan in December 1979; and (2) in early 1982 by President Ronald Reagan following the imposition, under Soviet pressure, of martial law in Poland in December 1981. More generally, US policy was particularly confrontational toward the Soviets in the first several years of the Reagan Administration. The Reagan Administration opposed deals finalised in late 1981 by France, Italy and West Germany to purchase large amounts of Soviet natural gas, fearing that West European dependence on the Soviet Union for vital energy supplies would leave these countries open to political pressure from the Soviets. The Reagan Administration also was concerned about the Soviets benefitting militarily from acquiring advanced Western technology. In fact, in the early 1980s the United States forced the Co-ordinating Committee for Multilateral Export Controls (CoCom), a group formed by the NATO members in 1949 to agree on joint controls on export of military technologies to the Soviet Union and its allies and later joined by Australia and Japan, to expand the export controls to include a much broader array of high technologies which could have military applications (Stokes, 1990).[15] Because trade with Eastern Europe and the Soviet Union was more important economically to many of the Western European countries than it was to the USA, this American pressure created tensions between the USA and many of its NATO allies. Indicative of these tensions, in 1983 and 1984 surveys the USA was consistently – and by wider margins than on other policy areas about which the question was asked – seen as uncooperative on the issue of trading with the Soviets by the publics in the four major West European countries.

West European publics generally opposed both economic sanctions against the Soviet Union and cutting their purchases of Soviet natural gas, both of which were major aspects of US policy in the early 1980s toward trade with the Soviets. In a January 1982 survey only a month after the imposition of martial law in Poland, a large plurality of West Germans, after being told that the USA had imposed economic sanctions against the Soviets, nevertheless preferred 'condemning the repression in Poland but taking no other action' (50 per cent) rather than imposing economic sanctions (26 per cent).[16] In February 1982, only 21 per cent in Britain, 17 per cent in France and 20 per cent in West Germany favoured economic sanctions on the Soviet Union, even though told the USA had done so.[17] Most picked the other three options on the list: condemn the repression in Poland but take no other action; do nothing, and wait and see what happens; strengthen efforts to improve relations with the USSR. Likewise, in April 1982, only minorities – 39 per cent in Britain, 32 per cent in France, 25 per cent in Italy and 27 per cent in West Germany – supported decreasing trade with the Soviets in view of the situation in Poland. The French,

German and Italian publics also predominantly: (1) opposed their country decreasing its purchases of Soviet natural gas; (2) believed that these purchases would not make their country substantially more vulnerable to Soviet political pressures; and (3) approved their country helping the Soviet Union to build the pipeline that would carry this gas.[18]

Opinion was more mixed in Western Europe during the 1980s on whether Western nations should impose 'tight restrictions on selling highly advanced technology to the Soviet Union', which was another important feature of the Reagan Administration's policy toward trade with the Soviets. Majorities in Britain and pluralities in West Germany favoured restrictions throughout the 1980s; in the case of West Germany, the plurality support narrowed in the late 1980s. In France, opinion was substantially divided throughout the 1980s, with between 14 and 31 per cent having no opinion. In Italy, bare pluralities in the 1981–84 period and majorities in surveys between 1985 and 1989 opposed such restrictions on hi-tech trade. However, in 1988 support for restrictions dropped in all four countries – from 52 to 35 per cent in Britain, from 36 to 17 per cent in France, from 30 to 14 per cent in Italy, and from 41 to 26 per cent in West Germany – when supporters were asked in a follow-up question whether they would still support restrictions if this meant 'the loss of important sales to the Soviet Union'. At the same time, opposition to Soviet trade restrictions decreased in 1988 by at least half in each of these countries when opponents were asked if they 'would still disagree with such restrictions if these highly advanced technologies would help the Soviet Union modernise its military force'.

There has been no consistent pattern in Western Europe during the 1980s in support for co-ordinating with the USA on trade policies toward the Soviet Union. When given two choices for their country's policy toward trade with the Soviet Union – 'for our country to make the best deal it can even if it harms relations with the USA' or 'to co-ordinate our trade policies with the USA even if it means trading less with the Soviet Union' – opinion has varied across the four major countries and from one year to another. The British widely favoured co-ordination in 1981 and 1982, more narrowly favoured co-ordination in 1984 and 1985, were divided in 1983, 1988 and 1989, and were broadly against co-ordination in 1987. In France, a plurality favoured co-ordination in the 1981–85 period, but opinion has been more divided since then. In West Germany, co-ordination was the plurality view in the 1981–83 and 1987–88 periods, making the best deal was the plurality view in 1984, and opinion was close to divided in 1985 and 1989. In Italy, except for divided opinion in 1982, majorities or pluralities have preferred making the best deal.

In sum, Western Europeans, who have broadly seen the USA as unco-operative on policies toward trade with the Soviet Union, have not consistently supported co-ordination with the USA over making the best trade deal with the Soviets. Opinion has been mixed on restricting hi-tech trade, with the British and Germans in support, the French divided and Italians opposed. The Western Europeans have, however, generally opposed economic sanctions against the Soviets as well as limiting purchases of Soviet natural gas.

CONCLUSIONS

Western Europeans clearly recognise the interdependence of their economy with that of the United States; they widely see the health of their own economy as at least fairly dependent on the health of the US economy, on the value of the US dollar, and on trade with the USA. Many see the economic interests of their country and the USA as similar, though few see them as *very* similar. In the mid-1980s, they widely believed that the USA took West European views into account at most only a little on economic decisions important to Western Europe, and only a minority thought that the US goal was to co-operate with Western Europe for mutual economic advantage. Western Europeans predominantly had little or no confidence in the USA to provide wise leadership on economic matters. Opinion is divided about whether they should co-ordinate with the USA when their self-interest is at stake.

West Europeans differ on how co-operative the USA is in trying to solve economic matters, but, when asked about specific policy areas in mid-1980s surveys, they predominantly did not consider the USA to be co-operative. Opinion also varies among West European publics on whether the USA is a free trader or protectionist. US economic policies were generally viewed as harmful rather than helpful or of little effect in the mid-1980s. In all four major West European countries, they were more often viewed as harmful during the first half of the 1980s than the second half. The number seeing US policies as harmful reached the majority level in Britain and West Germany in the mid-1980s, a level markedly higher than earlier or later in the decade. In the later 1980s, opinion was more mixed across Europe about the effects of US policies. However, even in the mid-1980s, US policies were not considered the major reason for their country's economic problems; in most countries, the worldwide recession and developments within their own country ranked ahead as principal causes.

In two areas of substantial conflict in the 1980s between the United States and Western Europe – agricultural trade and East–West trade – West European publics have often disagreed with the USA. On agriculture, Western Europeans generally sympathise with farmers and, contrary to US policy in the Uruguay Round, support a variety of forms of protectionism in agricultural trade. On East–West trade, the West European publics opposed economic sanctions on the Soviets in the early 1980s, while during the decade they have varied over time and among the four major countries on co-ordinating their policy with the USA and on hi-tech restrictions.

Economic issues will more and more be at the top of the agenda for US–West European relations now that security issues in the post-Cold War world do not hold the same priority they once did. International economic issues will continue to impact directly on domestic politics, and domestic politics will continue to play a major role in international economic issues.

10 Conclusion

The Reagan Administration, which presided over both the final contest of the Cold War – INF deployment – and the improvement in US–Soviet relations which eventually brought about the end of the Cold War, placed a greater emphasis on West European public opinion than previous Administrations in the postwar era. While foreign public opinion did not play the leading role in the formulation of US foreign policy, it was given a great deal of attention particularly regarding sensitive security policy decisions. For example, West European opinion was critical in the Allies' serious pursuit of arms control discussions.

Compared to previous US Administrations, the Reagan White House was especially sensitive to the role of the media in influencing public opinion and the policy process. Throughout the Reagan Administration, the White House was widely successful in staging presidential speeches to have the greatest impact on American television viewing audiences. To a large extent, this same strategy was tried in an effort to influence West European public opinion. Using carefully choreographed public appearances by President Reagan and Vice President Bush, along with US government television and radio communications and the more traditional tools of US public diplomacy, the United States set out to influence West European public attitudes on issues such as support for INF deployment and military retaliation against Libya. While these efforts did not fundamentally change West European attitudes, they did elevate public diplomacy to new heights in US–West European relations.

Many key West European public attitudes impacting US–West European relations, such as broad support for NATO and an overall positive image of the United States, remained fairly constant during the Reagan years. As well, West European publics continued to indicate their reluctance to support military responses to international problems, especially out-of-area issues. On security matters, while the Western Europeans continued their support for NATO, they consistently opposed the major aspects of NATO policy: the flexible response doctrine and increased defense spending. On economic issues, the West European publics generally supported trade restrictions and agricultural subsidies. On other issues, opinion changed over the decade – in some cases fluctuating and in others in a consistent manner. The most dramatic change in West European attitudes in the 1980s was the great improvement in the Soviet image during the second half of the decade.

AMERICAN IMAGE IN WESTERN EUROPE

A fundamental miscalculation by American policy makers and the mass media was their exaggerated perception of a deteriorated American image in Western Europe. Extensive survey data indicate that, in contrast to much of the traditional analysis of Western Europeans during the 1980s, pacifism, neutralism and anti-Americanism did not sweep Europe in the 1980s. In many cases, observers of West European politics confused Allied public dissatisfaction with specific US foreign policies such as INF deployment and the American role in Central America, or general anti-nuclear feelings, with more basic attitudes toward the United States as a society. Anti-Americanism, which is a more fundamental rejection of the United States and its society, is found only among a limited minority of Western Europeans. In fact, in contrast to conventional wisdom that President Reagan served as a lightning rod for increased anti-Americanism, after eight years of the Reagan Administration, anti-Americanism was no more apparent in the late 1980s than at the beginning of the decade. Furthermore, US fears that the Western Europeans perceived the moral equivalence between the USA and the USSR in the first half of the 1980s were greatly exaggerated. Confidence in US foreign policy, however, was generally lower throughout the 1980s in Britain, Italy and West Germany as compared to the previous two decades. In contrast, the French were somewhat more confident in US foreign policy during the Reagan years than during previous Administrations. The biggest changes during the 1980s in attitudes toward the USA occurred in France, where overall opinion of the USA and its foreign policy actually became more positive, and in Britain, where some attitudes became more negative. However, even in Britain, as in France, Italy and West Germany, overall opinion of the USA remained predominantly favourable throughout the 1980s.

President Reagan, the first American President to serve two full terms since Dwight D. Eisenhower, generated mixed attitudes in Western Europe. By the end of his eight years in office, favourable opinion of President Reagan clearly prevailed only in France and, to a lesser degree, in West Germany. Opinion was closely divided in Italy. By contrast, in a number of other West European countries, majorities or near majorities held unfavourable views of Reagan. The lack of consistent West European survey data throughout the 1980s makes it difficult to assess whether Reagan's image declined or improved over his eight years in office. Ronald Reagan, who did well among West European publics compared to the Soviet leaders Brezhnev and Andropov, suffered by comparison to Gorbachev. However, this may not be a completely fair comparison, given the novelty of Gorbachev and the question of whether Western Europeans used the same criteria to judge each leader.

Attitudes on Economic Matters

Over the course of the decade, concern over unemployment remained at the top of the publics' agenda as the most important problem. This concern was directly reflected in support for trade protectionist policies designed to protect domestic jobs. In fact, while the principle of free trade was consistently supported by large majorities, many fewer favoured free trade when it meant a loss of jobs in their country. West European sympathy for the farmer, a small minority of the population, is widely reflected in public support for the several mechanisms used to subsidise or protect agricultural products. These long-held attitudes must be taken into consideration as the USA and the EC struggle to bring about international economic policy reforms such as the continuing conflict in the GATT negotiations over agricultural protectionism. Attitudes toward US economic policies were most negative in the mid-1980s when the US dollar reached a postwar high.

Attitudes on Defense Issues

In general, while Western Europeans have habitually supported NATO over the past three decades, they did not endorse major NATO policies such as flexible response and INF deployment, and did not express support for higher defense spending during the 1980s. Except for the British and French, both of whom have their own nuclear arsenals, Western Europeans are predominantly opposed to nuclear deterrence. Nevertheless, despite Soviet propaganda efforts, the mass demonstrations, and sizeable public opposition, INF deployment occurred. Furthermore, the concept of neutralism was generally opposed, and the USA continued to be seen as an integral part of the West European defense equation throughout the 1980s. However, given the new East–West relations and the resulting NATO identity crisis in the post-Cold War era, West Europeans may begin to rethink the defense role of the United States, especially the necessity of American troops stationed in Europe. At the same time, the evidence suggests the Europeans are unlikely to question the fundamental US–Western European link.

In fact, during the Persian Gulf conflict – the first major international crisis of the post-Cold War period – most Western European publics broadly viewed NATO as essential to their country's security. Moreover, in a number of these European countries, public support for NATO in early 1991 was at its highest levels of recent years.

CHANGING ATTITUDES IN THE 1980S

Although many basic West European attitudes remained fairly constant during the 1980s, several fundamental attitudes, such as the assessment of US–Soviet relations and the perception of the Soviet Union, underwent dramatic change. In fact, the change in the West European publics' perception of the Soviet Union is the most striking change in West European attitudes on international affairs in the past 40 years. Survey data clearly indicate that Mikhail Gorbachev was the driving force behind the improved overall Soviet image among Western Europeans. Prior to the Gorbachev era, Western Europeans held predominantly negative views of the Soviet Union and its foreign policy, although, at least in the 1980s and possibly before, they did not generally perceive the USSR as a serious threat. However, as the 1980s drew to a close, Western Europeans overwhelmingly viewed Gorbachev in a favourable light, and attitudes toward the Soviets were more positive than at any time in the history of the postwar period. However, although Western Europeans held a new and improved image of the Soviet Union by the close of the decade, it did not mean they gave carte blanche approval of Soviet society or all its foreign policies. For example, despite Gorbachev's positive image, Western Europeans remained critical of the lack of human rights in the Soviet Union. However, as democratic developments continue in the Soviet Union in the 1990s, even these West European attitudes toward Soviet society are likely to change.

Caught in the midst of superpower politics, Western Europeans have encouraged improved relations between the two superpowers, especially if this contributes to a lessening of tensions and, perhaps more importantly, a reduction in nuclear stockpiles. The image of superpower relations improved substantially with the onset of a series of highly-publicized Reagan–Gorbachev summits, culminating in the INF Treaty in December 1987. As US–Soviet relations improved, the fear of war among the general public declined greatly compared to the early 1980s.

US–West European Relations in the 1990s.

In some ways the Cold War provided Allied policy makers with an anchor for managing East–West, and, to a great degree, US–West European, relations. Each nation's position in the scheme of international relations was fairly well established. Friend was easily distinguished from foe. Nevertheless, West European publics were uneasy about this arrangement, including the role of nuclear weapons and the fact that the USA wielded a great deal of power over their security affairs. Furthermore, though broadly supporting their Alliance with the USA, Western Europeans remained skeptical that the United States was protecting their interests in negotiating with the Soviets. The West European general public was particularly uncomfortable with the 'evil empire' rhetoric of the early Reagan Administration, and did not share the American perception of the Soviet threat. Nor did they support the US call to impose economic sanctions against the Soviet Union or to halt the purchase of Soviet natural gas.

While almost no one could have predicted the revolutionary changes that swept through Eastern Europe in 1989 and the USSR in 1991, these changes necessitate new security and economic policies. In many cases, these policies will be easier for the public to endorse than for many Western elites, since the public already opposed increased defense spending and had broadly anti-nuclear attitudes. As a result of NATO's July 1990 Summit call for a strategic review, six NATO countries (Britain, Canada, Denmark, Italy, the Netherlands, West Germany and the USA) announced they were going to reduce or freeze their level of troops and/or defense expenditures. Seven other NATO members were reviewing their defense expenditures. The July 1990 NATO Summit also greatly modified the long-held flexible response doctrine due, in part, to the broad public opposition to nuclear weapons.

Conclusion

In the wake of the Cold War, a new set of issues will take priority in defining US–West European relations. It is most plausible that economics will quickly overtake security issues as the primary concern throughout the Alliance. The EC will play a greater role in foreign affairs and possibly security questions as economic issues come to dominate the international agenda. With the end of the Cold War, and further steps toward economic integration within the EC, Western Europe may become a more independent actor on the world stage. In fact, some observers contend that the role of the superpowers in European affairs will decrease as arms control issues become less important. However, the evolving new security and economic environment does not, in the view of the West European publics, signal the demise of the US–Western European special relationship. The West European publics generally consider the bilateral relations with the USA as favorable, although many Western Europeans believe that the United States is not sensitive enough to their country's interests. Nevertheless, as the Reagan Administration and the decade of the 1980s came to a close, there was no indication that Western Europeans wanted to weaken their relations with the United States. Support for this relationship was further demonstrated in 1991 by the broad West European public support for US–West European co-operation during the Gulf conflict.

Epilogue: The Gulf Conflict

The Gulf conflict – from the Iraqi invasion of Kuwait on 2 August 1990 to the ceasefire on 27 February 1991 after the liberation of Kuwait – was the first major international crisis of the post-Cold War era and, therefore, the first test of the US–West European relationship in the changing landscape of world politics. Though international agreement on the steps to be taken against Iraq did not always come easily, the changed nature of the international system was key in ultimately enabling the United States to mobilise broad support. Even many Arab countries, the Soviet Union, and China joined in approving measures for, first, isolating Iraq through a trade embargo and, second, setting a 15 January 1991 deadline for Iraq to withdraw from Kuwait or face the use of force to expel it. A multinational coalition of almost 30 countries provided naval, air and/or ground forces for use in enforcing the embargo and in combat or support roles once the fighting against Iraq actually started.

If Saddam Hussein hoped that the multinational coalition would crumble rather than support the use of force against Iraq, clearly he miscalculated. Certainly, he was wrong in the case of Western Europe. Though not every NATO member agreed completely with every aspect of US policy at each stage between August 1990 and January 1991, for example on how much chance to give the Soviet mediation efforts, overall cooperation was excellent between the US and its NATO allies. The West European countries firmly supported the trade embargo against Iraq, the military containment effort, and ultimately the use of force to liberate Kuwait. Furthermore, nearly all West European NATO members provided some form of support to the military effort. Three West European countries directly participated in the war: British and French forces played major roles in both the bombing campaign and the ground war; while Italy's air force took part in the bombing of Kuwait and Iraq. These three countries plus seven other West European NATO members sent naval forces to the Persian Gulf. Virtually every one of the 14 West European NATO members also provided other forms of support, including material and logistical aid, use of bases and airports, financial contributions to those countries actually doing the fighting, or the stationing of planes in Turkey as a symbol of the NATO commitment to its defence.

If Saddam Hussein placed his hopes on public opinion for a weakening of West European resolve, he was clearly also wrong on this. Not only did the governments of America's West European NATO allies give key support to the military and diplomatic efforts of the United States, but most of the West European publics surveyed, including the British, French, Italians, and West Germans, also backed the trade embargo and the military containment of Iraq and ultimately the war. The major exception in support for the coalition's military efforts was the Spanish public.

A month prior to the start of the fighting against Iraq by the international coalition, West European opinion on the use of military force was mixed: military steps short of an actual attack were supported by most West European publics, but many publics did not yet favor an attack against the Iraqis even if the 15 January deadline passed without Iraq leaving Kuwait. In a mid-December survey in these five countries, large majorities in Britain (77 per cent) and France (65 per cent) and large pluralities in Italy (49 per cent) and West Germany (49 per cent), but only a minority (36 per cent) in Spain, supported the containment effort (President Bush's sending of armed forces to Saudi Arabia and the Persian Gulf). In addition, majorities in Britain (73 per cent) and France (65 per cent) and a plurality (53 to 39 per cent) in Italy were willing to see their country's forces remain in the Gulf for 'as long as is necessary'. Furthermore, majorities in all but Spain supported the United Nations resolution calling for the use of force to expel Iraq from Kuwait if it had not withdrawn by January 15. However, in mid-December, only in Britain (67 per cent) and France (56 per cent) did majorities actually support 'the use of military force to get Iraq to withdraw from Kuwait, if Iraq does not do so before January 15'. Majorities in West Germany (58 per cent) and Spain (58 per cent) and a 52-to-36 per cent plurality in Italy still opposed the use of force.[1] Of course, the British and French were the key publics, since, of all the Western Europeans, their forces would have by far the largest role in the war.

In any case, once the war actually started, support for it became even greater in Britain and France and solidified in Italy and West Germany. Only the Spanish among these five publics did not give clear majority approval to the war after it began. According to a USIA-sponsored telephone survey conducted in Britain, France, Italy, Spain, and West Germany on 24–25 January, 1991 (about a week after the war against Iraq started):

- Except in Spain (where 51 per cent supported the use of military force against Iraq and 46 per cent opposed it), the war was widely approved, with the majorities reaching 61 per cent in Italy and 64 per cent in West Germany and fully 76 per cent in France and 84 per cent in Britain.
- Furthermore, majorities in Britain (82 per cent), France (80 per cent), and Italy (63 per cent) – the three West European countries involved in combat – supported the use of their own military forces in it, with those *strongly* approving numbering fully 53 per cent in Britain and 50 per cent in France.[2] (Surveys in West Germany both before and after 15 January showed the public generally supporting (1) financial contributions to the US and other western countries doing the fighting and (2) the sending of German planes to Turkey, but widely opposing any involvement of German forces in the fighting in Kuwait.)[3]

A variety of other surveys in these five countries between late January and late February confirmed these findings. In Britain, support for both the war and British participation in it numbered three-quarters or more in all surveys; fully 79 per cent favoured continuing the war even 'if there are many casualties'. Public support for the war was at the same levels as the support in 1982 for the Falklands War.[4] In France, support for both the war and the French role in it totalled 70 per cent or more in all surveys.[5] In Italy, a 56-to-36 per cent majority supported the war in an early February telephone survey, while Italian approval of the participation of its forces in the war grew from a large plurality (49 per cent) to a clear majority (57 per cent) in three successive telephone surveys between 11 February and 26 February.[6] In West Germany, two surveys showed between 60 and 66 per cent believing the war just.[7] Spain was again the exception, with 65 per cent in late January saying the war was not fully justified.[8]

The US was not blamed for the war and was generally viewed as having made a serious effort to bring about the liberation of Kuwait by means other than military force. According to a late January survey:

- Except in Spain (where opinion was close to divided), large majorities ranging from 65 to 78 per cent saw the war as a conflict between Iraq and many nations of the United Nations rather than only a United States–Iraq conflict.

Epilogue: The Gulf Conflict

- Except in Spain, where a 45 per cent to 37 per cent plurality thought that President Bush handled the Persian Gulf crisis well, large majorities ranging from 61 to 82 per cent said this of President Bush.
- Majorities in Britain (74 per cent), France (70 per cent), and Italy (60 per cent) and pluralities in Spain (52 per cent) and West Germany (51 per cent) believed that the USA had done all it reasonably could to avoid war; between 23 and 39 per cent in these countries said that America was too quick to use force.[9]

Saddam Hussein was widely disliked by the West European publics and was seen as the one at fault in the Gulf conflict. In late January, large majorities of all five publics surveyed, including even the Spanish, wanted the international forces to 'seek to remove Saddam Hussein from power' rather than allowing him to remain in power once Iraq was completely out of Kuwait.[10] In other words, the West European publics favoured an objective far beyond the goals of the UN resolution authorising the use of force after 15 January.

In sum, during the Gulf conflict, the US-West European relationship functioned well, and most West European publics showed a great deal of support for cooperating with the United States to liberate Kuwait.

Appendix 1: Chronology of Events in US–West European Relations, 1979–89

18 June 1979 – SALT II Treaty signed by Brezhnev and Carter

28–29 June 1979 – Tokyo Economic Summit

4 November 1979 – US Embassy in Iran seized, hostage crisis begins

12 December 1979 – NATO decision in support of INF deployment

late December 1979 – Soviet invasion of Afghanistan

23–24 June 1980 – Venice Economic Summit

4 November 1980 – Ronald Reagan elected President, assumes office on January 20, 1981

30 March 1981 – President Reagan wounded in assassination attempt

May 1981 – François Mitterrand elected France's first Socialist President

19–21 July 1981 – Ottawa Economic Summit

October 1981 – Major anti-INF demonstrations in West Europe

18 November 1981 – President Reagan makes 'zero-option' INF proposal

30 November 1981 – INF negotiations begin in Geneva

13 December 1981 – Martial law imposed in Poland

April–June 1982 – Argentine–British War in the Falklands

30 May 1982 – Spain joins NATO, first new member since 1955

4–6 June 1982 – Versailles Economic Summit

8 June 1982 – President Reagan speaks to British Parliament

July 1982 – France and Italy announce intent to defy the USA on the Soviet pipeline contracts

October 1982 – Helmut Kohl replaces Helmut Schmidt as West German Chancellor

November 1982 – Soviet leader Leonid Brezhnev dies, is replaced by Yuri Andropov

8 March 1983 – President Reagan's 'evil empire' speech on the USSR

Appendix 1: Chronology of Events

23 March 1983 – President Reagan announces the Strategic Defence Initiative (SDI)

March 1983 – Christian Democrats win major victory in West German parliamentary elections and CDU–FDP coalition stays in power

28–30 May 1983 – Williamsburg Economic Summit

June 1983 – Conservatives win solid majority in British paliamentary elections

June 1983 – Five-party centre-left coalition retains majority in Italian elections and stays in power

1 September 1983 – Soviets shoot down Korean airliner (KAL 007)

late October 1983 – Major anti-INF demonstrations in Western Europe

25 October 1983 – US intervention in Grenada

23 November 1983 – Soviets walk out of Geneva INF negotiations

December 1983 – INF deployment begins in Britain, the FRG and Italy

February 1984 – Soviet leader Yuri Andropov dies and is replaced by Konstantin Chernenko

6 June 1984 – President Reagan speaks at Normandy to commemorate 40th Anniversary of D-Day

7–9 June 1984 – London Economic Summit

6 November 1984 – President Reagan re-elected for second term

February 1985 – Dollar reaches all-time high against the German Mark and the Japanese Yen

March 1985 – Soviet leader Konstantin Chernenko dies and is replaced by Mikhail Gorbachev

April 1985 – Daily Worldnet service to West Europe begins

2–4 May 1985 – Bonn Economic Summit

May 1985 – President Reagan visits Bitburg cemetery in the FRG, where Nazi soldiers, including some from the SS, are buried

22 September 1985 – Plaza Accord on the dollar among G-5 nations

October 1985 – VOA Europe begins broadcasting in West Europe

October 1985 – Italian ship *Achille Lauro* hijacked by Palestinian terrorists

19–20 November 1985 – US–Soviet Geneva Summit

27 December 1985 – Co-ordinated attacks by Palestinian terrorists at Rome and Vienna airports

January 1986 – US imposes economic sanctions on Libya, USA naval force begins maneuvers in Mediterranean north of Libya

5 April 1986 – Bombing of West Berlin nightclub frequented by US soldiers, USA claims Libya responsible

Appendix 1: Chronology of Events

15 April 1986 – US bombing raid on Libya
26 April 1986 – Chernobyl nuclear plant explosion
4–6 May 1986 – Tokyo Economic Summit
11–12 October 1986 – US–Soviet Reykjavik Summit
November 1986 – Iran-Contra Affair becomes public
April–December 1987 – INF agreement reached
8–10 June 1987 – Venice Economic Summit
8–11 December 1987 – US–Soviet Washington Summit, INF Treaty signed
29 May–2 June 1988 – US–Soviet Moscow Summit
19–21 June 1988 – Toronto Economic Summit
November 1988 – George Bush elected US President, assumes office January 20, 1989
14–16 July 1989 – Paris Economic Summit

Appendix 2: List of USIA Surveys used in this Book, 1976–91

The bulk of the data used in this book comes from surveys commissioned by the US Information Agency. The questionnaires for all surveys were prepared by the USIA Office of Research, while the fieldwork was conducted by reputable West European survey research firms. All are stratified random samples representative of the adult population (in most cases aged 18 years and older, in a few 15 and older). Where necessary, weighting by sex, age, region, and/or education was done by the fieldwork contractors.

Prior to November 1985, all USIA surveys were done through personal interviews. Since then, USIA has commissioned both personal interview and telephone surveys. As we have done in analysing trends in this book, we present the personal interview and telephone surveys in separate lists. An additional list in this Appendix shows all Eurobarometer surveys in the 1979–88 period in which USIA included questions; these are all also personal interview surveys.

A few long-term trend tables in Chapter 4 include USIA data from the 1950s and 1960s. The many surveys used in these few tables are not listed here. All, however, were personal interview surveys conducted by reputable West European contractors. Most had samples of roughly 1000 adults aged 18 and older.

In the following lists, the number of respondents for each country appears in parentheses.

PERSONAL INTERVIEW SURVEYS

June 1976 Puerto Rico Economic Summit Survey – Britain (1040), France (515), West Germany (953)

March 1977 London Economic Summit Survey – Britain (1830), France (1020), West Germany (1006)

July 1977 Human Rights Survey – Britain (1739), France (970), Italy (944), West Germany (959)

May–June 1978 Bonn Economic Summit Survey – Britain (1813), France (967), Italy (1127), West Germany (948)

April 1979 Tokyo Economic Summit Survey – Britain (1724), France (954), West Germany (934)

Appendix 2: List of USIA Surveys

March 1980 Multiregional Security Survey – Britain (987), France (1000), West Germany (941)

April 1980 Venice Economic Summit Survey – Britain (1002), France (964), Italy (1004), West Germany (1017)

April–May 1980 Afghanistan and Iran Issues Survey – Britain, France (957), West Germany

February 1981 International Issues Survey – Britain, France, West Germany

March 1981 Security Survey – Britain (986), France (959), Italy (1114), the Netherlands (1024), Norway (1002), West Germany (1000)

April 1981 Ottawa Economic Summit Survey – Britain (838), France (974), Italy (1075), West Germany (950)

April 1981 Soviet Peace Initiatives Survey – Britain, France, the Netherlands

July 1981 NATO Survey – Britain (896), France (967), Italy (1019), the Netherlands (854), West Germany (1065)

October 1981 Security Survey – Belgium (944), Britain (1006), France (985), Italy (1062), the Netherlands (770), Norway (1005), West Germany (989)

December 1981 INF Survey – Britain (997), the Netherlands (1009), West Germany (1211)

January 1982 West German Security Survey – West Germany (1003)

February 1982 Poland–INF Survey – Britain (1007), France (946), West Germany (923)

February 1982 Belgian Security Survey – Belgium (453)

April 1982 Versailles Economic Summit Survey – Britain (802), France (938), Italy (995), West Germany (953)

May 1982 and June 1982 British Before and After Presidential Visit Surveys – Britain

July 1982 Security Survey – Britain (967), France (915), Italy (1053), the Netherlands (1287), West Germany (923)

October 1982 INF Survey – Britain (888), France (934), Italy (991), the Netherlands (1073), West Germany (923)

December 1982 Correlation of Forces Survey – Britain (990), France (956), Italy (1040), West Germany (923)

April 1983 Williamsburg Economic Summit Survey – Britain (960), France (946), Italy (1080), West Germany (923)

April 1983 INF Survey – Britain (960), Italy (1080), the Netherlands (939), West Germany (923)

June 1983 INF Survey – Belgium (504), Britain (1058), Italy (1068), the Netherlands (1198), West Germany (924)

Appendix 2: List of USIA Surveys

July–August 1983 INF Intensive Survey – Britain (2296), Italy (1984), West Germany (2055)

December 1983 INF Survey – Britain (960), Italy (1095), West Germany (923)

February 1984 Middle East Issues Survey – Britain (994), Italy (1092), West Germany (918)

March 1984 London Economic Summit Survey – Britain (996), France (940), Italy (1071), West Germany (923)

May–June 1984 Security Survey – Belgium (1018), Britain (1131), Denmark (978), Italy (1040), the Netherlands (1219), Norway (929), West Germany (1033)

June–July 1984 Central American Issues Survey – Britain (977), Italy (1062), the Netherlands (1171), Spain (1857)

October–November 1984 International Issues Survey – Britain (888), Italy (1053), the Netherlands (1191), West Germany (918)

February 1985 Arms Control Survey – Belgium (1003), Britain (1073), Denmark (924), Italy (1077), the Netherlands (1354), West Germany (924)

February 1985 Bonn Economic Summit Survey – Britain (837), France (940), Italy (1077), West Germany (924)

March–April 1985 Terrorism Survey – Britain (992), France (940), Italy (1186), West Germany (924)

May 1985 Security Survey – Britain (1798), Italy (1054), West Germany (924)

June–July 1985 Baseline Survey – Britain (988), Denmark (1022), France (940), Italy (1035), the Netherlands (987), Norway (1034), West Germany (924)

September 1985 Security Survey – Britain (759), France (940), Italy (1032), West Germany (924)

December 1985 Geneva Summit Survey – Britain (964), France (956), Italy (1013), West Germany (924)

March 1986 Tokyo Economic Summit Survey – Britain (1011), France (947), Italy (1113), West Germany (922)

June 1986 Terrorism Survey – Britain (970), France (937), Italy (1056), Portugal (962), Spain (1007), West Germany (994)

July 1986 Arms Control Survey – Britain (994), France (956), Italy (1085), West Germany (994)

February 1987 Security Survey – Britain (963), France (939), Italy (977), West Germany (922)

March 1987 Security Survey – Britain (931), France (959), Italy (986), West Germany (940)

April 1987 Venice Economic Summit Survey – Britain (1027), France (961), Italy (1067), West Germany (938)

Appendix 2: List of USIA Surveys

September 1987 Security Survey – Britain (964), France (961), Italy (1061), West Germany (1022)

September–October 1987 American Image Survey – Britain (975), France (1053), Italy (1000), Spain, West Germany (1076)

October 1987 Scandinavian Survey – Denmark (845), Finland (1057), Norway (1008), Sweden (915)

November 1987 Security Survey – Britain (964), France (1053), Italy (1000), West Germany (1074)

April 1988 Toronto Economic Summit Survey – Britain (947), France (1004), Italy (1002), West Germany (960)

July 1988 Security Survey – Belgium (1027), Britain (1027), France (940), Italy (988), the Netherlands (1063), West Germany (1077)

February 1989 Image Survey – Britain (968), France (939), Italy (1018), West Germany (1001)

March 1989 Security Survey – Britain (1019), France (1000), West Germany (975)

May 1989 Paris Economic Summit Survey – Britain (1010), France (1004), Italy (1020), West Germany (965)

TELEPHONE SURVEYS

November 1985 Pre-Geneva Summit Telephone Survey – Britain (511), France (514), Italy (508), the Netherlands (505), West Germany (504)

December 1985 Geneva Summit Telephone Survey – Britain (504), France (500), the Netherlands (504), Italy (501), West Germany (510)

April 1986 Pre-Libya Raid Telephone Survey – Britain (975), France (504), West Germany (513)

April 1986 Post-Libya Raid Telephone survey – Britain (1012), France (499), West Germany (501)

June 1986 Security Telephone Survey – Britain (973), France (509), West Germany (500)

July 1986 Terrorism Telephone Survey – Britain (993), France (511), West Germany (510)

October 1986 Post-Reykjavik Summit Telephone Survey I – Britain (786), France (5050, West Germany (504)

October–November 1986 Post-Reykjavik Summit Telephone Survey II -Britain (993), France (501), West Germany (501)

January 1987 Security Telephone Survey – Britain (1002), France (509), West Germany (498)

Appendix 2: List of USIA Surveys

May 1987 INF Telephone Survey – Britain (939), France (505), West Germany (501)

July 1987 INF Telephone Survey – Britain (1016), France (504), West Germany (493)

September 1987 Reagan–Gorbachev Telephone Survey – Britain (1008), France (502), West Germany (496)

November 1987 Pre-Washington Summit Telephone Survey – Britain (946), France (505), West Germany (499)

December 1987 Post-Washington Summit Telephone Survey – Belgium (513), Britain (502), France (503), Italy (503), the Netherlands (536), West Germany (505)

March 1988 Pre-Moscow Summit Telephone Survey – Britain (979), France (1009), West Germany (989)

June 1988 Post-Moscow Summit Telephone Survey – Britain (505), France (501), West Germany (500)

January 1991 Persian Gulf War Telephone Survey – Britain (500), France (507), Italy (504), Spain (500), West Germany (584)

EUROBAROMETER SURVEYS

This list includes surveys in which USIA commissioned questions, listing countries in which USIA had questions.

April 1979 – Britain, France, Italy, West Germany

April 1980 – Belgium, Britain, France, Italy, the Netherlands, West Germany

October 1980 – Belgium, Britain, France, Italy, the Netherlands, West Germany

March–May 1982 – Britain, France, Greece, Italy, West Germany

October–November 1984 – Belgium, Britain, France, Greece, Ireland, Italy, the Netherlands, Portugal, Spain, West Germany

October–November 1985 – Belgium, Britain, Denmark, France, Greece, Ireland, Italy, the Netherlands, Portugal, Spain, West Germany

April 1987 – Belgium, Britain, Denmark, France, Greece, Ireland, Italy, the Netherlands, Portugal, Spain, West Germany

September–October 1987 – Belgium, Britain, Denmark, France, Greece, Ireland, Italy, the Netherlands, Portugal, Spain, West Germany

October 1988 – Belgium, Britain, Denmark, France, Greece, Ireland, Italy, the Netherlands, Portugal, Spain, West Germany

Appendix 3:
Additional Data Tables

Table A.1 Confidence in US foreign policy (per cent)

Britain

	May 1960	Jan. 1961	Jun. 1962	Jan. 1963	May 1965	Apr. 1968	Dec. 1968	Sep. 1969	Jun. 1970	Jul. 1971	Jan. 1972	Mar. 1972	Jun. 1972	Oct. 1974	May 1975
Great deal	8	15	11	16	19	14	9	14	9	14	17	22	15	18	12
Fair amount	27	38	32	35	45	50	36	46	27	43	47	51	42	51	38
Subtotal	35	53	43	51	64	64	45	60	36	57	64	73	57	69	50
Not very much	35	23	32	25	23	21	32	17	23	17	22	16	23	23	30
None at all	16	9	12	8	6	5	11	9	27	14	10	7	14	5	11
Subtotal	51	32	44	33	29	26	43	26	50	31	32	23	37	28	41
Don't know	14	15	13	16	7	10	13	14	14	12	5	5	6	3	8
Total	100	100	100	100	100	100	101	100	100	100	101	100	100	100	99

cont.

	Mar. 1981	Oct. 1981	Dec. 1981	Apr. 1982	Jul. 1982	Dec. 1982	Jun. 1983	Jul. 1983	Dec. 1983	May 1984	Oct. 1985	Feb. 1985	May 1985	Sep. 1985	Dec. 1985
Great deal	10	10	8	10	9	12	13	9	6	9	7	7	6	7	5
Fair amount	43	37	35	38	46	44	34	44	26	46	40	30	31	38	36
Subtotal	53	47	43	48	55	56	47	53	32	55	47	37	37	45	41
Not very much	32	37	38	37	31	35	36	35	42	34	36	42	39	36	38
None at all	8	12	14	13	10	7	15	10	22	8	11	18	18	12	15
Subtotal	40	49	52	50	41	42	51	45	64	42	47	60	57	48	53
Don't know	8	4	5	2	3	3	2	2	3	4	6	3	6	7	7
Total	101	100	100	100	99	101	100	100	99	101	100	100	100	100	101

Britain

	Mar. 1986	Feb. 1987	Jul. 1988	Feb. 1989	Oct. 1989
Great deal	7	6	7	10	12
Fair amount	33	30	42	48	46
Subtotal	40	36	49	58	58
Not very much	45	43	34	32	29
None at all	13	17	11	7	8
Subtotal	58	60	45	39	37
Don't know	3	4	6	3	5
Total	101	100	100	100	100

269

France

	May 1960	Jun. 1961	Jun. 1982	Jan. 1963	May 1965	Apr. 1968	Dec. 1968	Sep. 1969	Jun. 1970	Jul. 1971	Jan. 1972	Mar. 1972	Jun. 1972	May 1973	Oct. 1974
Great deal	5	8	4	5	5	4	4	9	5	8	6	4	2	6	8
Fair amount	38	37	31	28	33	27	34	48	31	47	31	49	30	34	38
Subtotal	43	45	35	33	38	31	38	57	36	55	37	53	32	40	46
Not very much	24	20	28	32	25	42	27	21	31	18	39	32	38	22	30
None at all	15	14	17	17	14	11	15	6	18	9	16	7	16	15	15
Subtotal	39	34	45	49	39	53	42	27	49	27	55	39	54	37	45
Don't know	18	21	20	18	23	16	20	16	15	18	8	8	14	22	9
Total	100	100	100	100	100	100	100	100	100	100	100	100	100	99	100

France

	May 1975	Mar. 1981	Oct. 1981	Apr. 1982	Sep. 1985	Dec. 1985	Mar. 1986	Feb. 1987	Jul. 1988	Feb. 1989	Oct. 1989
Great deal	3	8	6	5	4	5	5	6	8	5	8
Fair amount	24	43	40	44	36	37	43	38	43	43	52
Subtotal	27	51	46	49	40	42	48	44	51	48	60
Not very much	30	26	28	37	25	28	23	27	29	25	25
None at all	19	8	13	9	10	10	9	16	9	6	8
Subtotal	49	34	41	46	35	38	32	43	38	31	33
Don't know	24	16	14	5	26	21	20	13	12	21	8
Total	100	101	101	101	101	101	100	100	101	100	101

cont.

270

Italy

	May 1960	Jun. 1961	Jun. 1962	Jan. 1963	May 1965	Dec. 1968	Oct. 1969	Jan. 1972	Mar. 1972	Apr. 1973	Mar. 1981	Oct. 1981	Apr. 1982	Jul. 1982	Dec. 1982
Great deal	16	15	21	24	28	14	18	22	23	22	22	23	17	14	27
Fair amount	30	38	34	37	36	33	43	39	48	47	48	38	45	46	44
Subtotal	46	53	55	61	64	47	61	61	71	69	70	61	62	60	71
Not very much	12	12	15	10	11	12	15	24	18	17	19	24	23	26	19
None at all	17	6	7	5	4	5	5	9	5	6	6	11	11	10	7
Subtotal	29	18	22	15	15	17	20	33	23	23	25	35	34	36	26
Don't know	25	29	23	24	21	36	19	6	6	8	4	4	4	5	2
Total	100	100	100	100	100	100	100	100	100	100	99	100	100	101	99

Italy

	Apr. 1983	Jun. 1983	Jul. 1983	Dec. 1983	May 1984	Nov. 1984	Feb. 1985	May 1985	Sep. 1985	Dec. 1985	Mar. 1986	Feb. 1987	Jul. 1988	Feb. 1989	Oct. 1989
Great deal	12	13	16	13	13	15	14	15	14	13	14	12	14	18	18
Fair amount	43	38	46	40	51	42	38	44	46	43	47	42	49	52	51
Subtotal	55	51	62	53	64	57	52	59	60	56	61	54	63	70	69
Not very much	28	29	26	29	26	27	30	25	27	31	27	31	26	20	23
None at all	14	18	9	15	8	12	15	13	11	10	11	13	8	7	3
Subtotal	42	47	35	44	34	39	45	38	38	41	38	44	34	27	26
Don't know	3	2	3	4	2	4	3	3	2	3	2	2	4	4	6
Total	100	100	100	101	100	100	100	100	100	100	101	100	101	100	101

West Germany

	May 1960	Jun. 1961	Jun. 1962	Jan. 1963	May 1965	Apr. 1968	Dec. 1968	Oct. 1969	Jun. 1970	Jul. 1971	Jan. 1972	Mar. 1972	Jun. 1972	Oct. 1974	May 1975
Great deal	21	28	24	37	19	17	7	23	8	16	9	18	8	17	8
Fair amount	36	51	48	38	45	44	34	58	36	55	39	57	39	47	36
Subtotal	57	79	72	75	64	61	41	81	44	71	48	75	47	64	44
Not very much	18	9	19	8	21	28	40	14	33	16	41	15	28	26	41
None at all	4	2	3	1	3	4	6	2	11	4	10	7	15	4	6
Subtotal	22	11	22	9	24	32	46	16	44	20	51	22	43	30	47
Don't know	21	10	6	16	12	7	14	3	12	9	1	4	11	6	10
Total	100	100	100	100	100	100	101	100	100	100	100	101	101	100	101

West Germany

	Mar. 1981	Oct. 1981	Dec. 1981	Jan. 1982	Apr. 1982	Jul. 1982	Dec. 1982	Apr. 1983	Jun. 1983	Jul. 1983	Dec. 1983	May 1984	Oct. 1984	Feb. 1985	May 1985
Great deal	13	8	6	7	13	4	7	5	4	5	5	3	3	11	10
Fair amount	40	35	28	30	42	36	41	30	27	30	29	38	31	33	30
Subtotal	53	43	34	37	55	40	48	35	31	35	34	41	34	44	40
Not very much	30	32	40	39	29	46	34	45	40	51	41	45	40	33	36
None at all	4	10	8	11	7	6	8	8	8	8	12	7	11	11	10
Subtotal	34	42	48	50	36	52	42	53	48	59	53	52	51	44	46
Don't know	13	15	18	12	10	9	9	12	20	5	13	6	15	12	14
Total	100	100	100	99	101	101	99	100	99	99	100	99	100	100	100

cont.

West Germany

	Sep. 1985	Dec. 1985	Mar. 1986	Feb. 1987	Jul. 1988	Feb. 1989	Oct. 1989
Great deal	5	6	5	8	9	4	16
Fair amount	30	35	35	30	38	42	56
Subtotal	35	41	40	38	47	46	72
Not very much	43	39	40	41	33	38	20
None at all	10	7	7	12	6	6	3
Subtotal	53	46	47	53	39	44	23
Don't know	12	13	13	9	14	10	5
Total	100	100	100	100	100	100	100

Question: In the 1980s, the following question was asked: How much confidence do you have in the United States to deal responsibly with world problems? Do you have a great deal of confidence, a fair amount, not very much, or none at all? In the 1960s and 1970s, the question, which had minimal wording differences over these two decades, was: How much confidence do you have in the ability of the United States to deal wisely with present world problems – a great deal, a fair amount, not very much or none at all?

Sources: USIA Surveys, except October 1989. See Appendix 2 for details on the USIA surveys in the 1980s. The October 1989 data are reported in *Eurobarometer*, no. 32 (December 1989), p. A38.

Table A.2 Effects of US policies (per cent)

Britain

	Apr. 1982	Jul. 1982	Apr. 1983	Jul. 1983	Dec. 1983	Feb. 1984	May 1984	Feb. 1985	May 1985	Jun. 1985	Sep. 1985	Dec. 1985	Mar. 1986	Jun. 1986	Jul. 1987	Nov. 1987	Mar. 1989
Promote peace	39	43	24	34	16	17	29	34	24	32	27	47	41	18	17	44	57
Risk war	39	35	57	52	70	64	52	48	56	47	53	30	40	66	64	44	27
Don't know	22	22	18	14	14	18	19	18	20	20	20	23	20	16	19	13	16
Total	100	100	99	100	100	99	100	100	100	99	100	100	101	100	100	101	100

France

	Apr. 1982	Jul. 1982	Jun. 1985	Sep. 1985	Dec. 1985	Mar. 1986	Jun. 1986	Jul. 1986	Nov. 1987	Mar. 1989
Promote peace	40	38	49	34	46	55	30	42	41	58
Risk war	44	28	24	26	18	16	36	28	33	16
Don't know	16	35	27	41	36	30	34	30	26	26
Total	100	101	100	101	100	101	100	100	100	100

Italy

	Apr. 1982	Jul. 1982	Apr. 1983	Jul. 1983	Dec. 1983	Feb. 1984	May 1984	Feb. 1985	May 1985	Jun. 1985	Sep. 1985	Dec. 1985	Mar. 1986	Jun. 1986	Jul. 1986	Nov. 1987
Promote peace	43	46	37	37	31	34	44	42	42	57	41	49	50	31	31	43
Risk war	44	38	52	47	57	54	43	44	46	30	46	36	39	58	60	44
Don't know	13	15	12	15	12	12	13	14	12	13	12	14	11	11	10	13
Total	100	99	101	99	100	100	100	100	100	100	99	99	100	100	101	100

cont.

West Germany

	Apr. 1982	Jul. 1982	Apr. 1983	Jul. 1983	Dec. 1983	Feb. 1984	May 1984	Feb. 1985	May 1985	Jun. 1985	Sep. 1985	Dec. 1985	Mar. 1986	Jun. 1986	Jul. 1986	Nov. 1987	Mar. 1989
Promote peace	46	32	31	27	26	19	33	42	39	41	34	46	48	24	34	54	62
Risk war	33	33	38	48	41	40	40	31	33	29	34	25	24	48	37	32	13
Don't know	21	35	31	25	33	40	26	26	28	30	32	29	28	28	30	14	25
Total	100	100	100	100	100	99	99	99	100	100	100	100	100	100	100	100	100

Question: On balance, do you think that US policies and actions during the past year have done more to promote peace or done more to increase the risk of war?

Sources: April 1982 Versailles Economic Summit Survey, July 1982 Security Survey, April 1983 INF Survey, July–August 1983 INF Intensive Survey, December 1983 INF Survey, February 1984 Middle East Issues Survey, May–June 1984 Security Survey, February 1985 Arms Control Survey, May 1985 Security Survey, June–July 1985 Baseline Survey, September 1985 Security Survey, December 1985 Geneva Summit Survey, March 1986 Tokyo Economic Summit Survey, June 1986 Terrorism Survey, July 1986 Arms Control Survey, November 1987 Security Survey, March 1989 Security Survey.

Table A.3 Overall opinion of the Soviet Union, 1981–89 (per cent)

	West Germany									
	Oct. 1981	Feb. 1982	Dec. 1982	Jun. 1985	Sep. 1987	Oct. 1987	Apr. 1988	Mar. 1989	May 1989	Oct. 1989
Very favourable	0	1	4	1	4	3	3	3	3	17
Somewhat favourable	8	19	17	23	50	38	53	57	52	54
Subtotal	8	20	21	24	54	41	56	60	55	71
Somewhat unfavourable	44	54	41	44	30	43	23	22	31	16
Very unfavourable	33	23	18	11	4	9	3	4	2	3
Subtotal	77	77	59	55	34	52	26	26	33	19
Don't know	16	4	20	20	12	6	19	14	12	9
Total	101	101	100	99	100	99	101	100	100	99

cont.

Britain

	Oct. 1981	Feb. 1982	Dec. 1982	Jun. 1985	Sep. 1987	Oct. 1987	Apr. 1988	Mar. 1989	May 1989	Oct. 1989
Very favourable	1	2	2	8	5	2	5	9	7	7
Somewhat favourable	11	12	15	46	43	34	53	56	55	52
Subtotal	12	14	17	54	48	36	58	65	62	59
Somewhat unfavourable	31	32	42	27	30	38	26	18	18	23
Very unfavourable	42	42	23	8	7	16	4	5	6	10
Subtotal	73	74	65	35	37	54	30	23	24	33
Don't know	16	12	18	11	15	9	12	13	13	8
Total	101	100	100	100	100	99	101	101	99	100

France

	Oct. 1981	Feb. 1982	Dec. 1982	Jun. 1985	Sep. 1987	Oct. 1987	Apr. 1988	Mar. 1989	May 1989	Oct. 1989
Very favourable	1	N/A	1	2	2	2	2	3	3	4
Somewhat favourable	18		18	26	25	25	43	48	48	41
Subtotal	19		19	28	27	27	45	51	51	45
Somewhat unfavourable	40		40	37	34	43	33	27	24	30
Very unfavourable	17		15	15	13	15	6	9	7	13
Subtotal	57		55	52	47	58	39	36	31	43
Don't know	23		26	20	26	15	17	13	18	11
Total	99		100	100	100	100	101	100	100	99

Italy

	Oct. 1981	Feb. 1982	Dec. 1982	Jun. 1985	Sep. 1987	Oct. 1987	Apr. 1988	Mar. 1989	May 1989	Oct. 1989
Very favourable	4	3	4	4	6	6	8	N/A	13	17
Somewhat favourable	17	10	25	36	36	34	54		52	48
Subtotal	21	13	29	40	42	40	62		65	65
Somewhat unfavourable	42	36	38	38	39	31	27		22	16
Very unfavourable	31	32	28	13	12	23	6		7	6
Subtotal	73	68	66	51	51	54	33		29	22
Don't know	6	19	6	9	8	6	6		7	13
Total	100	100	101	100	101	100	101		101	100

Question: What is your overall opinion of the Soviet Union – do you have a very favourable, somewhat favourable, somewhat unfavourable, or very unfavourable opinion of the Soviet Union?

Sources: October 1981 Security Survey, February 1982 Poland–INF Survey, December 1982 Correlation of Forces Survey, June–July 1985 Baseline Survey, September 1987 Security Survey, September–October 1987 American Image Survey, April 1988 Toronto Economic Summit Survey, March 1989 Security Survey, May 1989 Paris Economic Summit Survey, October 1989 Eurobarometer Survey.

Table A.4 Confidence in Soviet foreign policy, 1982–89 (per cent)

Britain

	Dec. 1982	Jun. 1983	Dec. 1983	May 1984	Oct. 1984	Feb. 1985	Sep. 1985	Dec. 1985	Mar. 1986	Feb. 1987	Jul. 1988	Feb. 1989	Mar. 1989	Oct. 1989
Great deal	5	3	2	4	5	3	5	2	3	3	10	15	7	6
Fair amount	29	18	17	27	28	21	29	30	28	36	48	49	50	44
Subtotal	34	21	19	31	33	24	34	32	31	39	58	64	57	50
Not very much	41	44	45	47	39	39	40	44	44	41	32	27	26	33
None at all	21	30	28	18	20	30	15	15	19	16	7	6	6	11
Subtotal	62	74	73	65	59	69	55	59	63	57	39	33	32	44
Don't know	4	4	8	4	8	7	11	9	6	5	3	3	10	6
Total	100	99	100	100	100	100	100	100	100	100	100	100	99	100

France

	Dec. 1982	Sep. 1985	Dec. 1985	Mar. 1986	Feb. 1987	Jul. 1988	Feb. 1989	Mar. 1989	Oct. 1989
Great deal	1	1	1	1	2	3	3	5	5
Fair amount	15	13	15	14	16	25	26	37	31
Subtotal	16	14	16	15	18	28	29	42	36
Not very much	47	29	37	40	33	35	30	33	37
None at all	27	30	26	25	35	21	17	14	17
Subtotal	74	59	63	65	68	56	47	47	54
Don't know	10	28	22	20	15	16	24	11	9
Total	100	101	101	100	101	100	100	100	99

Italy

	Dec. 1982	Dec. 1983	May 1984	Nov. 1984	Feb. 1985	Sep. 1985	Dec. 1985	Mar. 1986	Feb. 1987	Jul. 1988	Feb. 1989	Oct. 1989
Great deal	7	4	4	8	5	8	6	7	7	11	16	15
Fair amount	29	19	28	24	21	33	33	34	37	49	49	51
Subtotal	36	23	32	32	26	41	39	41	44	60	65	66
Not very much	37	41	39	34	38	35	40	38	35	26	20	21
None at all	23	32	26	30	32	21	18	18	18	9	10	6
Subtotal	60	73	65	64	70	56	58	56	53	35	30	27
Don't know	3	4	3	4	4	3	3	3	4	5	5	8
Total	99	100	100	100	100	100	100	100	101	100	101	101

West Germany

	Dec. 1982	Dec. 1983	May 1984	Oct. 1984	Feb. 1985	Sep. 1985	Dec. 1985	Mar. 1986	Feb. 1987	Jul. 1988	Feb. 1989	Mar. 1989	Oct. 1989
Great deal	4	0	1	2	3	3	2	1	2	4	2	5	14
Fair amount	14	5	10	9	10	12	23	18	11	27	41	42	54
Subtotal	18	5	11	11	13	15	25	19	13	31	43	47	68
Not very much	49	45	60	44	48	47	46	46	51	37	38	36	22
None at all	23	35	21	28	28	24	16	20	25	13	6	7	4
Subtotal	72	80	81	72	76	71	62	66	76	50	44	43	26
Don't know	11	15	8	17	11	13	13	15	11	19	13	10	5
Total	101	100	100	100	100	99	100	100	100	100	100	100	99

cont.

Question: How much confidence do you have in the ability of the Soviet Union to deal responsibly with world problems? Do you have a great deal of confidence, a fair amount, not very much or none at all?

Sources: December 1982 Correlation of Forces Survey, June 1983 INF Survey, December 1983 INF Survey, May–June 1984 Security Survey, October–November 1984 International Issues Survey, February 1985 Bonn Economic Summit Survey, September 1985 Security Survey, December 1985 Geneva Summit Survey, March 1986 Tokyo Economic Summit Survey, February 1987 Security Survey, July 1988 Security Survey, February 1989 Image Survey, March 1989 Security Survey, October 1989 Eurobarometer Survey.

Table A.5 Effects of Soviet foreign policies, 1982–89 (per cent)

Britain

	Apr. 1982	Jul. 1982	Apr. 1983	Jul. 1983	Dec. 1983	May 1984	Feb. 1985	May 1985	Jun. 1985	Jul. 1985	Sep. 1985	Dec. 1985	Mar. 1986	Jul. 1986	Nov. 1987	Mar. 1989
Promote peace	9	18	11	18	10	10	27	32	33	24	25	50	49	43	65	85
Increase risk of war	75	52	60	60	62	64	46	40	36	37	47	23	30	26	20	7
Don't know	16	31	29	22	27	26	27	28	31	39	28	27	22	31	15	7
Total	100	100	100	100	99	100	100	100	100	100	100	100	100	100	100	99

France

	Apr. 1982	May 1984	Jun. 1985	Jul. 1985	Sep. 1985	Dec. 1985	Mar. 1986	Nov. 1987	Mar. 1989
Promote peace	11	11	24	18	17	32	40	35	66
Increase risk of war	75	60	43	34	38	27	27	36	12
Don't know	14	29	33	48	45	41	33	29	22
Total	100	100	100	100	100	100	100	100	100

Italy

	Apr. 1982	Apr. 1983	Dec. 1983	May 1984	Feb. 1985	May 1985	Jun. 1985	Jul. 1985	Sep. 1985	Dec. 1985	Mar. 1986	Jul. 1986	Nov. 1987	Mar. 1989
Promote peace	11	16	20	12	13	25	26	33	31	26	39	49	46	56	N/A
Increase risk of war	76	71	61	74	68	58	57	51	53	57	42	36	39	28	
Don't know	13	13	18	14	19	18	18	16	16	17	19	15	15	16	
Total	100	100	99	100	100	101	101	100	100	100	100	100	100	100	

cont.

West Germany

	Apr. 1982	Jul. 1982	Apr. 1983	Jul. 1983	Dec. 1983	May 1984	Feb. 1985	May 1985	Jun. 1985	Jul. 1985	Sep. 1985	Dec. 1985	Mar. 1986	Jul. 1986	Nov. 1987	Mar. 1989
Promote peace	9	15	17	14	9	11	18	19	22	20	20	35	37	31	51	78
Increase risk of war	68	52	49	60	56	60	49	47	42	43	45	31	32	37	31	3
Don't know	23	33	34	26	35	29	33	34	37	37	35	35	31	32	18	19
Total	100	100	100	100	100	100	100	100	101	100	100	101	100	100	100	100

Question: On balance, do you think Soviet policies and actions during the past year have done more to promote peace or more to increase the risk of war?

Sources: April 1982 Versailles Economic Summit Survey, July 1982 Security Survey, April 1983 INF Survey, July–August 1983 INF Intensive Survey, December 1983 INF Survey, May–June 1984 Security Survey, February 1985 Security Survey, May 1985 Security Survey, June–July 1985 Baseline Survey, September 1985 Security Survey, December 1985 Geneva Summit Survey, March 1986 Tokyo Economic Summit Survey, July 1986 Arms Control Survey, November 1987 Security Survey, March 1989 Security Survey.

Table A.6 US–Soviet relations, 1985–88 (per cent)

Britain

	Nov. 1985	Dec. 1985	Oct. 1986	Nov. 1986	Jan. 1987	Nov. 1987	Dec. 1987	Mar. 1988	Jun. 1988
Very good	0	2	2	1	1	3	6	3	12
Fairly good	48	58	46	33	34	74	78	77	77
Fairly bad	41	31	38	46	45	18	11	13	6
Very bad	9	5	8	7	9	2	2	2	1
Don't know	2	4	7	13	11	3	2	5	4
Total	100	100	100	100	100	100	99	100	100

France

	Nov. 1985	Dec. 1985	Oct. 1986	Nov. 1986	Jan. 1987	Nov. 1987	Dec. 1987	Mar. 1988	Jun. 1988
Very good	4	3	1	0	1	1	5	2	4
Fairly good	44	57	48	33	41	61	73	69	74
Fairly bad	43	29	34	45	41	17	12	18	7
Very bad	4	3	3	3	3	2	1	1	1
Don't know	4	8	14	19	14	19	11	10	4
Total	99	100	100	100	100	100	100	100	100

cont.

	Italy			Italy	The Netherlands		
	Nov. 1985	Dec. 1985	Dec. 1987	Nov. 1985	Dec. 1985	Dec. 1987	
Very good	5	9	18	1	—	5	
Fairly good	51	59	76	35	48	83	
Fairly bad	27	15	4	53	41	7	
Very bad	9	4	1	9	6	1	
Don't know	8	13	2	2	6	4	
Total	100	100	101	100	101	100	

	West Germany					
	Nov. 1985	Nov. 1986	Jan. 1987	Nov. 1987	Dec. 1987	Mar. 1988	Jun. 1988
Very good	2	2	1	5	10	6	7
Fairly good	33	37	22	68	74	73	81
Fairly bad	54	53	60	21	13	14	9
Very bad	8	5	9	2	1	1	2
Don't know	4	3	8	5	2	6	2
Total	101	100	100	101	100	100	101

Question: How would you describe the current relations between the Soviet Union and the United States? Would you say relations between these two countries are very good, fairly good, fairly bad or very bad?

Sources: November 1985 Pre-Geneva Summit Telephone Survey; December 1985 Geneva Summit Telephone Survey; October 1986 Post-Reykjavik Summit Telephone Survey I; November 1986 Post-Reykjavik Summit Telephone Survey II; January 1987 Security Telephone Survey; November 1987 Pre-Washington Summit Telephone Survey; December 1987 Post-Washington Telephone Survey; March 1988 Pre-Moscow Summit Telephone Survey; June 1988 Post-Moscow Summit Telephone Survey.

Table A.7 Effects of US economic policies (per cent)

	Belgium		
	Oct. 1984	Oct. 1985	Oct. 1988
More helpful	15	21	34
More harmful	47	30	26
Little effect	27	32	24
Don't know	12	17	15
Total	101	100	99

	Britain											
	Jun. 1978	Apr. 1982	Apr. 1983	Mar. 1984	May 1984	Oct. 1984	Feb. 1985	Jun. 1985	Oct. 1985	Mar. 1986	Apr. 1987	Apr. 1988	Oct. 1988	May 1989
More helpful	28	15	10	11	10	7	6	13	15	16	22	17	20	23
More harmful	12	32	36	39	37	57	58	46	38	36	31	33	32	26
Little effect	32	34	39	32	38	25	20	29	33	36	34	31	30	35
Don't know	28	19	15	18	16	11	16	12	15	13	14	19	17	16
Total	100	100	100	100	101	100	100	100	101	101	101	100	99	100

cont.

Denmark

	Jun. 1985	Oct. 1985	Oct. 1987	Oct. 1988
More helpful	14	23	16	17
More harmful	51	29	27	18
Little effect	17	21	35	41
Don't know	18	27	21	23
Total	100	100	99	99

France

	Jun. 1978	Apr. 1982	Apr. 1983	Mar. 1984	Feb. 1985	Jun. 1985	Oct. 1985	Mar. 1986	Apr. 1987	Apr. 1988	Oct. 1988	May 1989
More helpful	21	11	8	8	7	15	11	13	24	18	20	11
More harmful	28	48	34	49	41	40	37	24	30	38	37	40
Little effect	20	27	27	20	23	15	32	33	24	23	29	29
Don't know	32	15	31	23	29	30	20	30	22	22	15	23
Total	101	101	100	100	100	100	100	100	100	100	101	101

Greece

	Oct. 1984	Oct. 1985	Oct. 1988
More helpful	11	19	22
More harmful	52	49	30
Little effect	19	12	16
Don't know	18	21	32
Total	100	101	100

Ireland

	Oct. 1984	Oct. 1985	Jun. 1985	Oct. 1985	Oct. 1988
More helpful	19	30	30	30	29
More harmful	27	15	15	15	14
Little effect	38	38	38	38	37
Don't know	16	17	17	17	20
Total	100	100	100	100	100

							Italy								
	Jun. 1978	Apr. 1982	Apr. 1983	Mar. 1984	May 1984	Oct. 1984	Feb. 1985	Jun. 1985	Oct. 1985	Mar. 1986	Apr. 1987	Apr. 1988	Oct. 1988	May 1989
More helpful	33	37	17	29	26	25	7	34	43	10	39	36	47	38
More harmful	30	34	37	35	28	41	34	38	22	38	25	20	19	24
Little effect	12	16	27	19	30	19	21	16	21	22	22	32	20	24
Don't know	25	13	19	18	16	16	38	12	14	31	14	12	14	14
Total	100	100	100	101	100	101	100	100	100	101	100	100	100	100

	The Netherlands				Portugal				Spain			
	Oct. 1984	Jun. 1985	Oct. 1985	Oct. 1988	Oct. 1984	Oct. 1985	Oct. 1988		Oct. 1984	Oct. 1985	Oct. 1988	
More helpful	27	27	40	34	17	31	30		13	20	18	
More harmful	37	43	25	25	21	12	8		43	30	29	
Little effect	22	15	19	17	8	12	19		15	13	21	
Don't know	14	15	17	25	55	44	42		29	37	31	
Total	100	100	101	101	101	99	100		100	100	99	

						West Germany							
	Jun. 1978	Apr. 1982	Apr. 1983	Mar. 1984	May 1984	Oct. 1984	Feb. 1985	Jun. 1985	Oct. 1985	Mar. 1986	Apr. 1987	Apr. 1988	Oct. 1988	May 1989
More helpful	19	22	13	15	10	20	5	16	35	13	23	18	37	20
More harmful	28	29	43	39	56	41	46	35	26	37	29	25	19	32
Little effect	29	27	23	29	31	26	27	29	26	28	27	33	29	30
Don't know	24	22	22	17	3	13	22	19	14	23	21	24	15	18
Total	100	100	101	100	100	100	100	99	101	100	100	100	100	100

cont.

Question: Do you think that the economic policies and actions of the United States have been more helpful or more harmful to the economic situation in our country, or have they had little effect on our country? (In 1983, the question asked about the effects of the economic policies and actions of President Reagan rather than the United States.)

Sources: Economic Summit Surveys from 1978 and 1982–89, May–June 1984 Security Survey, June–July 1985 Baseline Survey, Eurobarometer Surveys from October–November 1984, October–November 1985, and October 1988.

Notes and References

2 NATO AND WESTERN SECURITY

1. July 1982 Security Survey, July 1988 Security Survey, and Table 2 in Adler and Wertman (1981a).
2. The data are reported in *Eurobarometer*, no. 32 (December 1989) pp. 150–63. The EC-wide numbers are based on a weighted average taking into account the relative population of each country. Portugal and Spain, which joined the EC only in 1986, are not included here. The 1977 data are for nine countries only because Greece was not then yet a part of the EC. Excluding Greece from these data does not seriously harm the trend since Greece represents only 4 per cent of the EC's total population.
3. While the numbers differed somewhat from one country to the next, the same general trends and largely the same results occurred among most of the ten publics.
4. July 1981 Security Survey, February 1982 Gallup Survey reported in *Newsweek*, 15 March 1982, p. 9, and April 1983 INF Survey.
5. October 1981 Security Survey, December 1985 Geneva Summit Survey.
6. September 1987 Security Survey.
7. March 1981 Security Survey, July 1981 NATO Survey, October 1981 Security Survey, December 1981 INF Survey, July 1982 Security Survey, June–July 1985 Baseline Survey.
8. October 1981 Security Survey, July 1988 Security Survey.
9. March 1981 Security Survey, July 1981 NATO Survey, May–June 1984 Security Survey, April 1987 Eurobarometer, September 1987 Security Survey, October 1987 Scandinavian Survey.
10. June–July 1985 Baseline Survey.
11. July 1981 Security Survey, July 1988 Security Survey.
12. We have data for all NATO members except Iceland.
13. See Adler and Wertman (1981a) for full trend data on Britain, France, Italy and West Germany.
14. On Denmark, see the Copenhagen newspaper *Berlingske Tidende*, 12 July 1981, p. 5. On Norway, see Waldahl (1985) pp. 308–10. On the Netherlands, see Everts (1985) pp. 264–6.
15. Various questions along these lines were asked repeatedly in USIA surveys between 1981 and 1989.
16. The data, from the October 1989 Eurobarometer, are reported in *Eurobarometer*, no. 32 (December 1989) p. A40.
17. The data, from the October 1989 Eurobarometer, are reported in *Eurobarometer*, no. 32 (December 1989) p. 33.

18. For the March 1990 survey, see *Der Spiegel*, 23 April 1990. The June 1990 survey, conducted by Allensbach Institute, is reported in *The American Enterprise*, Vol. 1, no. 5 (September–October 1990), p. 98.
19. March 1981 Security Survey, September 1987 Security Survey, November 1987 Security Survey, July 1988 Security Survey, March 1989 Security Survey.
20. July 1981 NATO Survey, April 1982 Versailles Economic Summit Survey, July 1982 Security Survey, July–August 1983 INF Intensive Survey, May–June 1984 Security Survey, May 1985 Security Survey, December 1985 Geneva Summit Survey, February 1987 Security Survey. See also surveys in note 19.
21. April 1987 Eurobarometer, September 1987 Security Survey, October 1987 Scandinavian Survey, October 1988 Eurobarometer.
22. The British data are not a pure trend, but are strongly suggestive. The earlier data come from two personal interview surveys: the March 1981 Security Survey and the May–June 1984 Security Survey. The 1990 data come from a mid–January 1990 telephone survey conducted by MORI among 504 adults and were reported in *The Economist*, 27 January 1990, p. 49. Question wording varied slightly among the three surveys.
23. This finding comes from a Sinus Institute survey commissioned by the Friedrich-Ebert-Stiftung and *Stern*.
24. The data come from a Gallup International Survey reported in *Newsweek*, 15 March 1982, p. 9.
25. October 1981 Security Survey.
26. This 1980 West German survey was conducted by the German Armed Forces Institute for Social Research and was reported in Schoenborn (1981).
27. July 1988 Security Survey.
28. May–June 1984 Security Survey.
29. March 1986 Tokyo Economic Summit Survey, July 1986 Arms Control Survey, February 1987 Security Survey, September 1987 Security Survey, July 1988 Security Survey.
30. May 1987 INF Telephone Survey and September 1987 Reagan–Gorbachev Telephone Survey.
31. For President Carter's version, see Carter (1982) pp. 225–9.
32. October 1981 Security Survey.
33. May–June 1984 Security Survey, February 1985 Arms Control Survey.
34. For a more detailed discussion of attitudes on SDI, including the impact of different question wordings, see Adler (1987). Based on an examination of a variety of questions on SDI, Adler also found a decline in West European support for SDI in the 1985–6 period.
35. May–June 1984 Security Survey.
36. March 1981 Security Survey.
37. May–June 1984 Security Survey.
38. The 1980 British findings come from a Gallup personal interview survey of 1063 adults aged 16 and older conducted 10–15 September 1980 and reported in *New Society*, 25 September 1980, p. 603–5. The 1989 findings are from a December 1989 USIA survey.

3 INF DEPLOYMENT IN WESTERN EUROPE

1. This chapter does not intend to give an extensive history of the INF issue, but rather presents a synthetic overview of the major events related to INF in the 1977–87 period as a background for the public opinion data used in it. Many different sources were consulted on the history of the INF issue. These include: Sorrels (1983), Sigal (1984), Talbott (1984), Treverton (1985), Langer (1986), Dean (1987; 1988), Joffe (1987), Hunter (1988), Freedman (1989), Nitze (1989; 1990), Goldberg (1990), US Department of State (1990) and Wirthlin (1990).
2. Data on the SS-20's capabilities come from 'The Heart of the Explosion', *The Economist*, 1 September 1984, p. 8 and from *Newsweek*, 31 January 1983, pp. 18–19.
3. Data on the Pershing II's capabilities come from *The Economist*, 1 September 1984, pp. 8–11 and from *Newsweek*, 31 January 1983, pp. 18–19.
4. The details of the 'walk in the woods' compromise are given in Talbott (1984, pp. 116–51) and Nitze (1989, pp. 375–91).
5. Paul Nitze, the chief US negotiator in the INF talks, admitted in an interview with the authors that he made the same miscalculation as the Soviets. In late 1983, he also expected the demonstrations to intensify after deployment. Rudig (1988, p. 27) also makes the point that protest activity declined considerably after deployment.
6. During this period, deployment continued. In Spring 1985, deployment began in Belgium. The Dutch government, despite intense internal opposition, also permitted site preparations to go forward with a target of deployment in 1988; the INF Treaty made deployment in the Netherlands unnecessary.
7. The INF Treaty, in fact, even went a little further than Reagan's original proposal. The 'zero option' proposal had called for the elimination of all longer-range INF systems with a range of 1000 to 5500 kilometres; the INF Treaty also provided for the elimination of shorter-range INF systems with a range of 500–1000 kilometres. The INF Treaty eliminated all production and flight testing of the INF missiles immediately upon coming into effect.
8. For discussions of the anti-INF protest movement, see: Alting von Geusau (1985), Ceadel (1985), Graf von Kielmansegg (1985), Joffe (1987), Rudig (1988) and Kriesi (1989).
9. For the data in this paragraph, see Crewe (1985a, p. 31), Everts (1985, p. 244) and the October 1982 INF Survey.
10. This same question was asked in three surveys: April 1983 INF Survey (all five basing countries), June 1983 INF Survey (all five basing countries), and July–August 1983 INF Intensive Survey (Britain, Italy, and West Germany). Because results were similar in all three surveys, data for only one is presented.
11. Given the small number of demonstrators interviewed (9 per cent of the Dutch and 2–3 per cent elsewhere), these findings should be treated as broadly suggestive. To increase the number of cases available for analysis

and, therefore, the level of confidence, samples of demonstrators interviewed in separate surveys have been combined within each country. Confidence is further enhanced by the similarity of findings within each country across all surveys. The total number of demonstrators interviewed was: Belgium (24), Britain (92), Italy (129), the Netherlands (180), and West Germany (107).

12. April 1983 INF Survey (Britain, Italy, the Netherlands, and West Germany) and December 1983 INF Survey (Britain, Italy, and West Germany). The nine items on the list from which two could be picked were: 'the high level of unemployment; threat of war between the Soviet Union and NATO; inflation and the high cost of living; growth of Soviet military power; crime, violence, and safety on the streets; stationing of new nuclear missiles in our country; cuts in social and medical services; high level of defence spending; unfair trade practices by Japan'.
13. July–August 1983 INF Intensive Survey.
14. The question on how closely one followed the INF issue was in both the July–August 1983 INF Intensive Survey and the December 1983 INF Survey. The question on talking about INF was in the July–August 1983 INF Intensive Survey.
15. June 1983 INF Survey, July–August 1983 INF Intensive Survey.
16. Data in this paragraph are from the following USIA surveys: February 1982 Belgian Security Survey, February 1982 Poland–INF Survey, October 1982 INF Survey, April 1983 INF Survey, and July–August 1983 INF Intensive Survey.
17. A MORI survey of 1907 British adults in January 1983 found 50 per cent saying they were aware when asked, 'Are you aware of any current negotiations taking place between the United States and the Soviet Union on nuclear disarmament?'
18. Rattinger (1987, p. 513) makes the same point in his analysis of information questions relating to INF asked in West Germany.
19. This question about the talks, asked in the December 1983 INF Survey, was the same one asked in earlier 1982–83 surveys, only this time the correct answer was different.
20. September 1987 Security Survey.
21. The number of warheads was constantly updated in the various questions used by USIA from 450 in July 1981 to 800 by July–August 1983.
22. Over the 1983–85 period, the preface to this question was changed slightly to reflect the changed situation as deployment occurred. In addition, while the April 1983, June 1983, July–August 1983 and December 1983 questions referred to stationing in their country, the May–June 1984 and February 1985 questions referred to stationing in Western Europe. Nevertheless, this was basically the same question throughout. In the April 1983, June 1983 and July–August 1983 surveys, the information on the number of Soviet warheads was given in 3, 6 and 9 questions prior respectively. This may have impacted on attitudes a little, but not as much as when the information was in the same question or only one question before.
23. Though the MORI questions of October 1981 and January 1983 (January 1983a in Table 3.6) do not directly mention the USA, the majority

opposition is undoubtedly because the fact that these were American missiles was strongly suggested by the question wording, which asked whether Britain should or should not 'allow cruise missiles to be placed in Britain'.

24. This analysis was helped by Adler (1983a) and Rattinger (1985; 1987).
25. The question in the survey conducted for *Newsweek* was: 'If the United States and the Soviet Union cannot agree on limiting nuclear weapons by the end of 1983, should NATO proceed with its plan to deploy Pershing II and cruise missiles in Western Europe?' In the Netherlands, 33 per cent said yes, while 51 per cent said no. *Newsweek*, 31 January 1983, p. 17.
26. This question was asked by NIPO, which provided the results to the authors.
27. These data are from the July–August 1983 INF Intensive Survey. Interestingly, in a January 1983 MORI survey in Britain, among those aware of cruise missiles (77 per cent of the sample), 57 per cent mistakenly said that the original proposal to deploy cruise missiles in Europe came from the USA rather than from the European NATO members. Only 20 per cent thought that the original idea came from the Europeans.
28. The preceding data in this paragraph come from: October 1981 Security Survey, October 1982 INF Survey and December 1983 INF Survey.
29. The data on the proposals are from the following surveys: April 1982 Versailles Economic Summit Survey, October 1982 INF Survey, April 1983 INF Survey and June 1983 INF Survey. The Reagan–Gorbachev question on credit for arms control comes from the following three telephone surveys: May 1987 INF Telephone Survey, September 1987 INF Telephone Survey and November 1987 Pre-Washington Summit Telephone Survey. The data on US–Soviet arms control are from the September 1987 Security Survey.
30. September 1987 Security Survey, December 1987 Post-Washington Summit Telephone Survey, March 1988 Pre-Moscow Summit Telephone Survey.
31. Some conservative elites in Western Europe would have preferred an agreement under which *some* American INF missiles would have remained in Western Europe. Of course, many of the post-INF Treaty concerns mentioned here have been altered significantly by the changes in the Soviet Union and Eastern Europe since then.

4 THE AMERICAN IMAGE

1. See the remarks of Michael Solomon of Warner Brothers reported in *Broadcasting*, 9 April 1990, p. 57.
2. As opposed to the many articles on the amount of anti-Americanism, there has been surprisingly little written on the concept of anti-Americanism. Among the limited literature, see Haseler (1987), Spiro (1988) and Thornton (1988).
3. October 1981 Security Survey.

4. A great deal has been written about the 'successor generation'. On the 'successor generation' and foreign policy, see The Atlantic Council (1981) and Szabo (1983).
5. Of those who answered both the pro-/anti-Americanism question and the favourable opinion question, only 10 per cent in West Germany, 14 per cent in France, 15 per cent in Italy and 17 per cent in Britain gave a positive response on one and a negative response on the other. Virtually all these cases were changes between 'somewhat' responses on the two questions. September–October 1987 American Image Survey.
6. Whether to include the 'neither' option in the question has been long debated by survey researchers, proponents arguing that it is an important substantive category, opponents that it provides respondents too easy an escape.
7. The proportion among different party identifiers giving the anti-American response in the July 1988 Security Survey was: (1) in Britain, 34 per cent of Labour voters and 18 per cent of Conservatives; (2) in France, 22 per cent of Socialists, 8 per cent of UDF voters, and 4 per cent of RPR voters; (3) in West Germany, 23 per cent of Social Democrats and 13 per cent of Christian Democrats; and (4) in Italy, 43 per cent of Communists, 16 per cent of Socialists and 10 per cent of Christian Democrats.
8. September–October 1987 Eurobarometer.
9. June–July 1985 Baseline Survey.
10. These results are reported in *Newsweek*, 11 July 1983, pp. 44–50. About 500 adults were interviewed in each country by Gallup affiliates, with the British and French surveys done by telephone and the West German survey in person.
11. West German results are reported in Gorder (1984), Italian results in Wertman (1984).
12. September–October 1987 American Image Survey.
13. September–October 1987 American Image Survey.
14. September–October 1987 American Image Survey.
15. *Eurobarometer*, No. 25, June 1986, pp. 43–4.
16. September–October 1987 American Image Survey.
17. This question was asked in the following surveys: October–November 1984 Eurobarometer, June–July 1985 Baseline Survey, October–November 1985 Eurobarometer, April 1987 Eurobarometer, September–October 1987 American Image Survey, November 1987 Security Survey, and March 1989 Security Survey.
18. October–November 1984 Eurobarometer and October–November 1985 Eurobarometer.
19. The only time this was asked in the 1980s was in the December 1982 Correlation of Forces Survey. Earlier findings are from USIA Office of Research Reports M-31–72, M-34–72, M-36–72, M-37–72 and R-20–76.
20. July 1988 Security Survey.
21. September–October 1987 American Image Survey.
22. March–May 1982 Eurobarometer, March 1984 London Economic Summit Survey, February 1985 Bonn Economic Summit Survey.
23. May–June 1984 Security Survey, February 1985 Arms Control Survey, December 1985 Geneva Summit Survey, March 1986 Tokyo Economic

Summit Survey, February 1987 Security Survey and April 1988 Toronto Economic Summit Survey.
24. September–October 1987 American Image Survey.
25. June–July 1985 Baseline Survey, April 1987 Eurobarometer.
26. This result was found in many surveys analysed by the USIA Office of Research during the 1980s.
27. December 1982 Correlation of Forces Survey, May–June 1984 Security Survey, and September–October 1987 American Image Survey.
28. September 1987 Security Survey, October 1987 Scandinavian Survey.
29. October–November 1984 Eurobarometer.
30. The British results are from surveys done by Social Surveys (Gallup Poll) Ltd. The French results are from surveys by Brule' Ville Associes, reported in *Public Opinion*, vol. 12, No. 1 (May/June 1989) p. 29. The West German results are from Allensbach surveys reported in *Public Opinion*, vol. 12, No. 1 (May/June 1989) p. 27.
31. All the Carter and Reagan results are from surveys done by Social Surveys (Gallup Poll) Ltd.
32. May 1987 INF Telephone Survey, September 1987 Reagan–Gorbachev Telephone Survey, and November 1987 Pre-Washington Summit Telephone Survey.
33. All or most of these five items were asked in the following surveys: November 1985 Pre-Geneva Summit Telephone Survey, December 1985 Geneva Summit Telephone Survey, March 1986 Tokyo Economic Summit Survey, July 1986 Arms Control Survey and February 1987 Security Survey. These surveys are used individually rather than as part of any single trend.

5 THE SOVIET IMAGE AND PUBLIC DIPLOMACY

1. 'The Gorbachev Effect', *The Economist*, February 17–March 4, 1988, p. 38.
2. Surveys conducted in 1954 and throughout 1955 in Great Britain, France, Italy and West Germany found about 15 per cent or less held good opinions of the Soviet Union. Similar figures were found in 1955 in Austria and Belgium. These data were reported in 'Trends in Attitudes Toward the U.S. and the USSR in the Wake of the Summit Conference', Report 12, USIA Research and Reference Service (16 September 1955).

Surveys conducted in Norway in December 1955, November 1957, and June 1960 indicated that only 15 per cent or less of the Norwegian public held a good opinion of the Soviet Union. A May 1960 personal interview survey in Britain (13 per cent), France (16 per cent), and West Germany (2 per cent) found very few with good opinions of the USSR. These findings were reported in 'Post-Summit Trends in Norwegian Opinion of the U.S. and the USSR'. USIA, Office of Research and Analysis, WE-66. (July 1960).

Based on USIA Research Report, R-12-83, the Soviet image between 1956 and 1980 remained in the following ranges: Italy (-14 to -20),

FRG (−57 to −68), France (+8 to −22) and the UK (−6 to −34). For an overview of the Soviet image in Western Europe from the 1950s to 1970s see 'The 28th Report of the United States Advisory Commission on Information', May 1977, Chapter V.

3. June–July 1985 Baseline Survey.
4. 1989 Eurobarometer survey reported in *Eurobarometer, Public Opinion in the European Community*, no. 32. December 1989.
5. September 1987 and July 1988 Security Surveys.
6. December 1983 INF Survey and February 1984 Middle East Issues Survey. This question was also asked in both these surveys in Britain, Italy and West Germany but the option to volunteer 'neither pro- nor anti-Soviet' was not provided in Britain and West Germany so the data are not precisely compatible with the 1983 and 1984 Italian results nor the 1987 and 1988 surveys and therefore do not appear in the accompanying table.
7. Eurobarometer April 1987 Survey of the European Community public. This question was not asked in Luxembourg.
8. October 1987 Scandinavian Survey.
9. British Gallup has asked the question 'Do you approve or disapprove of the role Russia is now playing in world affairs?' since 1983 in Britain. The most recent data, as reported in *Public Opinion*, May/June 1989, showed a dramatic increase in the number of British who said they approved of Russia's role, from 7 per cent in August 1983 to 49 per cent in December 1988.
10. September 1985 Security Survey and December 1985 Geneva Summit Survey.
11. 'Gorbachev Becomes Mover and Shaker of Markets', *The Washington Post*, February, 1991. p. G1.
12. September 1987 Security Survey.
13. September Security Survey 1987.
14. December 1985 Geneva Summit Telephone Survey.
15. October–November 1986 Post-Reykjavik Summit Telephone Survey II.
16. June 1988 Post-Moscow Summit Telephone Survey.
17. October 1987 Scandinavian Survey.
18. March 1989 Security Survey.
19. September 1987 Reagan–Gorbachev Telephone Survey.
20. October 1987 Scandinavian Survey and the September 1987 Security Survey.
21. July 1988 Security Survey.
22. May 1989 Paris Economic Summit Survey.
23. March 1988 Pre-Moscow Summit Telephone Survey.
24. July 1987 INF Telephone Survey.
25. April–May 1980 Afghanistan and Iran Issues Survey.
26. September–October 1987 American Image Survey.
27. A March 1980 Gallup survey found that the British (62 per cent) and French (56 per cent) did not think their own country should boycott the 1980 Moscow Olympics because of the Russian invasion of Afghanistan. The prevailing opinion among Germans was that West Germany should

boycott the Olympics. Reported in 'W. Germans, British Want to See Limits on Support for U.S' *The Washington Post,* 17 April 1980, p. A33.
28. April–May 1980 Afghanistan and Iran Issues Survey.
29. October–November 1984 Eurobarometer survey in Belgium, France, Great Britain, Greece, Ireland, Italy, the Netherlands, Portugal, Spain and West Germany.
30. February 1987 Security Survey.
31. July 1987 INF Telephone Survey.
32. June 1988 Post-Moscow Summit Telephone Survey.
33. June–July 1985 Baseline Survey.
34. October 1987 Scandinavian Survey.
35. Eurobarometer telephone survey reported in *European Community News,* no. 39/90, 18 October 1990.
36. Soviet disinformation campaigns were particularly prevalent throughout the Third World. The Soviets frequently circulated stories that charged the USA with cultivating the AIDS virus, developing a bacteriological weapon that would kill Cubans and Africans and arranging for South American babies to be kidnapped so their organs could be sold for transplants. The baselessness of these stories became so apparent and widespread that during the end of the Reagan Administration, the Soviets agreed to relent. See 'Soviets Back Off Disinformation Drive', *The Washington Post,* 24 October 1989, p. D34.
37. Soviet disinformation and propaganda measures over the years have been well documented by a variety of governmental and private sources including Romerstein and Levchenko (1989), Ebon (1987) and US State Department (1987) 'Soviet Influence Activities: A Report on Active Measures and Propaganda 1986–1988'.
38. The terms propaganda and public diplomacy are used interchangeably here. See Chapter 1 for discussion of these terms.
39. 'How to Spot a Stuffed Dove', *The Economist,* 14 March 1981, p. 19.
40. The Soviets' constant reference to their commitment to peace and no first use of nuclear weapons even made its way into a well-publicised exchange between American schoolgirl Samantha Smith and Soviet leader Andropov. In a letter to Smith, the Soviet leader stated 'the Soviet Union solemnly declared to the world that it will never, but never, be the first to use nuclear weapons against any country'. 'Andropov Assures Maine Girl That His Nation Seeks Peace', *The New York Times,* 26 April 1983.
41. April 1981 Soviet Peace Initiatives Survey.
42. May–June 1984 Security Survey.
43. Mikhail Gorbachev, 'The International Community and Change: A Common European Home', Speech delivered to the Council of Europe, Strasbourg France, 6 July 1989. As reprinted in *Vital Speeches of the Day,* vol. LV, no. 23, 15 September 1989.
44. February 1987 Security Survey
45. September 1987 Reagan–Gorbachev Telephone Survey.
46. June–July 1985 Baseline Survey
47. 'Public Opinion in the European Community', *Eurobarometer,* no. 25, June 1986, p. 40. The Eurobarometer has asked the trustworthiness question regarding different people since the 1970s.

48. March 1986 Tokyo Economic Summit Survey.
49. July 1986 Arms Control Survey.
50. June–July 1985 Baseline Survey.
51. 'Bloodless Coup: Russians Are Coming to Bonn, and Germans Are Positively Aglow', *The Wall Street Journal*, 3 June 1988, p. 1.
52. '*Soviet Military Power: An Assessment of the Threat*', 1988, (Washington, DC: U.S. Government Printing Office) p. 20.
53. See chapter 1 of US Department of Defense, *Soviet Military Power*, 1990.
54. *Time*, 1 January 1990.

6 US–SOVIET RELATIONS

1. A SINUS survey of West Germans commissioned by Frederick-Ebert-Stiftung and *Stern* magazine in September 1988 found a similar improvement in West German perceptions of East–West relations. In 1983 only 9 per cent said East–West relations were good, 18 per cent in 1986 and 49 per cent in 1988.
2. March 1989 Security Survey.
3. US Information Agency, Research and Reference Service. 'General Conference Expectations and Confidence in Conference Participants'. Report 9, 11 July 1955. Question wording for reported data, 'In the forthcoming Four-Power Conference, what are the chances, in your opinion, of achieving beneficial results?' Sample size was approximately 800 in each country.
4. US Information Agency, Research and Reference Service. 'Opinion Reactions in Western Europe to the Four-Power Conference' SR-2, August 3, 1955. Personal interview survey conducted among 325–500 respondents during the week of 25 July 1955. Question wording: How much, if at all, do you think the conference contributed to the relaxation of international tensions – very much, somewhat, very little, or not at all? Results of combined 'very much' and 'somewhat' are Britain (80 per cent), Austria (75 per cent), Italy (65 per cent), West Germany (55 per cent) and France (54 per cent).
5. US Information Agency, Research and Reference Service. 'Flash Survey of Reactions in Major World Opinion Centers To Forthcoming Eisenhower–Khrushchev Visits', SR-11, 31 August 1959. This report provides 'the results of a co-ordinated series of Flash surveys of public reactions to the projected Eisenhower–Khrushchev visits in major world opinion centers in 16 countries. In most cases, the sampling was done in the capital or major city, although [three surveys provide] national coverage. Interviewing for these small samples [ranging from 200 to 348] was conducted 18 and 25 August 1959, by the international network of affiliated Gallup institutes in the following areas: Great Britain, Italy, Switzerland, Paris, Berlin, Oslo, Helsinki, The Hague, Athens'. Given the small sample sizes, the original author recommended that results should be taken more as suggestive than conclusive.

6. US Information Agency, Office of Research and Analysis. 'Post-Summit Trends in West German Opinion of the U.S. and the U.S.S.R.', WE-65, July 1960.
7. US Information Agency, Research and Reference Service. 'The Impact of the Kennedy–Khrushchev and Kennedy–De Gaulle Conferences on West European Public Opinion', A Preliminary Note (14 July 1961). Question wording for reported data: How much do you feel the conference accomplished in settling disputes between the Western powers and the Soviet Union – a great deal, some, only a little, hardly anything? Asked only of those who had heard of the conference. Data represent the preliminary returns from the first one-third of 600 case national samples. The personal interview surveys were conducted June–July, 1961. Data reported are combination of 'great deal' and 'some'.
8. US Information Agency, Office of Research and Assessment. 'Awareness and Anticipated Impact of the President's Visit to the Soviet Union', R-26-72 (16 May 1972).
9. A thorough analysis of US–Soviet relations during this time period is provided by Garthoff (1985).
10. British Prime Minister Margaret Thatcher described Gorbachev, after first meeting him in 1984, as someone that the West 'could do business with'.
11. December 1985 Geneva Summit Telephone Survey.
12. December 1985 Geneva Summit Telephone Survey.
13. December 1985 Geneva Summit Telephone Survey.
14. Although the superpowers did not reach an arms control agreement at Geneva, they did sign six bilateral agreements 'pledging co-operation on cultural and scientific exchanges, improved air safety, consular exchanges, research and environmental protection'. 'Recent US–Soviet Summits' *The Washington Post*, 1 November 1989, p. A20.
15. March 1986 Tokyo Economic Summit Survey.
16. *The Economist*, 11 October 1986, p. 24.
17. The events at Reykjavik have been recounted in the numerous memoirs written by arms control experts and former Reagan Administration officials. These include Nitze (1989); Talbott (1988); Mandelbaum and Talbott (1986) and Adelman (1989).
18. Nitze (1989, p. 435) writes 'For President Reagan, confining research, development, and testing of SDI to the laboratory was synonymous with consigning it to the trash heap. And that was what Gorbachev wanted to get out of the President at Reykjavik. There were, of course, many other problems still undecided, but the meeting broke up on that issue'.
19. According to Nitze (1990), the US Administration considered the Reykjavik a tremendous success, even though the press built up Reykjavik as a disaster.
20. Numerous books written about the Reagan Administration describe White House efforts to manage public opinion and media coverage. For example, Schieffer and Gates (1989) Mayer and McManus (1988) and Hertsfaard (1988).
21. See Robert C. Kaiser, 'Europe Loves the Bomb', *The Washington Post*, 16 November 1986 p. K5.

22. October 1986 Post-Reykjavik Summit Telephone Survey I.
23. October–November Post-Reykjavik Summit Telephone Survey II.
24. October 1986 Post-Reykjavik Summit Telephone Survey I. Those who were familiar with the Reykjavik summit are defined as those who said they had hear or read at least something about the summit.
25. July 1987 INF Telephone Survey.
26. February 1987 Security Survey.
27. December 1987 Post-Washington Summit Telephone Survey.
28. December 1987 Post-Washington Summit Telephone Survey. Personal interview surveys conduced by MORI in Britain (November 1987) and the Sample Institute in West Germany (December 1987) found that 61 per cent in Britain and 57 per cent in Germany thought the USA would honour an agreement with the Soviet Union to limit nuclear weapons. Likewise, 68 per cent in Britain and 55 per cent in Germany said it likely that the Soviet Union would honour such a treaty with the United States.
29. December 1987 Post-Washington Summit Telephone Survey.
30. UK: The Harris Centre, National sample of 1005; France: The Lou Harris Survey, National sample of 901; West Germany: EMNID Institut, National sample of 1000. Survey data reported in *World Opinion Update*, vol. XII, Issue 1, January 1988, pp. 2–3.

    Question: As you know, the INF treaty abolishing US and Soviet intermediate nuclear forces was signed at the summit. To stabilise international relations, which *one* do you think is the *most* critical and urgent issue to address after the summit from the list I am now going to read to you – further bilateral (US and Soviet) reduction of strategic and tactical nuclear weapons; reduction of conventional weapons (by the U.S. and Soviets); solution of regional conflicts such as the war between Iran and Iraq, and the fighting in Afghanistan and Nicaragua; human rights issues; or relations between industrialised nations and third world nations, such as economic development aid?
31. June 1988 Post-Moscow Summit Telephone Survey.
32. June 1988 Post-Moscow Summit Telephone Survey.

7 US PUBLIC DIPLOMACY EFFORTS IN WESTERN EUROPE

1. Charles Z. Wick (March 1988) statement before US House Appropriations Committee.
2. National Security Decision Directive 77, 14 January 1983 as reprinted in full in *Staar*, 1986, pp. 297–299.
3. US Information Agency Fact Sheet, February 1989, p. 1.
4. For several examples of US successful information campaigns, especially the INF deployment in Europe, see Thompson (1987) pp. 302–316.
5. An example of the importance of site selection was revealed by Michael Deaver, the Reagan White House image maker, when he said, referring to the Economic Summit hosted in Williamsburg, 'one reason we picked Williamsburg was because of the visuals'. *National Journal*, 6 June 1990, p. 1420.
6. USIA Factsheet, February 1989.

7. USIA news release, 26 March 1990.
8. 'WORLDNET: Putting Satellite Technology to Work for Global Understanding' (undated) USIA Worldnet.
9. 'USIA's WorldNet Promotes "Good Guys", but Who's Watching?' *Washington Post*, 1 June 1988.
10. 1989 Annual Report of the US Advisory Commission on Public Diplomacy, p. 44.
11. 1989 Annual Report of the US Advisory Commission on Public Diplomacy, p. 44.
12. 'Proposed USIA/TV's Strategic Objectives and Priorities' (1990) Office of the Director, Television and Film Service, USIA.
13. 'Bush's Initiatives Implemented, USIA Officials in Hungary,' Daily News of the Hungarian News Agency MTI, Budapest. October 7, 1989. Provided by USIA Film and Television Service.

8 COMBATTING INTERNATIONAL TERRORISM

1. For an in-depth description of the many terrorist groups operating in Western Europe and throughout the Middle East, see *Terrorist Group Profiles*, November 1988 (Washington, DC: Government Printing Office).
2. *The Economist*, 6 February 1982 p. 43–44.
3. *Terrorist Group Profiles* (1988) (Washington, DC: U.S. Government Printing Office).
4. For a discussion of West European government attitudes on US-sponsored economic sanctions, see Palmer (1988, p. 14–15). During the 1980s the USA asked its West European allies to apply economic sanctions against the Soviet Union for the imposition of martial law in Poland. Following martial law in Poland in December 1981, the Reagan Administration embargoed the shipment of oil and gas equipment to the Soviet Union. As well, President Reagan extended this embargo to American licensed equipment sold by European companies. This struck at the economic heart of the European–Soviet siberian natural gas pipeline project. Not surprisingly, this US action caused ill will among West Europeans.
5. March–April 1985 Terrorism Survey.
6. March–April 1985 Terrorism Survey.
7. March-April 1985 Terrorism Survey.
8. June 1986 Terrorism Survey. Figures reported are total of moderate and great threat. Similar results were found in the April 1987 Venice Economic Summit Survey.
9. New York Times/CBS News personal interview survey conducted by MORI in February 1986. Reported in *The New York Times*, 9 March 1986, p. 1. Question wording: (Show Card) Which, if any, of these countries and organizations are involved in the planning and financing of international terrorist attacks such as airplane hijackings, bomb attacks and so on?
10. March–April 1985 Terrorism Survey.

11. Speech delivered by President Reagan 14 April 1986 as reprinted in *Vital Speeches of the Day*, vol.LII, no.14, 14 May 1986.
12. US Information Agency, Foreign Media Reaction Report, 7 April 1986.
13. US Information Agency, Foreign Media Reaction Report, 12 April 1986.
14. *The Times*, 15 April, 1986, p. 7.
15. USIA Foreign Media Reaction, 9 April 1986.
16. April 1986 Pre-Libya Raid Telephone Survey.
17. *The Economist*, 19 April 1986, p. 18. For a complete analysis of the US airstrike against Libya and the events leading up to it, see Davis (1989).
18. *The Economist*, 19 April, 1986, p. 11.
19. USIA, Special Foreign Media Reaction Report, 16 April 1986.
20. USIA, Foreign Media Reaction Report, 11 April 1986.
21. USIA, Foreign Media Reaction Report, 16 April 1986.
22. USIA, Special Foreign Media Reaction Report. 24 April 1986.
23. USIA Special Foreign Media Reaction Report. 21 April 1986.
24. USIA Special Foreign Media Reaction Report, 24 April 1986.
25. For a round-up on reaction of West European governments to the US air strike, see *The Economist*, 19 April 1986, pp. 23–25.
26. *The Times*, 19 April 1986, p. 1.
27. Speech delivered by President Reagan on 14 April 1986, as reprinted in *Vital Speeches of the Day*, Vol. LII, no. 14, 1 May 1986.
28. *The Times*, 16 April 1986, p. 1.
29. The MORI telephone poll was conducted 15–16 April, 1986 and reported in *The Times*, 17 April 1986. Question wording: Do you think that Mrs Thatcher was right or wrong to give President Reagan permission to for American bombers to fly from British bases to participate in the attack on Libya? The Gallup telephone survey of 1095 adults was conducted 15–16 April 1986, and reported in the *Daily Telegraph*, 17 April 1986. The question wording Do you think that the Government was right or wrong to allow the Americans to use air bases in Britain for their attack on Libya?
30. Telephone survey conducted by Centrum in Amsterdam on 15 April 1986 among 600 adults age 18 and over. Survey results reported in the *Algemeen Dagblad*, 17 April 1986, p. 1.
31. Swiss survey of 1011 adults conducted by Aktueller ISOP -Forschungs-sauftrag in May 1986. Reported in *World Opinion Update*, vol. X, no. 7, July 1986, p. 74.
32. April 1986 Post-Libya Raid Telephone Survey.
33. A great deal of debate took place during this time period over Libya's exact role in supporting terrorism abroad. Several years later, on 26 October 1989, the *New York Times* (p. A6) reported that during an interview with a Cairo weekly magazine, Colonel Qaddafi admitted to supporting terrorist groups. He is reported to have said 'At one point, we supported some of these groups without meticulously examining their aims and role. But when we discovered that these groups were causing more harm than benefit to the Arab cause, we halted our aid to them completely and withdrew our support'. The *New York Times* further quotes Qaddafi from the Cairo source as saying 'We erroneously thought that these groups could be part of the national liberation movement. But

we found out that they were practicing terrorism for the sake of terrorism and for other objectives that had nothing to do with our national cause'. Furthermore, information surfaced in public sources confirming a Libyan role in the night club bombing as East German intelligence agents defected to West Germany in 1990 prior to scheduled German unification and 'provided independent confirmation of previous US intelligence that agents based at the Libyan embassy in East Berlin provided logistical help' for the bombing. The *Washington Post* 'East German Defectors Bring Intelligence Lode'. 21 June 1990, p. A27.
34. April 1986 Post-Libya Raid Telephone Survey.
35. Some concern for terrorist retaliation against Western countries was justified. For example, immediately after the US air strike, Libya attacked a radar installation used by the US on the Italian island of Lampedusa. However, no casualties were reported, *The Times*, 16 April 1986, p. 1.
36. June 1986 Terrorism Survey.
37. June 1986 Terrorism Survey.
38. June 1986 Terrorism Survey.
39. *Terrorist Group Profiles*, 1988, (Washington, DC: U.S. Government Printing Office), p. 3.
40. June 1986 Terrorism Survey.
41. April 1987 Venice Economic Summit Survey.
42. *Terrorist Group Profiles*, 1988, (Washington, DC: Government Printing Office), p. 24.
43. *The Economist*, 5 December 1987, pp. 54–55; and 12 December 1987, p. 52.
44. For a discussion of President Reagan's stated policy of not negotiating for hostages, see Regan (1988), p. 34.
45. For greater detail on US operations and objectives in Lebanon, see Woodward (1987).
46. A MORI poll in Britain and a Sample poll in West Germany conducted December 1986 asked the question 'Generally speaking, do you approve or disapprove of President Reagan's dealings with Iran?' Data reported in Robert M. Worcester, 'Attitudes to America, Americans, American Foreign and Defence Policy and to American Multinational Companies in Britain'. Paper prepared for Institute of US Studies, Institute of Historical Research, University of London, 10 November 1989.
47. July 1987 INF Telephone Survey.
48. *The Economist*, 11 November 1986, p. 20.

9 US–WEST EUROPEAN ECONOMIC RELATIONS

1. This chapter is a revised, expanded version of Smith and Wertman (1989). Unlike the article, however, this chapter does not include American, Canadian, or Japanese public opinion.
2. The twelve members of the European Community are Belgium, Denmark, France, Greece, Ireland, Italy, Luxembourg, the Netherlands, Portugal, Spain, the United Kingdom and West Germany.

3. For an overview of the origins and development of the Economic Summits, see Bayne (1987), Merlini (1984), and Putnam and Bayne (1984). On the logistics and procedures of the Economic Summits, see Wallis (1990).
4. USIA conducted a survey on economic issues before every Economic Summit between 1976 and 1989. Except where noted, the data in this chapter come from these surveys. More details on all USIA surveys are given in Appendix 2.
5. December 1982 Correlation of Forces Survey, September–October 1987 American Image Survey.
6. October–November 1984 Eurobarometer. The six choices in the list, from which only one could be picked were: 'Worldwide recession', 'Developments within our own country', 'American economic policies', 'Japanese economic policies', 'EEC economic policies', and 'Low cost imports from the less developed countries'.
7. April 1983 Williamsburg Economic Summit Survey, March 1984 London Economic Summit Survey, and October 1983 survey co-ordinated for the Atlantic Institute by Louis Harris France. The number of cases for the Atlantic Institute survey was: Britain (1036), France (1023), Italy (956) and West Germany (943).
8. The data come from the *OECD Monitoring and Outlook Report* and are reported in US Department of Agriculture (1990), p. 5.
9. The OECD is the Organization for Economic Co-operation and Development. The data are reported in *Financial Times*, 14–15 July 1990, p. 6, and *International Herald Tribune*, 9 July 1990, p. 5.
10. The Spring 1987 data reported in this section on agriculture come from an in-depth series of questions included in the European Community's Eurobarometer conducted in March–April 1987 in all twelve member countries. The percentages given in this section for the EC public as a whole are weighted averages taking into account the relative population of each of the twelve member countries.
11. The two questions used in this paragraph are: (1) in the April 1987 and April 1988 Economic Summit Surveys, 'Do you think (Survey Country) should subsidise farmers to guarantee them a certain price for their products, or do you think we should not give government subsidies to our farmers because we cannot afford such subsidies?'; and (2) in the October 1988 Eurobarometer and May 1989 Paris Economic Summit Survey, 'Now some questions about the agricultural policy of the European Community. Do you favour or oppose the agricultural policy of the European Community which guarantees farmers a certain price for their products? Is that strongly or somewhat?'
12. October–November 1985 Eurobarometer. The question is: 'Some people say that we should not impose customs duties on food imports from outside the European Community because that increases the price we must pay for our food. Others say that these duties on imported food are necessary to protect our farmers from foreign competition and to avoid becoming dependent on imported food. Which of these views is closer to your own?'

13. April 1983 and February 1985 Economic Summit Surveys. The question is: 'Do you think (Survey Country) should subsidize our farmers to make it easier for them to sell (Survey Country's) farm products outside Europe, or do you think our farmers should not receive government subsidies even if that means some loss of sales outside Europe?'
14. March–April 1987 Eurobarometer. The question asked the respondent if he/she agreed or disagreed with the following statement: 'If we are going to continue to sell our farm products in world markets, we must, if necessary, subsidise them with the taxes we pay'.
15. Following the sweeping changes in Eastern Europe and the Soviet Union, the USA, under pressure from many West European governments, agreed in June 1990 to cut many high technologies from the restricted list.
16. January 1982 West German Security Survey.
17. February 1982 Poland–INF Survey.
18. April 1982 and April 1983 Economic Summit Surveys.

EPILOGUE: THE GULF CONFLICT

1. All findings in this paragraph come from coordinated telephone surveys conducted in mid-December in Britain, France, Italy, Spain, and West Germany by local Gallup affiliates. Approximately 500 adults aged 18 and older were interviewed in each country. In Germany, only those in the former West Germany were interviewed. In Spain, the survey was conducted only in major urban areas.
2. January 1991 Gulf War Telephone Survey. In Germany, only those in the former West Germany were interviewed. In Spain, the survey was conducted only in major urban areas.
3. The surveys in West Germany, all done by telephone, which reported these findings were: (1) 12–15 November 1990 survey by Forchungsgruppe Wahlen on behalf of ZDF German Television and *Suddeutsche Zeitung*; (2) mid-December survey by Emnid reported in note 1; (3) 21–23 January Emnid survey reported in *Der Spiegel*, 28 January 1991, pp. 32–8; and (4) early February Infas survey on behalf of Cologne Westdeutscher Rundfunk Network.
4. The surveys in Britain, all done by telephone, which found these results were: (1) 30 January–1 February 1991 survey of 1,042 adults by NOP reported in *The Sunday Times*, 3 February 1991, p. 2; (2) early February 1990 Gallup survey reported in *Daily Telegraph*, 8 February 1991, p. 4, which also reports the Gallup finding on the Falklands War; (3) 8–9 February 1991 survey by ICM (International Communications and Marketing Research) reported in *The Guardian*, 14 February 1991, p. 1; and (4) 8–11 February 1991 Gallup survey reported in *The American Enterprise*, Vol. 2, No. 2 (March/April 1991), p. 83.
5. The surveys in France were: (1) 23 January 1991 SOFRES survey of 800 adults aged 18 and older reported in *Le Figaro*, 25 January 1991, p. 6; (2) 26 January 1991 BVA survey reported in *Liberation*, 5 February 1991, p. 9; (3) 13 February 1991 SOFRES survey of 500 adults aged 18 and older

reported in *Le Figaro*, 15 February 1991, p. 6; (4) 24 February 1991 BVA survey reported in *The American Enterprise*, Vol. 2, No. 2 (March/April 1991), p. 81; and (5) 28 February–1 March 1991 BVA survey of 1,005 adults aged 18 and older reported in *Liberation*, 4 March 1991, pp. 9–10. The two surveys by SOFRES were done by telephone. The sources did not specify whether the BVA surveys were done in person or by telephone.

6. The 4–5 February 1991 survey was conducted by telephone by DOXA and reported in *La Repubblica*, 12 February 1991, p. 7. The three successive telephone surveys, conducted by SWG on 11–12 February 1991, 19–20 February 1991, and 26 February 1991, are reported in *Panorama* on 24 February 1991, p. 49; 3 March 1991, p. 51; and 10 March 1991, p. 53, respectively.
7. Both surveys were done by telephone: (1) 21–23 January Emnid survey reported in *Der Spiegel*, 28 January 1991, pp. 32–8; and (2) early February Infas survey on behalf of Cologne Westdeutscher Rundfunk Network.
8. These Spanish findings come from a 31 January 1991 Demoscopia survey conducted among 800 adults aged 18 and older by telephone in municipalities throughout the country with 2,000 or more inhabitants. The survey was reported in *El Pais*, 1 February 1991, p. 9.
9. January 1991 Gulf War Telephone Survey.
10. January 1991 Gulf War Telephone Survey.

Select Bibliography

Abshire, D. (1989) 'Don't Muster Out NATO Yet: Its Job is Far from Done', *The Wall Street Journal*, 11 December 1989, p. A14.
Adelman, K. (1986) 'The Road from Reykjavik', *World Affairs*, vol. 149, no. 1, p. 11.
Adelman, K. (1989) *The Great Universal Embrace: Arms Summitry – A Skeptic's Account* (New York: Simon and Schuster).
Adler, K. (1983a) 'New German Polls Show Widespread and Increasing Opposition to INF Stationing', USIA Office of Research, 25 November 1983.
Adler, K. (1983b) 'Text of INF Questions Asked in West Germany, Summer 1983', USIA Office of Research.
Adler, K. (1984a) 'Polling the Attentive Public', *The Annals of the American Academy of Political and Social Science*, vol. 472 (March 1984), pp. 143–54.
Adler, K. (1984b) 'West Europeans See Many Similarities in Superpower Actions, But Continue to View U.S. Less Negatively Than USSR', Report M-10/3/84, USIA Office of Research.
Adler, K. (1987) 'West European Opinion on SDI: Questions Plain and A La Mode', Paper presented at the Annual Conference of the American Association of Public Opinion Research, May 1987.
Adler, K. and D. Wertman (1981a) 'West European Security Concerns for the Eighties: Is NATO in Trouble?', Paper presented at the Annual Conference of the American Association of Public Opinion Research, May 1981.
Adler, K. and D. Wertman (1981b) 'Is NATO in Trouble? A Survey of Public Attitudes', *Public Opinion*, vol. 4, no. 4, pp. 8–12, 50.
Allen, C. and P. Diehl (1988) 'The Defence Issue in West Germany: Constraints on Increased Military Allocations', *Armed Forces and Society*, vol. 15, no. 1, pp. 93–112.
Alting von Geusau, F.A.M. (1985) 'Pacifism in the Netherlands', in W. Lacquer and R. Hunter (eds), *European Peace Movements and the Future of the Atlantic Alliance* (New Brunswick, NJ: Transaction Books) pp. 191–217.
The Atlantic Council, Working Group on the Successor Generation (1981) *The Successor Generation* (Washington, D.C.: The Atlantic Council).
Bayne, N. (1987) 'Twelve Years of Summits: A Balance-Sheet', Paper presented at the Istituto per gli Studi di Politica Internazionale, Milan, Italy, 27 May 1987.
Bergsten, C.F. (1988) *America in the World Economy: A Strategy for the 1990s* (Washington, D.C.: The Institute for International Economics).
Bissell, R. (1986) 'Research on Public Diplomacy', in R. Staar (ed.), *Public Diplomacy: USA Versus USSR* (Stanford, CA: Hoover Institution Press), pp. 210–25.
Brandt, W. (1983) 'Willy Brandt's Plea: It's Not Too Late for an Arms Deal', *The Washington Post*, 7 August 1983, p. C2.

Bundy, M., G. Kennan, R. McNamara, and G. Smith (1982) 'Nuclear Weapons and the Atlantic Alliance', *Foreign Affairs*, vol. 60, no. 4, pp. 753–68.
Cannon, L. (1991) *Ronald Reagan: The Role of a Lifetime* (New York: Simon & Schuster).
Capra, F. and C. Spretnak (1989) *Green Politics* (New York: E.P. Dutton, Inc.).
Carter, J. (1982) *Keeping Faith: Memoirs of a President* (New York: Bantam Books).
Ceadel, M. (1985) 'Britain's Nuclear Disarmers', in W. Lacquer and R. Hunter (eds), *European Peace Movements and the Future of the Atlantic Alliance* (New Brunswick, NJ: Transaction Books) pp. 218–44.
Cockburn, L. (1987) *Out of Control: The Story of the Reagan Administration's Secret War in Nicaragua, the Illegal Arms Pipeline, and the Contra Drug Connection* (New York: Atlantic Monthly).
Converse, P. (1987) 'Changing Conceptions of Public Opinion in the Political Process', *Public Opinion Quarterly*, vol. 51 (Winter Supplement) pp. 512–24.
Crespi, L. (1977) 'Some Indications of Trends and Current Opinions About the U.S. in Western Europe', in *The 28th Annual Report of the United States Advisory Commission on Information*, pp. 91–105.
Crespi, L. (1982a) 'West European Perceptions of the U.S.' Paper presented to the conference of the International Society of Political Psychology, Washington, D.C.
Crespi, L. (1982b) 'U.S. Standing in West European Public – Some Long Term Trends', Report R-13–82, USIA Office of Research, July 1982.
Crespi, L. (1983) 'Does West European Public Opinion Support the NATO Doctrine of Flexible Response?', Special Report, USIA Office of Research, October 1983.
Crespi, L. (1984) 'Comparative Effectiveness of Themes for Promoting Support for INF in Western Europe', Report R-7-84, USIA Office of Research, February 1984.
Crewe, I. (1985a) 'Britain: Two and a Half Cheers for the Atlantic Alliance', in G. Flynn and H. Rattinger (eds.), *The Public and Atlantic Defence* (Totowa, NJ: Rowman and Allanheld) pp. 11–68.
Crewe, I. (1985b) 'How to Win a Landslide Without Really Trying: Why the Conservatives Won in 1983', in A. Ranney (ed.), *Britain at the Polls, 1983: A Study of the General Election* (Durham, NC: Duke University Press) pp. 155–96.
Crewe, I. (1987) 'Why the British Don't Like Us Anymore', *Public Opinion*, vol. 9, no. 6, pp. 51–6.
Davis, B. (1989) *Qadaffi, Terrorism, and the Origins of the U.S. Attack on Libya* (New York: Praeger).
Dean, J. (1987) *Watershed in Europe: Dismantling the East–West Military Confrontation* (Lexington, Massachusetts: Lexington Books).
Dean, J. (1988) 'The INF Treaty Negotiations', in *SIPRI Yearbook 1988* (London: Oxford University Press) pp. 375–94.
Deibel, T. (1989) 'Reagan's Mixed Legacy', *Foreign Policy*, no. 75, pp. 34–55.
Den Oudsten, E. (1987) 'Public Opinion on Peace and War', in *SIPRI Yearbook 1986* (London: Oxford University Press) pp. 17–35.

Ebon, M. (1987) *The Soviet Propaganda Machine* (New York: McGraw Hill).
Ederma, V. (1986a) 'West European Press Critical of US, But Also of European Inaction After U.S. Strike at Libya', Report FMA- 4/24/86, USIA Office of Research.
Ederma. V. (1986b) 'West European Press Judge Strike Against Libya Misguided: Only a Few Note Qaddafi Quiescent', Report FMA- 8/4/86, USIA Office of Research.
Ederma, V. (1986c) 'West European Press on US–Iran: The President Regains Some Credibility During a 'Crisis of Confidence'', Report FMA-12/10/86, USIA Office of Research.
Ederma, V. (1987) 'West European Press Apprehensive That the Iran Affair May Paralyze U.S. Foreign Policy', Report FMA-1/21/87, USIA Office of Research.
Ederma, V. (1988a) 'Even Conservative West European Press Supports INF Treaty, Opposition Strongest in France', Report FMA-4/5/88, USIA Office of Research, 5 April 1988.
Ederma, V. (1988b) 'West European Papers Call Moscow Summit 'The Good Atmosphere Summit'', Report FMA-6/10/88, USIA Office of Research.
Eichenberg, R. (1982) 'Pacifism or Pragmatism? Public Opinion on National Security Issues in Western Europe and the United States', Paper presented at the Annual Meeting of the International Studies Association, 24–28 March 1982.
Eichenberg, R. (1983) 'The Myth of Hollanditis', *International Security*, vol. 8, no. 2, pp. 143–159.
Elliot, K. (1989) 'Too Many Voices of America', *Foreign Policy*, no. 76, pp. 113–131.
Everts, P. (1985) 'Public Opinion on Nuclear Weapons, Defence, and Security: The Case of the Netherlands', in G. Flynn and H. Rattinger (eds), *The Public and Atlantic Defence* (Totowa, NJ: Rowman and Allanheld) pp. 221–74.
Flynn, G. (1985) 'Poltics, Publics, and Changing Images of Security', in G. Flynn, E. Moreton, and G. Treverton, *Public Images of Western Security* (Paris: The Atlantic Institute for International Affairs) pp. 7–14.
Flynn, G., E. Moreton, and G. Treverton (1985) *Public Images of Western Security* (Paris: The Atlantic Institute for International Affairs).
Flynn, G. and H. Rattinger (1985) 'The Public and Atlantic Defence', in G. Flynn and H. Rattinger (eds), *The Public and Atlantic Defence* (Totowa, NJ; Rowman and Allanheld) pp. 365–88.
Freedman, L. (1989) 'The Future of NATO's Deterrent Posture: Nuclear Weapons and Arms Control', in S. Sloan (ed.), *NATO in the 1990s* (Washington, D.C.: Pergamon-Brassey's) pp. 263–97.
Fritsch-Bournazel, R. (1985) 'France: Attachment to a Nonbinding Relationship', in G. Flynn and H. Rattinger (eds), *The Public and Atlantic Defence* (Totowa, NJ: Rowman and Allanheld) pp. 69–100.
Garthoff, R. (1985) *Detente and Confrontation: American–Soviet Relations from Nixon to Reagan* (Washington, D.C.: The Brookings Institution).
Gibson, D. (1988) 'Listening to VOA Europe in Munich, W. Germany', Report R-8-88, USIA Office of Research.
Gibson, D. (1989) 'Listening to VOA Europe in Oslo, Norway', Report R-11-89, USIA Office of Research.

Gibson, D. (1990) 'Listening to VOA Europe in Milan, Italy', Report R-4-90, USIA Office of Research.
Gladdish, K. (1987) 'The Centre Holds: The 1986 Netherlands Election', *West European Politics*, vol. 10, no. 1, pp. 115-19.
Goldberg, A. (1990) 'Moscow's INF Experience', in M. Mandelbaum (ed.), *The Other Side of the Table: The Soviet Approach to Arms Control* (New York: Council on Foreign Relations Press) pp. 89-120.
Golden, J. (1982) *NATO Burden-Sharing: Risks and Opportunities* (New York: Praeger).
Gorder, C. (1984) 'West German's 'Successor Generation': Views of American Society', Report M-3/8/84, USIA Office of Research, 8 March 1984.
Gordon, M. (1987) 'Dateline Washington: INF – A Hollow Victory', *Foreign Policy*, no. 68, pp. 159-79.
Graf von Kielmansegg, P. (1985) 'The Origins and Aims of the German Peace Movement', in W. Lacquer and R. Hunter (eds), *European Peace Movements and the Future of the Atlantic Alliance* (New Brunswick, NJ: Transaction Books) pp. 318-38.
Grant, S. (1986) 'Soviet Public Diplomacy and the 27th Party Congress', Report M-4/24/86, USIA Office of Research.
Green, F. (1988) *American Propaganda Abroad* (New York: Hiprocene Books).
Hansen, A. (1989) *Public Diplomacy in the Computer Age* (New York: Praeger).
Haseler, S. (1987) *The Varieties of Anti-Americanism* (Washington, D.C.: Ethics and Public Policy Center).
Henning, C.R. (1987) *Macroeconomic Diplomacy in the 1980s: Domestic Politics and International Conflict Among the United States, Japan, and Europe* (Atlantic Paper No. 65) (London: Croom Helm).
Hertsgaard, M. (1988) *On Bended Knee: The Press and the Reagan Presidency* (New York: Farrar Straus Giroux).
Hinckley, R. (1988) 'Public Attitudes Toward Key Foreign Policy Events', *Journal of Conflict Resolution*, vol. 32, no. 2, pp. 295-318.
Hinckley, R. (1990) 'Information Technology and Foreign Policy', in *Paradigms Revisited: The Annual Review of Communications and Society*, The Institute for Information Studies, pp. 45-76.
Hitchcock, D. (1988) *U.S. Public Diplomacy* (Washington, D.C.: The Center for Strategic and International Studies).
Hopmann, P.T. and F. Barnaby (eds) (1988) *Rethinking the Nuclear Weapons Dilemma in Europe* (London: Macmillan).
Hormats, R. (1989) 'Redefining Europe and the Atlantic Link', *Foreign Affairs*, vol. 68, no. 4, pp. 71-91.
Howard, M. (1988) 'A West European Perspective on Reagan', *Foreign Affairs*, vol. 67, no. 1, pp. 478-93.
Hughes, R. (1990) *SDI: A View from Europe* (Washington: National Defense University Press).
Hunter, R. (1988) 'After the INF Treaty: Keeping America in Europe', *SAIS Review*, vol. 8, no. 2, pp. 151-71.
Hunter, R. (1990) 'The Future of European Security', *The Washington Quarterly*, vol. 13, no. 4, pp. 55-68.

Huntington, S. (1983) 'Conventional Deterrence and Conventional Retaliation in Europe', *International Security*, vol. 8, no. 3, pp. 32–56.
Huygen, M. (1986) 'Dateline Holland: NATO's Pyrrhic Victory', *Foreign Policy*, no. 62, pp. 167–85.
Imbert, C. (1989) 'The End of French Exceptionalism', *Foreign Affairs*, vol. 68, no. 4, pp. 48–60.
Joffe, J. (1987) 'Peace and Populism: Why the European Anti- Nuclear Movement Failed', *International Security*, vol. 11, no. 4, pp. 3–40.
Johnson, P. (1989) 'Europe and the Reagan Years', *Foreign Affairs*, vol. 68, no. 7, pp. 28–38.
Kaplan, L. (1988) *NATO and the United States: The Enduring Alliance* (Boston: Twayne Publishers).
Kegley, C. and E. Wittkopf (1982) *American Foreign Policy: Pattern and Process* (Second Edition) (New York: St. Martin's Press).
Kellner, P. (1985) 'The Labour Campaign', in A. Ranney (ed.), *Britain at the Polls, 1983: A Study of the General Election* (Durham, NC: Duke University Press) pp. 65–80.
Kriesi, H. (1989) 'The Political Opportunity Structure of the Dutch Peace Movement', *West European Politics*, vol. 12, no. 3, pp. 295–312.
Langer, P. (1986) *Transatlantic Discord and NATO's Crisis of Cohesion* (Washington, D.C.: Pergamon-Brassey's).
Lyne, R. (1987) 'Making Waves: Gorbachev's Public Diplomacy, 1985–1986', in R. Laird (ed.), *Soviet Foreign Policy* (Montpelier, Vermont: Capital City Press) pp. 235–53.
Mako, W. (1983) *U.S. Ground Forces and the Defence of Central Europe* (Washington, D.C.: The Brookings Institution).
Mandelbaum, M. (1984) 'The Anti-Nuclear Weapons Movement', *PS*, vol. XVII, no. 1, pp. 24–32.
Mandelbaum, M. and S. Talbott (1986) 'Reykjavik and Beyond', *Foreign Affairs*, vol. 65, no. 2, pp. 215–35.
Markovits, A. (1989) 'Anti-Americanism and the Struggle for West German Identity', in P. Merkl (ed.), *The Federal Republic of Germany at Forty* (New York: New York University Press).
Mayer, J. and D. McManus (1988) *Landslide: The Unmaking of the President 1984–1988* (Boston: Houghton Mifflin Company).
Merlini, C. (ed.) (1984) *Economic Summits and Western Decision-Making* (London: Croom Helm).
Merritt, R. and D. Puchala (1968) *West European Perspectives on International Affairs* (New York: Praeger).
Moisi, D. 'French Foreign Policy: The Challenge of Adaptation', *Foreign Affairs*, vol. 67, no. 1, pp. 151–64.
Mueller, J. (1973) *War, Presidents, and Public Opinion* (New York: John Wiley).
Nitze, P. (1989) *From Hiroshima to Glasnost: At the Center of Decision - A Memoir* (New York: Grove Wiedenfeld).
Nitze, P. (1990) Interview with the authors, Washington, D.C., 2 April 1990.
Olds, H. (1988) 'Soviet Cultural and Information Activities in Western Europe: Glasnost Expands in 1987', Report M-5/25/88, USIA Office of Research.

Palmer, J. (1987) *Europe Without America? The Crisis in Atlantic Relations* (London: Oxford University Press).
Parisot, L. (1988) 'Attitudes About the Media: A Five-Country Comparison', *Public Opinion*, vol. 10, no. 5, pp. 18–19.
Penniman, H. (ed.) (1987) *Italy at the Polls, 1983: A Study of the National Elections* (Durham, NC: Duke University Press).
Putnam, R. and N. Bayne (1984) *Hanging Together: The Seven-Power Summits* (Cambridge: Harvard University Press).
Rattinger, H. (1985) 'The Federal Republic of Germany: Much Ado About (Almost) Nothing', in G. Flynn and H. Rattinger (eds), *The Public and Atlantic Defence* (Totowa, NJ: Rowman and Allanheld) pp. 101–74.
Rattinger, H. (1987) 'Change Versus Continuity in West German Public Attitudes on National Security and Nuclear Weapons', *Public Opinion Quarterly*, vol. 51, no. 4, pp. 495–521.
Regan, D. (1988) *For the Record: From Wall Street to Washington* (New York: St. Martin's Press).
Romerstein, H. and S. Levchenko (1989) *The KGB Against the Main Enemy* (Lexington, KY: Lexington Books).
Rossi, S. (1985) 'Public Opinion and Atlantic Defence in Italy', in G. Flynn and H. Rattinger (eds), *The Public and Atlantic Defence* (Totowa, NJ: Rowman and Allanheld) pp. 175–220.
Rudig, W. (1988) 'Peace and Ecology Movements in Western Europe', *West European Politics*, vol. 11, no. 1, pp. 26–39.
Rush, M. (1989) 'The War Danger in Soviet Policy and Propaganda', *Comparative Strategy*, vol. 8, no. 1, pp. 1–9.
Schieffer, B. and G. Gates (1989) *The Acting President* (New York: E. P. Dutton).
Schoenborn, M. (1981) 'Perceptions of National Security of the U.S. and the Federal Republic of Germany', Paper presented at the Annual Conference of the American Association of Public Opinion Research, May 1981.
Shapiro, R. and B. Page (1988) 'Foreign Policy and the Rational Public', *Journal of Conflict Resolution*, vol. 32, no. 2, pp. 211–47.
Shultz, R. and R. Godson (1984) *Dezinformatsia* (Washington, D.C.: Pergamon-Brassey's).
Sigal, L. (1984) *Nuclear Forces in Europe: Enduring Dilemmas, Present Prospects* (Washington, D.C.: The Brookings Institution).
Smith, G. (1991) *Reagan and Thatcher*, (New York: W.W. Norton and Company).
Smith, S. (1985) 'West European and Japanese Television News Coverage Applauds Summit for Easing Superpower Tensions', Report FMA-12/3/85, USIA Office of Research.
Smith, S. and D. Wertman (1989) 'Summing Up Before the Economic Summit', *Public Opinion*, vol. 11, no. 6, pp. 41–5.
Soofer, R. (1988) 'SDI and Deterrence: A West European Perspective', *Comparative Strategy*, vol. 7, pp. 17–38.
Sorrels, C. (1983) *Soviet Propaganda Campaign Against NATO* (Washington, D.C.: U.S. Arms Control and Disarmament Agency).
Speakes, L. (1988) *Speaking Out: Inside the Reagan White House* (New York: Charles Scribner's Sons).

Spiro, H.J. (1988) 'Anti-Americanism in Western Europe', *The Annals of the American Academy of Political and Social Science*, vol. 497 (May 1988), pp. 120–32.
Staar, R. (ed.) (1986) *Public Diplomacy: USA Versus USSR* (Stanford, CA: The Hoover Institution Press).
Stokes, B. (1990) 'Opening Eastern Gates', *National Journal*, 23 June 1990, pp. 1531–4.
Szabo, S. (ed.) (1983) *The Successor Generation: International Perspectives of Postwar Europeans* (London: Butterworths).
Szabo, S. (1989) 'Public Opinion and the Alliance: European and American Perspectives on NATO and European Security', in S. Sloan (ed.), *NATO in the 1990s* (Washington, D.C.: Pergamon- Brassey's) pp. 143–72.
Talbott, S. (1984) *Deadly Gambits: The Reagan Administration and the Stalemate in Nuclear Arms Control* (New York: Alfred A. Knopf).
Talbott, S. (1988) *The Master of the Game: Paul Nitze and the Nuclear Peace* (New York: Vintage Books).
Thompson, W.S. (1987) 'Some Elements of an American Strategy', in W.R. Kintner (ed.), *Arms Control: The American Dilemma* (Washington, D.C.: The Washington Institute Press) pp. 302–16.
Thompson, W.S. (1988) 'Anti-Americanism and the U.S. Government', *The Annals of the American Academy of Political and Social Science*, vol. 497 (May 1988), pp. 20–34.
Thornton, T. (1988) 'Preface', *The Annals of the American Academy of Political and Social Science*, vol. 497 (May 1988), pp. 9–19.
Treverton, G. (1983) 'Is There a Crisis in US–European Relations?', in A. Platt (ed.), *The Atlantic Alliance: Perspective from the Successor Generation* (Santa Monica, CA: The Rand Corporation), pp. 71–86.
Treverton, G. (1985) *Making the Alliance Work: The United States and Western Europe* (Ithaca, NY: Cornell University Press).
Tucker, R. (1989) 'Reagan's Foreign Policy', *Foreign Affairs*, vol. 68, no. 1, pp. 1–27.
US Department of Agriculture (1990) *The GATT Negotiations*, July 1990 (Washington, D.C.).
US Department of Defense (1988) *Soviet Military Power* (Washington, D.C.: Government Printing Office).
US Department of Defense (1990) *Soviet Military Power* (Washington, D.C.: Government Printing Office).
US Department of State (1985) *Contemporary Soviet Propaganda and Disinformation: A Conference Report*; June 1985 (Washington, D.C.).
US Department of State (1987) *Soviet Influence Activities: A Report on Active Measures and Propaganda 1986–1987*, August 1987 (Washington, D.C.).
US Department of State (1989) *Terrorist Group Profiles* (Washington, D.C.: Government Printing Office).
US Department of State (1990) *GIST on the INF Treaty*, May 1990 (Washington, D.C.).
US Information Agency (1990) *A Chronology of United States Arms Control and Security Initiatives 1946–1990*, May 1990 (Washington, D.C.).
Veen, H. (1990) 'German Unity: Public Opinion and Voting Trends', *The Washington Quarterly*, vol. 13, no. 4, pp. 177–89.

von Staden, A. (1989) 'The Changing Role of the Netherlands in the Atlantic Alliance', *West European Politics*, vol. 12, no. 1, pp. 99–111.
Waldahl, R. (1985) 'Norwegian Attitudes Toward Defence and Foreign Policy Issues', in G. Flynn and H. Rattinger (eds), *The Public and Atlantic Defence* (Totowa, NJ: Rowman and Allanheld), pp. 275–320.
Walker, M. (1986) *The Waking Giant: Gorbachev's Russia* (New York: Pantheon Books).
Wallis, W.A. (1990) 'A Sherpa's View of Economic Summits', *The American Enterprise*, vol. 1, no. 4, pp. 63–9
Weihmiller, G. and D. Doder (1986) *US–Soviet Summits* (New York: University Press of America).
Wertman, D. (1984) 'The Successor Generation in Italy: Their Values and Attitudes', Report R-22–84, USIA Office of Research.
Wettig, G. (1986) 'Public Diplomacy, Soviet Style', in R. Staar (ed.), *Public Diplomacy: USA Versus USSR* (Stanford, CA: The Hoover Institution Press) pp. 273–81.
Whelan, J. (1990) 'USIA: Sink or Swim? Trimming Sails in Western Europe Would let the Agency Ride the Winds of Change', *Foreign Service Journal*, September 1990, pp. 26–9.
Wirthlin, R. (1990) Interview with the authors. McLean, Virginia, April 12, 1990.
Woodward, R. (1987) *Veil: The Secret Wars of the CIA 1981–1987* (New York: Simon and Schuster).
Worcester, R. (1989) 'Attitudes to America, Americans, American Foreign and Defence Policy and to American Multinational Companies in Britain', Paper presented at the conference 'The American Presence in Britain', Institute of United States Studies, Institute of Historical Research, London, 10 November 1989.

Index

Abshire, David, 51
Abu al Abbas, 214
Achille Lauro, terrorist attack on, 214
Afghanistan, Soviet invasion of, 1, 10–11, 19, 53, 124, 131, 150–2, 165, 168, 243, 296
agricultural trade, 2, 229, 238, 240–3, 247, 304–5
Andropov, Yuri, 89, 126–7, 250
Antenne-2, 204
anti-Americanism, 3, 12, 17, 91–103, 128, 188–90, 249, 293–4
arms-control initiatives, 53–7, 87–90

Ban the Bomb movement, 3, 93
Belgian Socialist Party, 59
Belgium, INF deployment in, 53, 57, 73, 291
Bissell, Richard, 3
Brandt, Willy, 91
Brezhnev, Leonid, 89, 126–7, 130, 142, 250
Britain, INF deployment in, 53, 55–6, 77, 78–9
British Parliament, speech by President Reagan to, 4, 187
British political parties
 Alliance (Liberals and Social Democrats), 62, 95
 Conservative Party, 55–6, 95
 Labour Party, 5, 10, 52, 55–6, 59, 62
Buckley, William, 214–15
Bush, George, 50, 116, 187, 193, 248

Campaign for Nuclear Disarmament (CND), 58–9
Canada, role of in G–7, 218–19
Carter, Jimmy, 10, 11, 39, 52, 126, 243

Central America, US policies towards, 124
Chernenko, Konstantin, 166
Chernobyl, 152, 154
Comiso, Sicily, 59
Coordinating Committee for Multilateral Export Controls (COCOM), 244
cruise missiles, ground-launched, 53, 54, 57
Cyprus, impact of on Greek attitudes towards the US, 95
Czechoslovakia, radio broadcasting in, 193

Daily Telegraph, 207
Deaver, Michael, 300
defence spending, 6, 9, 10, 12, 43, 46–8, 52–3
Diario, 16, 207
Die Welt, 207
dual track decision, 4, 10, 52–4, 57, 66, 70, 73
Dutch Christian Democratic Appeal (CDA), 57
Dutch Interchurch Peace Council (IKV), 59
Dutch Labour Party (PvdA), 59, 62

East–West trade, 243–6, 247
economic summits
 general, 218–19, 304
 Houston 1990, 240
 London, 1991, 218
Economist, The, 207, 290, 291
Eisenhower, Dwight D., 124, 164, 207
elections
 1983 British elections, 5, 55–6, 61–2
 1983 Italian elections, 5, 55–6, 61

elections (*cont.*)
  1983 West German elections, 5, 55–6, 61
European Community, 146, 154, 204, 206–8, 231–3, 250, 253, 303
  bilateral discussions with USA, 2, 218
  Common Agricultural Policy (CAP), 218, 240–3
  Project 1992, 218–19, 234–5

Falklands War, 5, 7, 256
Financial Times, The, 204, 206
Finlandisation, 16–17
Ford, Sergeant Kenneth, 204
Franco, Francisco, 95
Frankfurter Allgemeine, 205, 216
French Socialist Party (PS), 59

G–5 countries, 219
G–7 countries, 218–19
GATT, 218, 250
  Uruguay Round, 2, 219–20, 233–4, 238, 240
German reunification, 1, 9, 27, 132
Gibraltar, Straits of, 206
Gonzalez, Felipe, 20
Gorbachev, Mikhail, 1, 51, 56–7, 89, 129–83, 207, 218, 250–2, 295–6, 299
  popularity in Western Europe, 126–8, 185
  public diplomacy efforts, 157–9
  and Ronald Reagan, 1, 124, 126–8, 164
Greenham Common, UK, 58
Grenada, US intervention in, 120
Gromyko, Andrei, 155
Guardian, The, 195
Gulf conflict, 28, 32, 251, 254–7, 305–6
Gulf of Sitre, 203

Hinckley, Ronald, 4
Howe, Geoffrey, 205
Hungary, radio broadcasting in, 193
Hussein, Saddam, 254–7

INF deployment, 1, 3, 4, 5, 6, 10, 31, 51–90, 92, 128, 155–6, 166, 178, 184, 187, 248–51, 291–3
  demonstrations and other protest activities about, 1, 3, 10, 11–12, 54, 58–64, 101, 155, 184, 291
  demonstrators, characteristics of, 62–4, 291–2
  Geneva negotiations about, 53–7, 64–6, 120
  INF Treaty, 11, 51, 57, 66, 89–90, 124, 164, 176–80, 183, 252, 291, 293
International Monetary Fund (IMF), 218
Iran–Contra affair, 2, 120, 124, 127, 213–17
Iran, terrorism and, 198, 202, 214–15
Iraq, role in Gulf War, 254–7
Israel, role in Iran–Contra affair, 215
Italian Communist Party (PCI), 20, 55, 59
Italian Radical Party (PR), 59
Italian Socialist Party (PSI), 59
Italy, INF deployment in, 5, 53, 55–6, 59, 73

Kennedy, John F., 165
Khrushchev, Nikita, 164–5
Kirkpatrick, Jeanne, 191
Korean airliner (KAL 007), Soviet downing of, 1, 120, 154, 165–6
Kuwait, invasion and liberation of, 254–7
Kvitsinsky, Yuli, 54

Lebanon, conflict in, 151, 214
Libya
  bombing of (April 1986), 2, 120, 203–12
  terrorism and, 2, 198–214, 248, 303
Louvre Accord, 219

McNamara, Robert S., 36
Mediterranean Sea, 203
Mitterrand, François, 133, 229
Molotov, Vyacheslav, 155

National Security Council, 4
NATO, 1, 4, 6, 9–50, 51–8, 70, 73, 81, 155, 157, 159, 198, 206–7, 220, 244, 248, 250–1, 254–5
  flexible response doctrine of, 6, 9, 35–8, 47, 248, 250
  London Summit (July 1990), 9, 35, 252
Netherlands, The, INF deployment in, 53, 57, 80–1, 291
neutralism, 3, 12, 17, 19–23, 24–8, 47, 50
neutron weapons, 7, 37, 39, 42, 52, 58
Newsweek, 93, 289, 291, 293
Nicaraguan contras, 215
Nitze, Paul, 36, 54, 154, 173, 291
Nixon, Richard M., 165
Normandy, speech of President Reagan at, 187
NSDD–77, 3, 185
nuclear freeze, 156
nuclear pacifists, 38, 87
nuclear weapons, 3, 6–7, 9, 10, 13, 35–43, 51–90

Organisation for Economic Cooperation and Development (OECD), 218, 241, 304

pacifism, 3, 12, 17, 36–7
Palestine Liberation Front, 214
Pershing II missiles, 53, 54, 57, 291
Plaza Agreement, 2, 219, 222
Poland, imposition of martial law in, 1, 10–11, 19, 165, 243–4, 301
protectionism, 222, 233–8
public opinion and foreign policy, 4–8, 248

Qaddafi, Muammar, 199–200, 203–7, 302–3
Quotidien, 207

Reagan, Ronald, 1, 3, 4, 17, 19, 30, 39, 42, 51, 53–4, 57, 66, 89, 106, 115–16, 118, 120–1, 146, 150, 165–6, 185–7, 204, 207–9, 214–20, 224, 235, 238, 240, 243–5, 248–50, 252–3, 300
  at Geneva summit, 11, 120, 165–71
  at Moscow summit, 180–1
  at Reykjavik summit, 172–5, 299
  at Washington summit, 51, 57, 176–80
  'evil empire' speech, 116, 120, 124, 165–6
  image in Western Europe, 124–8

SALT I Treaty, 165
SALT II Treaty, 52–3, 165–6
Schmidt, Helmut, 39, 52, 56
South Africa, 151
Soviet Military Power (US Department of Defense), 12, 159
Soviet Union
  human rights in, 129, 147–50, 180–1
  missiles: SS-4, 52, 54; SS-5, 52, 54; SS-20, 51, 52, 54, 57, 70, 77, 80, 142, 155, 166, 291
  public diplomacy, 154–9, 250, 297; charm offensive, 154; peace offensive, 1, 3, 130, 142, 154–7
Spain
  and US bombing of Libya, 184, 198, 205
  referendum on NATO membership held in, 20
START Agreement, 180–1
Strategic Defense Initiative (SDI), 1, 42–5, 120, 161–83, 187, 290, 299
successor generation, 3, 62–3, 93
Syria, terrorism and, 198, 214

terrorism, 198–247
terrorist groups
  Action Directe, 198
  Irish Republican Army, 198, 202
  November 17, 198
  Red Army Faction, 198
  Red Brigades, 198
Thatcher, Margaret, 7, 55, 208, 299
Times, The, 204, 208
Tripoli, Libya, 206

United Nations, role in Gulf
  conflict, 254–7
United States Information Agency
  (USIA), 185, 191–2
  Office of Research, xii, 3, 67, 73,
    100, 261–5
US–Soviet relations, 87–9, 161–83,
  250–1
US–Soviet summits
  Four Power Conference, July
    1955, 162, 164
  Camp David Meeting, September
    1959, 162, 164–5
  Paris Conference, May 1960, 162,
    165
  Vienna, June 1961, 162
  Geneva, November 1985, 88,
    162–3, 167–71
  Reykjavik, October 1986, 120,
    162–3, 172–5, 183
  Washington, DC, December
    1987, 51, 57, 162, 176–80
  Moscow, June 1988, 162, 164,
    180–3
US News and World Report, 93

Vietnam War, 3, 29, 92
Voice of America (VOA), 185, 188–90
  VOA Europe, 3, 188–90;
    listenership in Western
    Europe of, 188–90

'walk in the woods', 54, 291
Warsaw Pact, 12, 35, 43, 90
West German political parties
  Christian Democratic Union
    (CDU/CSU), 55–6, 241
  Free Democratic Party (FDP), 52,
    55–6
  Green Party, 59, 62, 184
  Social Democratic Party
    (SPD), 10, 52, 55–6, 59, 62
West German TV-Two, 207
West Germany, INF deployment
  in, 5, 53, 55–6, 77, 80, 81–2
Wick, Charles Z., 185, 190
Wirthlin, Richard, 4
Worldnet Television, 3, 185, 190–3

ZDF Television, 167
zero option, 54–5, 57, 66, 291